T0282924

FARNSWORTH'S
CLASSICAL ENGLISH ARGUMENT

Farnsworth's

CLASSICAL
ENGLISH
ARGUMENT

by

WARD FARNSWORTH

GODINE

BOSTON · MASSACHUSETTS

PUBLISHED IN 2024 BY

GODINE

BOSTON, MASSACHUSETTS

COPYRIGHT © 2024 BY WARD FARNSWORTH

Library of Congress Cataloging-in-Publication Data is found on the last printed page of this book

FIRST PRINTING, 2024
PRINTED IN THE UNITED STATES OF
AMERICA

* *
*

Contents

Preface

THIS BOOK is about the art of argument. It collects useful tools of reasoning and rhetoric and illustrates them with examples from the heyday of public debate in England and America. The result is partly meant for instruction; it's a chance to learn about the *reductio ad absurdum* from Edmund Burke, about the slippery slope from Abraham Lincoln, and about other classic ideas from writers and talkers of the first rank. The book is also meant for fun. It shows masters of the language crossing analytical swords and exchanging abuse when those things were done with more talent and dignity than is common today. They made argument a spectator sport of lasting value and interest.

* * *

That summary states the general aims of this book. For those wanting elaboration, here's a more detailed account.

↬ *Patterns.* We learn how to argue by seeing it done. These days that means most people learn about argument from social media, a kind of virtual campus on which the subject is taught badly indeed. This book is an alternative school. It uses old examples to explain and illustrate patterns in debate—the range of moves that get made in arguments about all sorts of subjects in all times and places. Some of the methods amount to ways of approaching an adversary or audience: irony and insult, displays of generosity or the will to fight, or the creation of an identity that makes the speaker more persuasive. Some of them are patterns of reasoning: ways to spot logical mistakes, think about evidence, or argue about the meaning of words. Some patterns are triumphs of rationality. Some are alternatives to rationality. Some are offenses against it.

This is the fourth book in a series about some of the knowledge embedded in the good speech and writing of an earlier age. As in the prior books, each theme to come is illustrated with a few examples that show how it has been used or discussed. I've sought illustrations that are reasonably short and have something in their wording to commend them to the reader—a dash of eloquence, passion, wit, flagrant error, or other source of interest or charm. More complex ideas receive more explanation; simpler ones get less. The entries are mostly brief in any event, and this regardless of whether the topic is large or small. Some topics are minor enough to need only brief coverage anyway. But some of them could support—some *have* supported—much longer treatments. In that case the book just serves to make introductions, like an encyclopedia with entries of modest length.

➤➤ *Sources*. The examples are typically drawn from British and American debate from the late eighteenth century to the early twentieth, with spillover once in a while in the timing at both ends—e.g., to catch some earlier examples from Swift or later ones from Churchill. That period is our focus because public argument was practiced at a high and distinctive level in those times and places. I don't necessarily say it was done better then than now (though sometimes it's hard not to think so). But it was done well enough, and differently enough, to reward attention from students of argument, which means all of us.

The book draws mostly from the same time period as the earlier ones in the series and from many of the same sources. But it also relies heavily on a set of sources used less in the others: debates in British and American legislatures. That shift follows from the change in subject matter. The most talented masters of argument haven't written fiction. Often they haven't written at all. They've stood and used the spoken word.

Since the illustrations are usually a century or two old, they use a dialect a little different from ours. That's the meaning of the book's title: *English* refers to the language, not the country, and *Classical* refers to an era in the life of that language, not to ancient times. Public speech and writing from the era considered here are often more formal and polite than what we'd find today, so the ideas to come will need some adaptation if you want to use them yourself. But for the discerning reader this difference will add to the pleasure of the

examples and what they teach. The writers and speakers we'll examine were able to disagree about important things without the quick
descent into savagery or imbecility that has become so familiar. They
were invested in good manners to an extent that can seem strange to
modern ears; they were protective of the dignity of their enterprise
and the parties to it. But that's not to say they were gentler. Those
customs sometimes let them vilify each other with more zing than is
common now while debasing themselves less.

↦ *Topics*. This book isn't comprehensive. Plenty of things can happen in an argument that aren't discussed or illustrated here. The
book just aims to show themes that were prominent in the time and
place that it considers. If you could travel back in time 200 years and
listen to a great deal of debate, you'd hear a lot of talk about issues
and details that are no longer important to you. But you'd also hear
many patterns of argument that don't depend on those details, that
are highly interesting, and that are as useful now as they were then.
If you jotted down examples of those patterns, your notes might
look like this book.

   The examples in the book come from debates about a wide range of
issues. Sometimes the context isn't quite visible. You'll see the form
of the argument but not that it's from, say, a debate about tariffs on
lemons. In other cases the topic is clear and still matters: the value
or meaning of liberty, or whether a utilitarian way of looking at
problems is the best one. And we'll glimpse many disputes that aren't
alive anymore but once burned fiercely—whether or not to ratify the
Constitution, who should have the right to vote, the pros and cons
of flogging criminals. The chance to revisit such controversies is an
edifying form of historical tourism.

↦ *Offense*. This book has examples in which people speak for great
causes and bad ones. I've deliberately included some that will now be
found loathsome. Those views are part of the history of the era, and
they teach valuable lessons about rhetoric. It's good to see solemn
and moving guarantees that turned out to be wrong, and well-worded

arguments for appalling views. They remind us not to mistake eloquence for truth. Only sometimes do those good things overlap.

That last point isn't taught firmly enough in schools. Rhetoric is, among other things, the art of making things sound true. Something said beautifully is more likely to be accepted as right. Eloquence is therefore a powerful aid to persuasion for those with a deserving cause but also with an undeserving one. So studying rhetoric is like the study of weaponry. It's important to know both sides of its potential. Some of it you study to use; some of it you study to beware. The book thus means to offer lessons in rhetoric and reasoning but also in skepticism. Some of its illustrations are offered for the sake of instruction, others for inoculation.

↦ *How to use the book*. The book is divided into 32 short chapters. The chapters are grouped into three sections. The first, Offense and Defense, is about the personal side of argument: the use of aggression and emotion and responses to them, the speaker's creation of a credible persona, and appeals to the better qualities of an audience or adversary. The second section, Inference and Fallacy, introduces tools for reasoning and hazards in carrying it out. The third section, Judgments and Tradeoffs, broadly involves weighing evidence and making choices about it.

These groupings by family aren't rigorous, nor are the groupings within the chapters. They just mean to collect topics that are interesting to read about near one another. The chapters can be read in any order by those who prefer to wander around, a practice I encourage. The book is meant as a reference, though a readable one—the kind in which learning (and entertainment, too) may be helped by some serendipity. The curiosities of the reader will be the best guide to what to read and when.

↦ *Acknowledgments*. For helpful comments and other assistance, I wish to thank Barbara Bintliff, Robert Chesney, Alexandra Delp, Janice Fisher, Ted Frank, David Greenwald, Andrew Kull, Richard Lanham, Brain Perez-Daple, Robert Pitman, Christopher Roberts, Nicholas Shackel, Matt Steinke, and Paul Woodruff.

FARNSWORTH'S
CLASSICAL ENGLISH ARGUMENT

I

Offense and Defense

AS THE preface explains, this book divides the activity of argument into three parts. We begin here with the more personal and sometimes less rational aspects of it: the withering attack, the attempt to endear, the appeal to emotion, etc. In later sections we'll consider the testing of logical claims and of evidence. Those last topics may seem more urgent; we need better reasoning more than we need better insults. (Yet we *do* need better insults.) But this section makes a good route into our subject. It shows some familiar things done with unfamiliar ability; and since its themes are sometimes light, it provides an easy way to get acclimated to the rhetorical setting in which our time will be spent.

1

Insult and Invective

↠ *Limited talents.* Observing deficiencies in the other side's wit or ability. This theme works best when the points aren't made in a spirit of accusation or relish. They're just matter-of-fact acknowledgments—friendly, even—that the adversary has meager capacities and is struggling with them. The first illustration here might serve in spirit as a keynote for the rest of the chapter.

> There was scarce a word he uttered that was not a violation of the privileges of the House; but I did not call him to order—why? because the limited talents of some men render it impossible for them to be severe without being unparliamentary. But before I sit down I shall show him how to be severe and parliamentary at the same time.

Grattan, *Invective Against Corry* (1800)

> But "it is impossible," says the Reviewer, "to define what are corporal pleasures." Our brother would indeed, we suspect, find it a difficult task; nor, if we are to judge of his genius for classification from the specimen which immediately follows, would we advise him to make the attempt.

Macaulay, *Utilitarian Theory of Government* (1829)

> LEWIS. Is the Prime Minister aware of the deep concern felt by the people of this country at the whole question of the Korean conflict?
> CHURCHILL. I am fully aware of the deep concern felt by the Honorable Member in many matters above his comprehension.

Exchange in the House of Commons (1952)

↠ *Pity.* Saying that you feel sorry for the other side. It's an insult dressed in compassion; you're pained by their behavior and the incompetence it displays. This kind of pity typically includes overtones of condescension and, like the previous theme, an implied assertion of status. You can only make this kind of judgment because you understand more than whoever receives it.

Paine, *The Rights of Man* (1791)	It is painful to behold a man employing his talents to corrupt himself. Nature has been kinder to Mr. Burke than he is to her.
Thurman, speech in the Senate (1871)	There are some things that are painful to see. It is not painful to see a weak man make a weak speech, but it is painful to see a man of ability sinking to the level of the weakest intellect that can be found in the land.
Allen, speech in the Senate (1894)	When the Senator from New York stands in this Chamber and says that the sugar tax is the only thing to be considered, I am sorry for him. He betrays more ignorance than I supposed he possessed.

➻*Low expectations*. Saying that your (or anyone's) expectations of the other side are low and were met. The insult is double: the subject of it has a bad reputation and the reputation was confirmed. And the low expectations make the new judgment in the foreground more convincing; if we expected incompetence, it's less controversial to say that we got it.

Macaulay, *Sadler's Law of Population* (1830)	We did not expect a good book from Mr. Sadler; and it is well that we did not; for he has given us a very bad one.
O'Connell, speech in the House of Commons (1832)	As respects the speech of the noble Lord who seconded the Amendment, much was not to be expected from him. I did not much mind the rabid argument of the noble Lord, because he is a young man of very little experience, and little skillful in debate.
Wood, speech in the House of Commons (1903)	In Ulster, of course, they were acquainted with the attitude taken up by the hon. and gallant Member for North Armagh. He had been true to his past career, and he was true to it today. They expected nothing better, and they were not disappointed.

It may follow that your antagonists give no offense because you're inured to their lack of ability.

Disraeli, speech in the House of Commons (1846)	The hon. and learned Gentleman has been extremely personal, so far as I am concerned, in the comments which he has

addressed to the House. I do not make that observation in the spirit of complaint against the hon. and learned Member. I am quite used to such treatment at his hands.

Let hon. Members attack the Government as much as they like. We are accustomed to it; it is our trade to listen to these comments, and we do so with the utmost philosophy.

Balfour, speech in the House of Commons (1900)

↦ *Sorrow.* You wish you didn't have to correct your adversaries or make your case in such a disagreeable manner. Maybe the audience is getting edgy because your arguments are long or obvious, or they'll find the matters to come distasteful. You turn that discomfort against the other side: if you're sorry to hear these points belabored, don't blame me; I'm sorry to have to *say* them, but can't do otherwise.

If, in the recital of the circumstances which I have to detail, I shall be under the painful necessity of bringing before your lordships scenes which must disgust every well-regulated mind—transactions which must offend the feelings of every honourable and virtuous person—I am sure your lordships will think that upon this occasion I ought to hold no reserve.

Gifford, speech in the House of Lords (1820)

Some [utilitarians] have, however, thought fit to display their ingenuity on questions of the most momentous kind, and on questions concerning which men cannot reason ill with impunity. We think it, under these circumstances, an absolute duty to expose the fallacy of their arguments. It is no matter of pride or of pleasure. To read their works is the most soporific employment that we know.

Macaulay, *Westminster Reviewer's Defence of Mill* (1829)

The "Mill" under attack by Macaulay, above and elsewhere, is James Mill, the father of John Stuart Mill. All quotations in this book attributed *to* "Mill" are from the son.

That is my reading of the Constitution. Have I read it to so little purpose as to be mistaken? Is not the Federal Union bound to guaranty to all the States a republican government? If so, how can a State without any kind of government be a

Dumont, speech in the House of Representatives (1866)

part of the Federal Union? It is a solecism I am ashamed to combat in the hearing of reasoning men.

➤➤ *Ridiculing followers.* The other side is receiving praise or will be soon; you say it figures, perhaps implying that those giving the applause and getting it deserve each other and are both contemptible. In addition to explaining away the acclaim, this discourages people on the fence from adding to it.

Wollstonecraft, *A Vindication of the Rights of Men* (1790)

The rich and weak, a numerous train, will certainly applaud your system, and loudly celebrate your pious reverence for authority and establishments—they find it pleasanter to enjoy than to think.

Macaulay, *Mill on Government* (1829)

They surrender their understandings, with a facility found in no other party, to the meanest and most abject sophisms, provided those sophisms come before them disguised with the externals of demonstration. They do not seem to know that logic has its illusions as well as rhetoric,—that a fallacy may lurk in a syllogism as well as in a metaphor. Mr. Mill is exactly the writer to please people of this description.

Stanley, speech in the House of Representatives (1908)

Said the gentleman from Pennsylvania, "I come here to sing no new song, to make no new speech." The grand exalted ruler of the Ancient Order of Stand-patters, the high priest of protection, never uttered a truer thing than that. He said, amid thunderous applause, that he was going to plant the factory beside the farm. Oh, how they applauded that!

➤➤ *Talking too much.* A rough kind of insult: ridiculing the length of an adversary's speech. This avoids the merits, embarrasses the other side, and (assuming the point is accurate) probably gains appreciation from the audience. They won't like being bored, and will be happy to hold it against the party responsible if they don't mind your bluntness.

Macaulay, *Burleigh and His Times* (1832)

On every subject which the Professor discusses, he produces three times as many pages as another man; and one of his pages is as tedious as another man's three.

The Attorney General, in his long, dull, stupid speech, which was a hybrid between a churchman's and a lawyer's, made an enormous deal of the matter.

Harris, speech in the House of Commons (1889)

I hope, Sir, that the hon. Gentleman has found ample compensation in the length of his speech for what has been irreverently termed the agonies of prolonged retention.

Davitt, speech in the House of Commons (1893)

Making the point in advance puts pressure on whoever speaks afterwards.

I would willingly hear the gentleman's explanation, if he would confine himself to that. I know the gentleman well. When he commences speaking, he seems unable to stop himself, but appears to be impelled onward by some power similar to that principle in physics which causes a body, when once put in motion, in the absence of any other resisting power, to move on in a straight line forever.

Rayner, speech in the House of Representatives (1842)

Compare:

He that is weary the first hour is more weary the second; as bodies forced into motion contrary to their tendency pass more and more slowly through every successive interval of space.

Johnson, *Lives of the English Poets* (1781)

➤➤ *Welcoming disapproval.* Sometimes criticism is welcome because of its source. A proposal thus can be praised for having all the right enemies.

We trust you will concur with us in thinking, that as the considerate approbation of *the wise and good* is a fair argument in favor of a public measure, so is its deliberate rejection by *the weak and wicked.*

Coxe, *Virginia's Power Under the Constitution and the Dangers of Failing to Ratify* (1788)

The point can also be made more personal: I'm pleased to hear disagreement from *this* person or quarter in particular. Saying so is a display of comfort with your own view and invites the audience to likewise be indifferent to disapproval. Relishing criticism is also a way to sidestep the merits of it, and of course it's a strong put-down.

Hamilton, *The Farmer Refuted* (1775) — I congratulate myself upon the sentiments you entertain of my last performance. Such is my opinion of your abilities as a critic, that I very much prefer your disapprobation to your applause.

Moore, speech in the House of Commons (1938) — With some I do not agree, and I do not agree especially with the hon. Member for East Wolverhampton. My disagreement with him, however, is so fundamental that I look upon a debate as having gone wrong if I find myself in agreement with him.

And then the reverse: you've gotten praise and are sorry for it.

Cobden, speech at London (1849) — Every species of abuse, every sort of misrepresentation, every kind of suppression, was resorted to by them, until we became strong; and when we were both strong and fashionable, we were beslavered with their praise; and I confess I liked it less than their abuse.

Benton, speech in the Senate (1846) — I want to ask the Senator from Michigan if, at seeing himself thus applauded by the London Times, he does not feel tempted, like the Athenian of old at seeing himself applauded by a rabble that he despised, to turn round to his friends, and ask what he had done amiss to bring this applause upon him?

The classical reference is to Phocion (*c.* 402–318 BC), a statesman of whom that anecdote is told in Plutarch's *Lives*.

Ansberry, speech in the House of Representatives (1914) — Mr. Speaker, I begin to doubt my own judgment when my position on pension legislation is endorsed by that arch enemy of all pension legislation, the gentleman from Texas.

Criticism by degrees. Climbing from one level of condemnation to the next. This lets you arrange the subjects of your criticism in relation to one another. A precise organization of such judgments makes them sound well founded. And it gives the most severe judgment a climactic push. The subject isn't just bad; it's on top of a mountain of ignominy.

> Taskmasters are bad, hired taskmasters are worse, hired political taskmasters are worst.
>
> McDougall, speech in the Senate (1864)

> This is the whole product of Poole as novelist: three novels, bad, worse, worst.
>
> Mencken, *Six Members of the Institute* (1919)

A case where the degrees are explained so the adversary can be placed at the summit:

> I condemn the person who, on a subject that supposes a knowledge of 100 facts, should generalize on ten or twelve. I condemn still more the person who generalizes on five or six: and the theorists who generalize on four, three, or two facts respectively, must be considered to be characterized by the positive, comparative, and superlative degrees of imbecility. But what shall we say of him who generalizes on one—who takes a single instance for the foundation of a theory? who on a single coincidence grounds a general rule? Surely he is the king of theorizers. Surely if anybody is a visionary speculatist, he is. That man is the honourable opener.
>
> Mill, *The British Constitution* (1826)

↦ *Hyperbole.* If you put a criticism in ultimate terms—*the worst ever*, etc.—the result probably won't survive literal scrutiny, but it can effectively convey how the matter *seems*. And like a wild demand in a negotiation, it can drag the listeners some way toward the exaggerated judgment.

> A greater absurdity cannot present itself to the understanding of man than what Mr. Burke offers to his readers.
>
> Paine, *The Rights of Man* (1791)

> With respect to the charge against Great Britain and the Algerines, it is the most whimpering, babyish complaint that ever disgraced the lips of manhood, and when a member of the House of Representatives made mention of it, he deserved to have his backside whipped.
>
> Cobbett, *A Little Plain English* (1795)

> Deliberately considering the Payne-Aldrich bill, I here state that, after most exhaustive analysis, in my judgment it is the most outrageous tax measure ever placed upon the statutes of any government in Christendom.
>
> Henry, speech in the House of Representatives (1910)

➤➤*Density of adjectives*. Good English style usually calls for a sparing use of adjectives. When you pack them densely, though, their effect can be striking and greater than the sum of the parts. It works well on those special occasions that call for high-grade invective.

Grey, speech in the House of Lords (1815)

In the worst transaction of the worst period of the worst government that ever existed—in the vilest deceit, the most infamous perfidy, the foulest crime that ever occurred—in the blackest record of fraud and imposture that is to be met with in the annals of the world, nothing can be found more flagrant and heinous—nothing more hateful for its treachery—nothing more contemptible for its baseness.

He was talking about correspondence exchanged during the Congress of Vienna.

Sheil, undated speech (c. 1827)

Thanks be to God, the hoary champion of every abuse—the venerable supporter of corruption in all its forms—the pious antagonist of every generous sentiment—the virtuous opponent of every liberal amelioration—the immaculate senator, who wept over the ruins of Grampound; the incorruptible judge, who declared the Princess of Wales to be innocent, the Queen of England to be guilty—Eldon, the procrastinating, canting, griping, whining, weeping, ejaculating, protesting, money-getting, and money-keeping Eldon, is out. This, after all, is something.

Windom, speech in the House of Representatives (1862)

The blood curdles in our veins, and we turn away with sickening disgust from the contemplation of their horrid crimes to inquire what gigantic iniquity it is that breeds such moral monsters. The answer is obvious. It is slavery that vitiated the conscience, destroyed the morals, brutalized the soul, and, in its own foul fens, generated these monsters of wickedness, whose mad attempt to destroy the Republic is characterized by the frightful excesses to which I have referred.

➤➤ *Words inadequate*. Language can't convey the severity of your judgment or do justice to the facts. Maybe the right words don't *exist*;

this invites the audience to try to think of words that do, to reflect on their inadequacy, and to feel horror, contempt, and the like.

> There are no words that can convey a correct idea of his meanness. He is the fellow that shot himself to make it appear that his life was in danger from Democrats.

Bogy, speech in the Senate (1877)

Or the words may exist but you don't have the ability to summon them. Again, the listeners can ask themselves how *they* might get the job done.

> Were I in fear of the hereafter, I would first go to Camp Cody for a preparatory course. It is an annex of Hades of which his Satanic Majesty is evidently ashamed, and why the War Department should have seen fit to select such a place in which to train 26,000 red-blooded young Americans I cannot understand. Had I the gift of a Dante I might do justice to the subject, but its true portrayal is beyond my poor power.

Knutson, speech in the House of Representatives (1918)

Or the words exist but can't be used *here*. Now the audience has the easiest job of all: fill in the gaps with obscenities.

> I can not find words which are appropriate to be spoken in this body under its parliamentary rules to express my utter contempt for such a speech as the Senator has made upon this question.

Miller, speech in the Senate (1887)

2

Irony

↦ *Ironic appreciation.* Complimenting your adversaries for bad qualities, or otherwise giving them thanks or praise for traits they'd rather not have. The mock flattery makes it a little easier to give the insult without seeming ill mannered, and a little more complicated for the other side to fend off.

Hamilton, *The Farmer Refuted* (1775)

You possess every accomplishment of a polemical writer which may serve to dazzle and mislead superficial and vulgar minds: a peremptory, dictatorial air, a pert vivacity of expression, an inordinate passion for conceit, and a noble disdain of being fettered by the laws of truth. These, sir, are important qualifications; and these all unite in you in a very eminent degree.

Clancy, speech in the House of Commons (1892)

I think the weakest reasons ever offered in opposition to this Bill have just been advanced by the hon. and learned Member for Mid Armagh. He has not been very long in this House; but I must congratulate him upon having, within the space of one week, acquired all the stock of cut-and-dried objections to Irish reform.

Churchill, speech in the House of Commons (1909)

I like the martial and commanding air with which the gentleman treats facts. He stands no nonsense from them.

Or you appreciate the damage they've done to their own side, or the help they've given to yours.

Mill, speech on parliamentary reform (1824)

That which I did not conceive to be possible has actually come to pass: I have been strengthened in my opinions by the discussion which they have undergone. It is not that any new evidence has been brought forward in their support, or that I have heard any thing advanced in their favor of which I was not previously aware. I knew all which could be said on

our side of the question; but I knew not, nor was it possible
to foresee, how little could be said on the other.

➤➤ *Glad they're happy.* More fake generosity: if they're pleased, I'm
pleased for them (but they shouldn't be). The usual idea is that your
adversaries are fooling themselves, though not the rest of us. They're
encouraged to keep at it. Maybe a weak or discredited claim seems
satisfying to them.

> Mr. Burke has talked of old and new whigs. If he can amuse
> himself with childish names and distinctions, I shall not in-
> terrupt his pleasure.

Paine, *The Rights of Man* (1791)

> If your lordships choose to believe this, far be it from me to
> interrupt an illusion so pleasing, even by calling it such; for
> it is delightful to have any such spot for the mind to repose
> upon. If your lordships can believe it, do so in God's name!

Brougham, speech in the House of Lords (1820)

Sometimes the point is more personal.

> This book, the fruit of Mr. Courtenay's leisure, is introduced
> by a preface in which he informs us that the assistance fur-
> nished to him from various quarters "has taught him the su-
> periority of literature to politics for developing the kindlier
> feelings, and conducing to an agreeable life." We are truly
> glad that Mr. Courtenay is so well satisfied with his new em-
> ployment, and we heartily congratulate him on having been
> driven by events to make an exchange which, advantageous
> as it is, few people make while they can avoid it.

Macaulay, *Sir William Temple* (1838)

> Mr. Morley is always in an attitude of watchful jealousy as
> regards the rights of the non-Christian world, and sees an
> implied affront to them in the most harmless remark. His
> little outburst of temper at such a very small overstatement
> reminds me of his trick of printing God with a 'g' as a sort of
> typographical intimation of his disagreement with common
> opinions on that subject. Every little bit helps, I suppose.

Stephen, *Liberty, Equality, Fraternity* (1873)

➤➤ *Surely you jest.* Saying that the other side's claim must have been a
joke. This provides them with an out if they want it; if not, it makes

the claim embarrassing to defend. Of course the idea that they were joking is itself probably less than earnest. Thus this account of a speech from Brougham (in the old third-person format):

Brougham, speech in the House of Lords (1838)

At first, he only thought this portion of his speech extremely stupid—(he spoke it with all respect)—very flat and tedious, and insipid, and, at so late an hour, somewhat of the most tiresome—but he soon perceived that it was all the while sarcasm in disguise. We had heard of "war in disguise," and this, it seemed, was "wit in disguise"—so thick a disguise indeed, that he questioned if all their Lordships, for whose behoof it was intended, had as yet pierced through to come at it.

Boteler, speech in the House of Representatives (1860)

When my friend from Tennessee made a speech in opposition to the amendment, I really thought at the time that he was in earnest. I had forgotten, sir, that he was a gentleman of "infinite jest, of most excellent fancy".... He could not have been in earnest, sir, in opposing my amendment; and I owe him an apology, which I now tender, for not having recognized that fact yesterday.

(His adversary replied: "I was never more earnest in my life.") From debate on a bill to hire spies who would watch American officials abroad:

Lore, speech in the House of Representatives (1887)

It is too improbable. It must be a joke. Perhaps the distinguished chairman of Foreign Affairs out of his abundant ability has been giving free reins to an exuberant fancy.

↠ *Let me help*. The offer or promise to do the other side a favor. They need instruction, or their case needs help, and you're game to provide it. This lets you make a criticism (they didn't do their job) but with a dash of magnanimity (I'll do it for them). It also positions you well as a matter of competence; you have the ability that they lack. And it justifies what you're about to say: it's what your adversary should have said.

Paine, *The Rights of Man* (1791)

As Mr. Burke has passed over the whole transaction of the Bastille (and his silence is nothing in his favor), and has entertained his readers with reflections on supposed facts distorted into real falsehoods, I will give, since he has not, some account of the circumstances which preceded that transaction.

I will do for the honorable gentlemen what they have failed to do for themselves. I will attempt to separate their different arguments from one another, and state them, fairly and distinctly one by one.

Mill, *The British Constitution* (1826)

Or you offer advice. This way of framing a criticism takes the criticism for granted and so doesn't invite immediate scrutiny of it. Instead of saying *you did X*, you say *let me suggest how to avoid doing X, or how to do it better.* This also makes an insult easier to pass off as parliamentary.

I would advise him, when he wishes to bring an elaborate indictment for grave inconsistency against a Member of this House, as he did against my right honorable Friend the Member for West Monmouth, that he should not spoil the effect of it by immediately pointing out that he has himself been even more inconsistent.

Campbell-Bannerman, speech in the House of Commons (1899)

Now he comes forward and says he is anxious to know whether it is really true that His Majesty's Government are in favor of children being brought up as atheists. If I might offer a little friendly advice to the noble Marquess, I would suggest that, when he takes these excursions into the country and into the realms of imagination, as a pure matter of stage management his efforts ought to bear a little more air of spontaneity.

Crewe, speech in the House of Lords (1906)

I hope the new Air Minister will imitate the example of Lord Baldwin, and when he makes a mistake blurt it out in the most appalling manner, so that, at any rate, whatever we may complain about, we cannot complain that we have been misled.

Churchill, speech in the House of Commons (1938)

↠ *Thanks anyway.* You graciously decline advice when it comes from a bad source. The simplest reply: I already have enough.

Kelley, speech in the House of Representatives (1863)

I remember to have once seen a beggar craving a sixpence. The good lady from whom he asked the boon declined making the gift, but proposed to give him, instead thereof, some advice. "Thank you, madam," said he, "I am full of it." I feel, I must confess, a little that way now. I have had quite enough of such advice as we have been getting today.

Or: I appreciate the concern, but will keep my own counsel all the same.

Wright, speech in the House of Representatives (1866)

They generously bestow their advice upon us here in our seats, and in this building, and at our hotels, telling us how we can best discharge our duty. All I can say is that we are very much obliged to them for their interest in our enlightenment, and we will act as we may deem best.

Or: excuse me for ignoring you.

Shaw, *The Irrational Knot* (1880)

You must pardon me if I hesitate to set aside my own judgment in deference to your low estimate of it.

↠ *Enemies to themselves.* Others are talking or acting (or are poised to do so) as though they were their own enemies; or they're doing all that their enemies could wish. This claim is powerful when it's plausible. If the other side makes your case for you, there's nothing left to be concerned about.

Paine, *The Rights of Man* (1791)

Had anyone proposed the overthrow of Mr. Burke's positions, he would have proceeded as Mr. Burke has done. He would have magnified the authorities on purpose to have called the right of them into question; and the instant the question of right was started, the authorities must have been given up.

Williams, speech in the impeachment of Andrew Johnson (1868)

What more do you want, then, to convict this man? If he had intended to make a case for you, could he have made it stronger?

The point can also be made in prospect and put hypothetically: you're about to act like your own enemy—or about to do what I'd wish if you were *my* enemy.

The new constitution in its present form is calculated to produce despotism, thraldom and confusion, and if the United States do swallow it, they will find it a bolus, that will create convulsions to their utmost extremities. Were they mine enemies, the worst imprecation I could devise would be, may they adopt it.

Philanthropos,
Antifederalist 7
(1787)

↦ *My mistake.* You admit that you made a mistake, but the effect is to put the blame elsewhere: you trusted others, or assumed the best of them, and were wrong. Blaming yourself hides the insult (a little) and makes it more credible: it's a mild admission against interest on your part. (See chapter 23.) And you aren't pointing a finger *directly* at anyone but yourself, which makes the implied criticism trickier to repel.

Having detected the frauds and falsehoods of this vile impostor Wood in every part, I foolishly disdained to have recourse to whining, lamenting, and crying for mercy, but rather chose to appeal to law and liberty and the common rights of mankind, without considering the climate I was in.

Swift,
Drapier's Letters
(1725)

I have been mistaken. I relied upon a willingness which the Democratic party does not possess, a readiness of which it is not capable, and a patriotism which it has never displayed.

Watson, speech
in the House of
Representatives
(1903)

The United States can, does, and ought to wash its hands of all of it. It can only say, as good men and good women have said, "I trusted one whom I thought to be honorable; I was mistaken."

Plumb, speech
in the Senate
(1890)

The party he had in mind was the State of Florida.

3

Demand, Response, and Neutrality

↠ *Admit or deny.* You set forth two answers and demand a choice between them: yes or no; admit or deny. This clarifies the issue and can force the other side to make an awkward election or awkwardly avoid it.

Webster, *Second Reply to Hayne* (1830)
I ask him to come forth and declare, whether, in his opinion, the New England States would have been justified in interfering to break up the embargo system under the conscientious opinions which they held upon it? Had they a right to annul that law? Does he admit or deny?

Vandiver, speech in the House of Representatives (1902)
Now, I ask you whether you approve of civilized soldiers torturing uncivilized people, as you call them, for the purpose of extorting confessions from them? Answer yes or no. Answer, or else take your seat.

This tactic smacks of the courtroom and is open to abuse, since a good answer often can't be given in a word. An old example is the demand for a yes-or-no reply to a compound or "loaded" question—i.e., a question that contains a controversial premise.

Granville, speech in the House of Lords (1871)
There never was a more hasty motion than that, and it would have placed the official Members of this House in the position of the witness in the legal Joe Miller, who was asked by counsel—"Answer me—yes or no, are you continuing to beat your wife?"

A "Joe Miller" meant a stale joke. It was an allusion to a collection of such jokes, *Joe Miller's Jests* (named after an English actor who wasn't responsible for most of the contents).

↠ *The right of reply.* Rejecting the choice described above. The other side has said something that calls for a response, but *how* you respond is up to you. It may be important to make that clear, as when the question boxes you in.

> If I were to admit all of the Senator's premise, of course I would answer "yes"; and if the Senator will permit me to frame a question in my own way, I can always compel him to answer "yes."

Reed, speech in the Senate (1914)

You may need to put aside the other side's question and address the issue in a way that suits you better. This is a natural response to demands for a yes-or-no answer when a question calls for different treatment.

> MR. PICKLER. Here is my question: do you indorse the indiscriminate suspension of pensions that has been made by this Administration before the soldier has been notified of any charges filed against him?
>
> MR. LIVINGSTON. You heard my remarks; and I will repeat them.
>
> MR. PICKLER. You can answer it, yes or no.
>
> MR. LIVINGSTON. You cannot frame a question and then frame my answer. You have not lived long enough for that.

Exchange in the House of Representatives (1893)

This approach is sometimes used to dodge embarrassing questions. At the end of the 19th century, South Carolina passed educational qualifications to vote. It was an open effort to suppress the influence of Black voters in elections. That led to this exchange in Congress between representatives from Oregon (Crumpacker) and South Carolina (Talbert).

> MR. CRUMPACKER. Is not the gentleman aware of the fact that local legislation in a great many of the States has disfranchised a large percentage of the male inhabitants over 21 years of age?
>
> MR. TALBERT. I assert, and the statement will be sustained by examination, that the laws of the States north of Mason and Dixon's line are much more restrictive and severe in respect to suffrage than those of the South, and the gentleman should

Exchange in the House of Representatives (1902)

inquire in that direction, and I advise him to sweep before his own door before he comes to mine.

MR. CRUMPACKER. That is not an answer to my question.

MR. TALBERT. The gentleman must understand that he must not stand up here and attempt to put words in my mouth. I must be allowed to answer in my own way, as I am accustomed to do in other things.

⇥ *Guided options.* Rather than demanding an admission or denial (or "yes or no" answer), you can present options and seek to force the discussion through the channels of reasoning provided. The result can resemble a verbal flow chart or process of elimination.

Burke, *Speech on Conciliation with the Colonies* (1775)

If, then, the removal of the causes of this spirit of American liberty be, for the greater part, or rather entirely, impracticable,—if the ideas of criminal process be inapplicable, or, if applicable, are in the highest degree inexpedient, what way yet remains? No way is open, but the third and last,—to comply with the American spirit as necessary, or, if you please, to submit to it as a necessary evil.

Lincoln, letter to James Conkling (1863)

You desire peace, and you blame me that we do not have it. But how can we attain it? There are but three conceivable ways. First, to suppress the rebellion by force of arms. This I am trying to do. Are you for it? If you are, so we are agreed. If you are not for it, a second way is to give up the Union. I am against this. If you are, you should say so plainly. If you are not for force, nor yet for dissolution, there only remains some imaginary compromise.

Again, of course, it's open to the other side to reject the offered framework.

Hale, speech in the Senate (1859)

They say, in their report, that there are three alternatives for Cuba: first, her possession by a foreign Power, which we would never submit to; secondly, her independence, which is impossible; thirdly, her acquisition by us, which is inevitable. Well, sir, those are curious alternatives. One never can be, the other never shall be, and the third is inevitable, and we are called upon today to appropriate $30,000,000 to bring about an inevitable consequence.

↠ *The denial.* Denying a claim straight out can be better than taking it apart. A jury likes to hear a defendant deny a charge directly; the audience to a debate likes the same. You can decide just what to deny and how to phrase it. And you can deny what anyone has said, even if it was said elsewhere and the author isn't named.

> It is said we cannot deny that the Budget is driving capital out of the country. I deny it absolutely.

Churchill, *The Budget and Property* (1909)

Denying a claim invites the listeners to agree without more discussion: maybe the claim is clearly wrong when you stop to think about it. We just needed someone with the nerve to say so.

> It is commonly said, and more particularly by Lord Shaftesbury, that ridicule is the best test of truth; for that it will not stick where it is not just. I deny it.

Chesterfield, letter to his son (1752)

Denials can also be piled up to fine effect. The hammer comes down until the table is cleared.

> Touching these English colonies, I do not wish to be misunderstood. I do not say of them or of America that they have not a future, or that they will not be great nations. I merely deny the whole established modern expression about them. I deny that they are "destined" to a future. I deny that they are "destined" to be great nations. I deny (of course) that any human thing is destined to be anything.

Chesterton, *Heretics* (1905)

↠ *No neutrals.* Most debates have bystanders. You can try to make them commit by saying that everyone is on one side or the other; you demand to know which it is. The reasoning can be practical: something is about to happen if there's no action, so staying out makes them responsible for the result.

> Whatever we may say about it, in the last analysis we must either adopt the President's course or by our refusal accept the Kaiser's course. There is no middle ground.

Stephens, speech in the House of Representatives (1917)

The point can be ethical. Failing to side with right is itself wrong: if you don't support us, you're the enemy. Of course this defines the position of the listeners in a way they may reject and find offensive. It's a popular argument in moral crusades.

Giddings, speech in the House of Representatives (1849)

Those who are not with us are against us. There can be no neutrals. Every man is in favor of this slave trade and its attendant crimes, or he is against it.

Or the claim can be conceptual: how can you *elect* to be neutral once you understand the choice?

Stephen, *Liberty, Equality, Fraternity* (1873)

I cannot understand how a man who is not a Roman Catholic can regard a real Roman Catholic with absolute neutrality. A man who really thinks that a wafer is God Almighty, and who really believes that rational men owe any sort of allegiance to any kind of priest, is either right—in which case the man who differs from him ought to repent in sackcloth and ashes—or else he is wrong, in which case he is the partisan of a monstrous imposture.

➻ *Against moderation.* Rejecting neutrality for *yourself*: the case is one-sided, or in any event you're committed to one side and it's wrong to pretend otherwise. You normally gain credibility by weighing both sides and acknowledging their strengths before making a decision. But a different kind of credit can be had by rejecting that approach. You say that showing a false respect toward the other side would gain you good will that you'd rather forfeit. This invites the audience to join you and commit without hedging.

Hamilton, *Federalist* 1 (1787)

I affect not reserves which I do not feel. I will not amuse you with an appearance of deliberation when I have decided. I frankly acknowledge to you my convictions, and I will freely lay before you the reasons on which they are founded.

Mill, *The British Constitution* (1826)

It would have been easy for me to have dealt in compromise, and trimming, and equivocation, to have talked a little on one side of the question, and then a little on the other.... I might thus have had the satisfaction (if satisfaction it could be deemed when thus purchased) of hearing every tongue sound the praises of my moderation and my candor: and I might have been pardoned even the odiousness of my opinions in favor of the lukewarmness with which I had defended them. But playing fast and loose with opinions is not to my taste.

I will be harsh as truth and as uncompromising as justice. On this subject I do not wish to think or speak or write with moderation. No! No! Tell a man whose house is on fire to give a moderate alarm; tell him to moderately rescue his wife from the hands of the ravisher; tell the mother to gradually extricate her babe from the fire into which it has fallen, but urge me not to use moderation in a cause like the present.

Garrison,
To the Public
(1831)

He was talking about slavery.

↦ *I wash my hands.* You've done your part and won't be blamed for what is about to occur, and so want nothing further to do with it; the reference is to Matthew 27:24. It's a preemptive strike that you can cite later when things go badly. It's also an ominous view of the future (there will be blame to distribute), which can discourage offenses now. Hence this defense of persistent but futile legislation to regulate beer:

I have brought this subject forward, prompted by a regard for the people, and a desire to see their morals and habits improved—I have moved the third reading of the bill; I now wash my hands of it. If it be thrown out by the non-attendance of those who pushed me forward to introduce it, I may regret having taken the trouble to introduce it, but I shall not be sorry for having done my duty; the evil will no longer lie at my door.

Brougham,
speech in the
House of Lords
(1839)

A similar defense of persistent but futile efforts to restrict slavery:

That majority may, if they will, defeat all action. They cannot prevent my ceaseless efforts to force action. If, through the course of that majority, I must finally fail—be it so. The

Dunn, speech in
the House of
Representatives
(1856)

consequences for good or ill, cannot, and shall not, attach to me either praise or blame.

Hands can be washed not just of consequences but of people : I'll have nothing further to do with *you*.

Wallace, speech
in the House
of Commons
(1887)

If you come to me and ask for help in restoring order I would certainly give you my help, and all the good advice in my power. That advice, however, would be to let order be restored by the Irish people themselves.... If on the other hand you say you do not want this sort of help from anyone to restore order in Ireland, but that you will use your own authority and your own power, then I say I will have nothing to do with it. I wash my hands of you altogether.

4

Belligerence

→ *Bidding defiance.* A tough way to respond to the other side: do your worst; I don't care, or in any event I'm ready. This shows faith in your position and a fine indifference to criticism. Sometimes defiance is an alternative to engagement when you've had enough of it.

> Those who still believe the lies that have been vomited forth against me are either too stupid or too perverse to merit further attention. I will, therefore, never write another word in reply to anything that is published about myself. Bark away, hell-hounds, till you are suffocated in your own foam.

Cobbett, *Remarks on the Pamphlets Lately Published Against Peter Porcupine* (1796)

Defiance might be called for because you're sure of victory and want the chance to earn it. You say, in effect, *bring it on.*

> I have returned to refute a libel, as false as it is malicious, given to the public under the appellation of a Report of a Committee of the Lords. Here I stand ready for impeachment or trial. I dare accusation. I defy the honorable gentleman. I defy the Government; I defy their whole phalanx. Let them come forth.

Grattan, speech in Parliament (1800)

Defiance may be better than argument because argument hasn't been offered. You've been hit with a threat or show of anger meant to produce fear. You reply with contempt.

> I thought your book an imposture; I think it an imposture still. For this opinion I have given my reasons to the public, which I here dare you to refute. Your rage I defy.

Johnson, letter to James Macpherson (1775)

> It is a miserable Bill, as I said before. I, too, have received threats from people who, I suppose, call themselves constituents of mine, and who tell me I shall be thrown out at the next Election if I do not support this Bill. I say—"Very well; be it so."

O'Gorman, speech in the House of Commons (1875)

Defiance can also be offered more calmly: resist if you like, or if you dare. I expect it and am at peace.

Bentinck, speech in the House of Commons (1847)

I will be responsible for the regeneration of Ireland; and if it fail, why then, as the responsible head of the Commission, I shall be liable to impeachment; and I now challenge the House to put that process in force against me. I say not this in any trifling spirit, or in any idle bravado. There are ready hands and willing hearts in this House, I doubt not, to put it in execution. There is a party in this House to whom I have shown no quarter; and it is meet and just that they should give no quarter to me.

Davis, speech in the Senate (1851)

I make no terms, I accept no compromises. If when I ask for an appropriation, the object shall be shown to be proper and the expenditure constitutional, I defy the gentleman, for his conscience's sake, to vote against it. If it shall appear to him otherwise, then I expect his opposition, and only ask that it shall be directly, fairly, and openly exerted. The case shall be presented on its single merit; on that I wish to stand or fall.

↠ *Prepared for battle.* Making clear that you're ready for a fight. It's a display of confidence and an offer of intimidation: all comers will be met with energy and won't like the result.

Douglass, speech at Rochester (1850)

This fugitive slave law stands alone in the annals of tyrannical legislation. I doubt if there be another nation on the globe having the brass and the baseness to put such a law on the statute-book. If any man in this assembly thinks differently from me in this matter, and feels able to disprove my statements, I will gladly confront him at any suitable time and place he may select.

These suggestions tend to be most ominous when made in decorous or indirect words.

Webster, *Second Reply to Hayne* (1830)

I shall not allow myself, on this occasion, I hope on no occasion, to be betrayed into any loss of temper; but if provoked, as I trust I never shall be, into crimination and recrimination, the honorable member may perhaps find, that, in that contest, there will be blows to take as well as blows to give; that others can state comparisons as significant, at least, as his own, and that his impunity may possibly demand of him whatever powers of taunt and sarcasm he may possess. I commend him to a prudent husbandry of his resources.

We are quite as little afraid of a contest in which quarter shall be neither given nor taken as he can be. But we would advise him seriously to consider, before he publishes the promised continuation of his work, whether he be not one of that class of writers who stand peculiarly in need of the candor which he insults, and who would have most to fear from that unsparing severity which he practices and recommends.

Macaulay, *Sadler's Law of Population* (1830)

You can make a challenge just because you know that no one will accept it. The class of brave opponents is empty. From a dispute about seating the successor to Henry Clay in the Senate, in which it was debated whether there was a vacancy to fill:

I ask for the party who denies in this case. Let him stand forth in the presence of the Senate of the United States, and of the American people. I ask, I challenge him to come upon the floor of the Senate of the United States, and deny that there is a vacancy. Who is he? Let him stand forth and he shall be heard. He comes not.

Seward, speech in the Senate (1852)

↠ *Now vs. later.* A decision has to be made: fight now or put it off until later. Fighting now spares others the hardship of it—especially successors, whether real or figurative children.

It was argued that, sooner or later, it was evident there must be a rupture with Great Britain; and that all that could be done was to delay it for a season. "Well," said he, "at any rate, let me have peace in my day!" How just and noble the sentiment of the writer, who remarks, that if that man had felt as a parent should, his language would have been far different; he would have said: "If war must come, let it come now, that my child may have peace."

Owen, speech in the House of Representatives (1846)

Or the job will get more expensive as time goes by—for example, because costs are accruing in the meantime or because criticism for being late will be added to the cost of performance. So the best time for action of whatever sort is now.

Jay, *Address to the People of New York on the Constitution* (1787)
It seems necessary to remind you, that some time must yet elapse, before all the States will have decided on the present plan. If they reject it, some time must also pass before the measure of a new Convention can be brought about and generally agreed to.... In the mean time our affairs are daily going on from bad to worse, and it is not rash to say that our distresses are accumulating like compound interest.

Wilson, address to Congress (1913)
The only question is, When shall we supply it—now, or later, after the demands shall have become reproaches that we were so dull and so slow?

Perhaps your ability to do the job may go down, or the strength of the other side may go up.

Henry, *Speech to the Virginia Convention* (1775)
They tell us, sir, that we are weak; unable to cope with so formidable an adversary. But when shall we be stronger? Will it be the next week, or the next year? Will it be when we are totally disarmed, and when a British guard shall be stationed in every house?

Churchill, radio broadcast to the United States (1938)
We have now at last got far enough ahead of barbarism to control it, and to avert it, if only we realize what is afoot and make up our minds in time. We shall do it in the end. But how much harder our toil for every day's delay!

The opposite claim: sufficient unto the day is the evil thereof; if we have to fight, better to postpone it. Perhaps our strength is improving, so the odds of success will improve if we wait.

Canning, speech in the House of Commons (1826)
If we are to be driven into war, sooner or later, let it be later: let it be after we have had time to turn, as it were, the corner of our difficulties—after we shall have retrieved a little more effectively our exhausted resources, and have assured our-

selves of means and strength, not only to begin, but to keep
up the conflict, if necessary, for an indefinite period of time.

Or delay might create a chance to avoid the fight entirely; and if not,
better for misery to come later than sooner.

> The hon. and learned Gentleman said we must fight the Rus-
> sians now, because if we did not we should have to fight them
> hereafter. I do not like arguing in the future tense, in that
> way especially, when such serious questions are concerned.
> By the same rule, a man might bring one a bowl of poison,
> and say—"You may as well take it now, because you will be
> sure to die some time."

Cobden, speech
in the House
of Commons
(1854)

↠ *The forward defense.* Saying that we should fight an evil while it's
still far away. The point can be literal: it's safer to do battle from a
distance.

> It is better to fight for the first inch of national territory than
> for the last. It is better to defend the door sill than the hearth
> stone—the porch than the altar.

Cass, speech
in the Senate
(1845)

> If we can meet and disable our enemy on foreign soil, let us
> vote men and money to do so. It is better to fight the enemy
> in Europe than in the United States.

Sherman, speech in
the Senate
(1917)

But arguments about distance can also be a metaphor for fights about
intangible things—e.g., protecting rights in cases that seem small
instead of waiting until the stakes are higher. We're afraid of an
advance by a principle, not an army.

> The chief danger to this purpose of the Republican party
> is not just now the revival of the African slave trade, or the
> passage of a Congressional slave code, or the declaring of a
> second Dred Scott decision, making slavery lawful in all the
> States. These are not pressing us just now. They are not quite
> ready yet. The authors of these measures know that we are
> too strong for them; but they will be upon us in due time,

Lincoln, speech
at Columbus
(1859)

and we will be grappling with them hand to hand, if they are not now headed off.

Smith, speech in the House of Commons (1898)

We shall have an attempt made to permit a Roman Catholic sovereign to sit upon the Throne. I think the country should face those things. It is a great deal better to fight this question a long way off than to wait until it comes upon us with irresistible power.

This point can also be turned around and made a warning about the strategy of your adversaries: they'll defend their minor offenses to stop you from reaching more serious ones. Thus Paine's argument about why it's so hard to get rid of a corrupt despot:

Paine, The Rights of Man (1791)

When once such a vicious system is established it becomes the guard and protection of all inferior abuses. The man who is in the receipt of a million a year is the last person to promote a spirit of reform, lest, in the event, it should reach to himself. It is always his interest to defend inferior abuses, as so many outworks to protect the citadel.

↦ *Distrust the enemy.* You're against something because your enemies are for it or recommend it. What they like, we should not do.

Burke, *Letters on the Proposals for Peace with the Regicide Directory of France* (1796)

How comes it, that now for the first time, men think it right to be governed by the counsels of their enemies? Ought they not rather to tremble, when they are persuaded to travel on the same road, and to tend to the same place of rest?

Tillman, speech in the House of Representatives (1886)

It is not the friends of silver but its avowed bitter enemies who ask for the total suspension of its coinage, and there is no safer maxim in war, in politics, and in the battles of private life than "never do anything your enemy wants you to do."

He's referring to Napoleon's 16th Maxim of War: "never to do what the enemy wishes you to do, for this reason alone, that he desires it." But this kind of argument can also be an *ad hominem* error (on which see chapter 14), and harmful to the person making it: a refusal to believe the truth or hear wisdom because it's said by the wrong person.

I will avail myself of the avuncular relationship which I hope
I may still possess in respect of the Government to put it to
the Prime Minister personally and even intimately, Has he
ever heard of Saint Anthony the Hermit? Saint Anthony the
Hermit was much condemned by the fathers of the church
because he refused to do right when the devil told him to.

Churchill, speech
in the House of
Commons
(1938)

The truth, it is felt, becomes untruth when your enemy utters
it. Recently I noticed that the very people who swallowed
any and every horror story about the Japanese in Nanking in
1937 refused to believe exactly the same stories about Hong
Kong in 1942. There was even a tendency to feel that the
Nanking atrocities had become, as it were, retrospectively
untrue because the British Government now drew attention to
them.

Orwell, *Looking
Back on the Spanish
War* (1942)

↦ *Losing battles.* A fight that you can't win may be worth fighting
anyway. Thus a protest against accepting the proposed constitution:

If, as the federalists say, there is a necessity of our receiving
it, for heaven's sake let our liberties go without our making
a formal surrender. Let us at least have the satisfaction of
protesting against it, that our own hearts may not reproach
us for the meanness of deserting our dearest interests.

Winthrop,
Agrippa XII
(1788)

Never again say, as I have heard said: "Don't quarrel with
the railroad, temporize with them or with money they will
beat us." Oh, fatal, false, perfidious words! Even if they were
true, could they speak who have gone before us, who have
passed to the "realms of shade," they would tell us as our own
manhood tells, that better, a thousand times better, to go down
fighting like free men, than to live in servitude, than to live
lifting to the gaze of mankind our wrists encircled with the
galling manacles of a willing degradation.

George, speech
in the House of
Representatives
(1886)

I know, as I have said, that it is a waste of time to protest
against this enormity. I take that back. It is a futile attempt,
but it is not a waste of time. It can never be a waste of time

Flood, speech in
the House of
Representatives
(1906)

to sound a note of warning against the action of an arrogant majority in trampling under foot the freedom of speech, the right of debate in this House.

↠ *Vindication later.* You'll win in the long run if you don't now. This can lift the morale of your allies; thoughts of glory in the future can shore up endurance in the present. Gesturing to the future is also a way to attack an adversary: you invite them to imagine how they will look in retrospect. One day the tables will be turned, and those on the wrong side will be shamed or worse.

McRoberts, speech in the Senate (1841)

You may refuse to do justice, but you shall not perform the fraudulent rite in silence. You shall be told of it to your face, in this Senate. You have an inexorable Federal majority, and can therefore oppress the new States; but you have no moral right to do so. The day will come—mark it, sir, the day will come—remember, another census, yes, ten years more, will bring that bright day; and my prayer is that I may live to be one of the men who will then right ourselves.

Phillips, speech at Boston (1853)

There is the jury of honest men to come! Before that jury we summon you. We are weak here,—out-talked, out-voted. You load our names with infamy, and shout us down. But our words bide their time. We warn the living that we have terrible memories, and their sins are never to be forgotten.

Sullivan, speech in the House of Commons (1878)

You will complain of my words; you will say I do not warn, but threaten; and you will prefer to believe those who tell you the Irish masses are contented and well affected, as enthusiastically ready as Englishmen could be to pour their blood in your defense. But I dare all risk of temporary misrepresentation and blame. I look into the future, and can await my vindication.

↠ *Let them fight.* When your adversaries fight with each other, it's best to encourage them or at least stay out of the way. In the Lincoln-Douglas debates, for example, Douglas was a Democratic senator and was in a feud with the sitting president, James Buchanan—also a Democrat. Lincoln, a Republican, saw nothing better than to urge them on.

[Douglas] was a little more severe upon the Administration than I had heard him upon any occasion, and I took pains to compliment him for it. I then told him to give it to them with all the power he had; and as some of them were present, I told them I would be very much obliged if they would give it to him in about the same way. I take it he has now vastly improved upon the attack he made then upon the Administration. I flatter myself he has really taken my advice on this subject. All I can say now is to re-commend to him and to them what I then commended,—to prosecute the war against one another in the most vigorous manner. I say to them again: "Go it, husband!—Go it, bear!"

Lincoln, debate with Stephen Douglas at Alton (1858)

Lincoln was referring to a frontier tale in which a woodsman's wife saw a bear attacking her husband. Her reaction was as described. A simpler expression of the idea:

Far be it from me to restrain any of the gentlemen on the other side when they are disposed to tell each other just what they think of each other.

Mondell, speech in the House of Representatives (1914)

These are cousins to a time-honored adage:

It is the law of war that the enemy of my enemy is my friend.

Gore, speech in New York (1918)

5

Justifying Aggression

↦ *Decorum and defense.* Insults, strong dissent, and other hard words can bring on the objection that they aren't fit for the place where they're used—a breach of decorum.

Hamilton, speech
in the House
of Commons
(1888)

I have to call your attention, Mr. Speaker, to the circumstance that an hon. Member has made use of the words "Tory skunks." I wish to ask you, Sir, whether such language is regular?

(The language was held to have been irregular.) You can meet complaints about decorum, in turn, by saying that the stakes are too high for such worries.

Cuthbert, speech
in the Senate
(1841)

That I must not dare to speak of a subject of this importance, because it does not comport with the Senator's notions of decorum! Can any man listen to this with patience? That the rights of the whole people are to be put in the scales with the Senator's ideas of delicacy and decorum? I laugh at it. I spurn at it. The interests of my constituents shall be defended by me on all occasions—by God they shall.

Perhaps you're acting from a passion that's justified under the circumstances.

Wellington, speech
in the House of
Lords (1830)

I trust that your Lordships will excuse me if, feeling warmly, I also speak warmly upon this subject.

Douglas, speech
in the Senate
(1856)

These attacks are heaped upon me by man after man. When I repel them, it is intimated that I show some feeling on the subject. Sir, God grant that when I denounce an act of infamy I shall do it with feeling, and do it under the sudden impulses of feeling, instead of sitting up at night writing out my denunciation of a man whom I hate, copying it, having it printed, punctuating the proof-sheets, and repeating it before the glass, in order to give refinement to insult, which is only pardonable when it is the outburst of a just indignation.

→→ *Returning fire.* You can justify aggression by saying the other side provoked it. What choice do you have when you're challenged?

> This is a hall for mutual consultation and discussion; not an arena for the exhibition of champions. I offer myself, sir, as a match for no man; I throw the challenge of debate at no man's feet. But then, sir, since the honorable member has put the question in a manner that calls for an answer, I will give him an answer.

Webster, *Second Reply to Hayne* (1830)

> Had the opposers of the bill chose to let it pass in silence, or, in this discussion, treated its friends and the general courteously, I would have been willing to let all the matters connected therewith rest in the grave of forgetfulness; but they have decided otherwise; and have indulged in flings at the character of Jackson, and questioned the motives of his friends. So be it, then. If they want war, war they shall have; and I, for one, say to them "Lay on Macduff, And damned be he who first cries hold! Enough!"

Kennedy, speech in the House of Representatives (1844)

(The allusion is to *Macbeth*, act 5, scene 8.) It's the same if the debate has gone in a bad direction: I don't like the turn it has taken, but that's the other side's doing, not mine, and it would be wrong to give up the fight on that account.

> I beg pardon, sir, for the scandalous, indecorous, and disgusting scene which I am now compelled to open to your view. But, sir, because my enemy, like the swine, which delight in nothing as much as but filth, has thought it convenient to seek a refuge in the quagmire of Billingsgate abuse, shall I let go the hold I have of him? No, sir, covered with dirt, it is true, but nobly covered with dirt, which, coming in contact with such an enemy, I cannot protect myself from, I will still hold him.

Fromentin, letter to John Quincy Adams (1821)

Billingsgate is a fish market in London with a long tradition of foul language.

Sometimes this theme has another element: you'll match the other side blow for blow and use the same tactics. They've started a game at which two can play. If it gets ugly, blame them.

Wood, speech in the House of Commons (1845)

I am quite prepared to meet the noble Lord on the ground which he himself has chosen; and I can assure the House that I am prepared not only to meet him on his own ground, but also to imitate him in the tone and temper in which he discussed this question.

Rapier, speech in the House of Representatives (1875)

If in the course of my remarks I should use language that may be considered inelegant, I have only to say that it shall be as elegant as that used by the opposition in discussing this measure; if undignified, it shall not be more so than my subject; if ridiculous, I enter the plea that the example has been set by the democratic side of the House, which claims the right to set examples.

The point applied to specific language:

Sullivan, speech in the House of Commons (1878)

Mr. Speaker, that hon and learned Gentleman said of the men amidst whom I stand that they were "masquerading as Home Rulers." Masquerading! The phrase is not offensive, I suppose, or he would not have applied it; so I may use it too, and say that the thing which is really intolerable is to see the grandson of the great Plunket masquerading on the floor of this House as an Imperialist.

↠ *Their dispute is not with me.* If you need to say something provocative, a good defense is simply that it's true and that you aren't responsible for its truth—indeed, that you regret it. As the saying now goes, don't shoot the messenger.

Webster, speech in the Senate (1840)

I'm sorry it is true. These are truths; not creditable to the country, but they are truths. I am sorry for their existence.

Let the friends of these gentlemen defend them now, or let the admission be conclusive that they cannot—I will, if it is more likely to call out a defense, say dare not. I am not here to use hard words or to deal in denunciation or abuse; I have no malice, indeed no feeling in this matter; but justice requires that I should lay the facts before the House and the country which rendered our report necessary.

Beck, speech in the House of Representatives (1874)

I do not mean to charge the Ohio statesman with misrepresentation or deception, but simply state the truth, offer the evidence, and rest this portion of the case. His difference is with the facts, not with me.

Stark, speech in the House of Representatives (1900)

The same approach can justify harsh judgments—i.e., sorry, but it's true. This time the equivalent saying is *if the shoe fits, wear it.*

From your own account of the matter we may justly draw these two conclusions: 1st, That you serve a monster; and 2d, That never was a messenger sent on a more foolish errand than yourself. This plain language may perhaps sound uncouthly to an ear vitiated by courtly refinements, but words were made for use, and the fault lies in deserving them, or the abuse in applying them unfairly.

Paine, *The American Crisis* (1783)

These are the Americans who thought it unbecoming a moral and religious people to rejoice over the success of the American arms. These may seem to be harsh and rather severe expressions. Agreed. Truth demands, and the occasion asks it; and if any man thinks the shoe fits him, he is welcome to wear it.

Kennedy, speech in the House of Representatives (1844)

If it be said that I have at any time used severe language, I answer to him who reproaches me as Antigone in the Greek play answered the tyrant: "Tis you that say it, not I. You do the deeds, And your ungodly deeds find me the words."

Mason, speech in the Senate (1902)

Instead of saying your adversaries are arguing against truth or fact, you can seek to position them against the audience, the record, past authors, etc.—anyone but you.

Rice, speech in the House of Commons (1837)

If I am guilty in giving a preference to the orders of the House over the claim of the hon. and learned Gentlemen, let the House so decide. If the House prefer his letter to my letter— his opinions to mine—be it so. It is not a question between him and me. Do not let the House think it is. It is a question between their own resolution and a single Member of Parliament, who rising in his place says, I claim that as a privilege which you (the House) say is not a privilege.

Bradbury, speech in the Senate (1852)

I propose to submit the bill for the action of the Senate. I prefer to let the twenty-eight favorable reports that have been made by committees of Congress advocate its justice. I prefer to let Marshall, Madison, Monroe, Livingston, and other distinguished men of that day, who were acquainted and identified with the facts, out of which the claims arose, speak in their behalf. If they are not heard, nothing that I can say will be likely to receive attention.

→→ *Confirmation by resistance.* Whatever you've said is justified, and this is shown by the response it provokes; the other side's strong reaction means you've hit the mark. This was Burke's view of those who resented disagreement with their policies toward the American colonies.

Burke, *Letter to the Sheriffs of Bristol* (1777)

All this rage against unresisting dissent convinces me, that, at bottom, they are far from satisfied they are in the right.

The framers of the Constitution were once described as "conspirators," and their objections to the term were likewise said to show its accuracy.

Bryan, *Centinel* XII (1788)

If any doubt had remained whether this epithet is merited, it is now removed by the very uneasiness it occasions; this is a confirmation of its propriety. Innocence would have nothing to dread from such a stigma.

This approach makes a criticism work like quicksand. If they accept the criticism, it's damaging; if they resist, it's worse.

A related theory: the other side's resistance is exaggerated and therefore insincere and unconvincing. Thus Gertrude's famous assessment in *Hamlet* of the overacting in a play (in which the Queen says she will never remarry if her husband dies): "The lady doth protest too much, methinks."

> But, verily, you on the other side do protest too much. You have overdone the thing, and have called attention, by the very vehemence of your announcement, to the glaring difference between your promises and your performances concerning the welfare of labor in the United States.

Benny, speech in the House of Representatives (1904)

↦ *Could be worse.* You say that you're restraining yourself. Usually this comes with hints about what you aren't saying or showing but could. Keeping things out of view makes them grow in the mind of the listener. This theme also positions you as a responsible type; you're trying to keep things civil. And it helps excuse what you do say: it could be worse.

> Pardon me, my dear Sir, if my expressions are strong. My feelings are so much more so, that it is with difficulty I reduce them even to the tone I use.

Jefferson, letter to Elbridge Gerry (1799)

> I hope the gentleman will not appeal to my patriotic fervor. I am holding down my patriotic fervor every moment for fear that in discussing this claim of a sailor of the United States Government I might make some mention of that pitiful occurrence when nearly 300 of our sailors were on a fateful night in a treacherous harbor blown to instant death. I am restraining and holding back the thoughts that swell in my breast lest I might inquire whether the honor of the Government of the United States has been upheld and is likely to be upheld in that matter. I trust the gentleman will not appeal to my patriotism. I am wild when I get on that subject.

Handy, speech in the House of Representatives (1898)

6

Deploying Emotion

➤➤ *Scare tactics.* Fear is a mighty persuader for the advocate who can conjure it up. For this purpose the recital of dire predictions—the parade of horribles—is the most classic method.

Coxe, *Virginia's Power Under the Constitution and the Dangers of Failing to Ratify* (1788)

Consider then, in the event of your rejection, in what a condition we shall be left—into what a situation we may be thrown! Thirteen jarring sovereignties—two or three contending confederacies—or a feeble union—will be the miserable and hopeless alternatives. The measure of foreign contempt will be filled up. Insult will naturally follow, and then injuries abroad—while the certain dangers to liberty, property and peace, at home, will sink every American, however firm, into despondency, or drive him to despair.

Stronger cases describe more personal threats that are said to face the audience.

Antifederalist 26 (1787)

If you should, at any time, think you are imposed upon by Congress and your great Lords and Masters, and refuse or delay to pay your taxes, or do anything that they shall think proper to order you to do, they can, and I have not a doubt but they will, send the militia of Pennsylvania, Boston, or any other state or place, to cut your throats, ravage and destroy your plantations, drive away your cattle and horses, abuse your wives, kill your infants, and ravish your daughters, and live in free quarters, until you get into a good humor, and pay all that they may think proper to ask of you, and you become good and faithful servants and slaves.

A description of horrors can have side effects beyond stirring up a desire to avoid them. The revulsion they cause can irrationally raise the listener's felt estimate of the chance that the predictions will come true.

You can inflate the sense of a threat by avoiding specifics about it. Painting the prospects for chaos and disaster in a general way leaves room for imagination to fill in the worst.

> These are short hints—they ought not to be more developed— you can easily in your own mind dilate and trace them through all their relative circumstances and connections.—Pause then for a moment, and reflect whether the matters you are disputing about, are of sufficient moment to justify your running such extravagant risks.

Jay, *Address to the People of New York* (1788)

Scare tactics can also be made stronger with metaphors. A comparison can link a risk that seems abstract to physical sensations of fear.

> You are on the brink of a dreadful precipice; in the name therefore of holy liberty, for which I have fought and for which we have all suffered, I call upon you to make a solemn pause before you proceed. One step more, and perhaps the scene of freedom is closed forever in America.

An Officer of the Late Army, *Independent Gazetteer* (1787)

> If we can stand up to him, all Europe may be free and the life of the world may move forward into broad, sunlit uplands. But if we fail, then the whole world, including the United States, including all that we have known and cared for, will sink into the abyss of a new Dark Age made more sinister, and perhaps more protracted, by the lights of perverted science.

Churchill, speech in the House of Commons (1940)

↦ *Humiliation.* Ridicule and contempt have great power to unify their objects and make them indignant. Sometimes it takes an advocate to point out these affronts, or to enlarge them by construing the facts in a way that goads the audience.

> Your situation is alarming indeed; yourselves and your petitions are despised and trampled under the feet of self-important nabobs; whose diabolical plots and secret machinations have been carried on since the revolution, with a view to destroy your liberties, and reduce you to a state of slavery and dependence; and alas! I fear they have found you off your guard, and taken you by surprise: these aspiring men

Workman, *Philadelphiensis* V (1787)

have seized the government, and secured all power, as they suppose, to themselves, now openly browbeat you with their insolence, and assume majesty; and even treat you like menial servants.

<table>
<tr><td>Walker, speech in the House of Representatives (1856)</td><td>And why, noble, generous, and highminded Whigs, do you submit to this flattery and friendship, without explanation for former insult? Have you lost your self-respect and dignity as gentlemen, so as now ignominiously to submit to their degrading and humiliating appeals to you? They will despise you when they have used you, and reproach you for your imbecility and folly.</td></tr>
</table>

Humiliation may effectively be described without emphasizing exactly who inflicts or observes it. It becomes just a mind game.

<table>
<tr><td>Orth, speech in the House of Representatives (1865)</td><td>Looking at these multiplied and increasing instances of foreign intervention in our affairs, we may well ask the question, can indignity and outrage go any further? And shall there not be a day of reckoning? Shall we longer submit to these humiliations and indignities without a murmur or word of complaint? God forbid!</td></tr>
<tr><td>Jones, speech in the Senate (1914)</td><td>With no information we are expected, in schoolboy fashion, to do as we are told and ask no questions. Mr. President, what is the foreign policy that requires such humiliating, cowardly, and craven action on our part? What are the delicate matters that demand this price?</td></tr>
</table>

It is a time-honored strategy to put the masculinity of the audience at issue.

<table>
<tr><td>Cox, speech in the House of Representatives (1884)</td><td>Are we not as brave as the English, and as skillful and as intelligent? Are we so emasculated by protection, so dwarfed in enterprise, that we fear, with our ten thousand natural advantages, to meet our ancient foe on the high seas?</td></tr>
<tr><td>Barlow, speech in the House of Representatives (1898)</td><td>Shame on American manhood! Shame on American spirit that would for a moment submit to such humiliation! I again assert that men who would be guilty of such nefarious designs, such</td></tr>
</table>

villainous schemes, are dangerous to society, are enemies to their race, the foes of progress, the agents of decadence and barbarism.

A related theme: *they're laughing at us*. This riles up listeners against whoever is said to be responsible or whoever is said to be laughing. It puts the audience in the mood for aggression.

> Look forward a little and anticipate the day when the last cow of the family may be taken to pay the enormous taxes of this war; then look at haughty, arrogant England chuckling at our divisions, insulting us with impunity; our glory obscured; our flag dishonored; and remembering the proud position we once occupied, tell me, if you can, what is an adequate punishment for those traitors who have brought all these evils upon our country?

Arnold, speech in the House of Representatives (1862)

> In showing the white feather under these humiliating circumstances with no greater foe than that bankrupt nation, we have achieved the great glory and the imperishable renown of being called cowards and made the laughingstock of the world. Shame, shame, a blistering and eternal shame! I repeat it, sir, I am for war.

Martin, speech in the House of Representatives (1898)

↠ *Consider the children.* Everyone wants to protect their children— any real and immediate ones but also their descendants more broadly understood. So audiences can be moved by appeals to protect future generations, and alarmed by the thought of injuring or burdening those who will follow.

> Let coming generations remember that I vainly struggled to apply a preventive to this gigantic evil, and vindicate rights. The representatives of the American people prefer that their children and their children's children shall apply the cure. Fearful will be that remedy; for the stain which you this day affix upon the nation is destined to be washed out only with their blood!

Levin, speech in the House of Representatives (1848)

Mills, speech
in the Senate
(1896)

Ordinarily, if unwise legislation is enacted in one Congress a subsequent Congress can remove the evil. But if we issue and sell bonds redeemable only after fifty years we place ourselves, our children, our children's children and our children's grandchildren and great grandchildren beyond the region of hope, for no power that Congress possesses can redeem them.

→→ *Being watched.* Saying that others are watching and waiting to see what we do. Again the onlookers may be imaginary, exaggerated, or a mix of fact and fiction. The thought of others watching can provoke strong feelings regardless: pride in the dream of impressing them, fear that they will think badly, guilt in imagining their disappointment.

Winthrop,
Agrippa X
(1788)

By adopting the form proposed by the convention, you will have the derision of foreigners, internal misery, and the anathemas of posterity. By amending the present confederation, and granting limited powers to Congress, you secure the admiration of strangers, internal happiness, and the blessings and prosperity of all succeeding generations.

Gurley, speech
in the House of
Representatives
(1861)

Liberty-loving men of all countries are watching us with the interest that more than seventy years of successful experiment has inspired in their minds; and for the action which we now take, civilization as well as history itself will hold us sternly responsible.

Robinson, speech
in the House of
Representatives
(1898)

Till today the eyes of nations are upon us, the eyes of trembling natives, 500,000 strong, with liberty kindled in their breasts, but hands not strong enough to strike—their eyes are upon us. All look this way to see if we will relapse into the pusillanimity of cowardice or assert our dignity and strength by a bold stroke of policy.

→→ *Being remembered.* The hope of being remembered later, especially after death, is a powerful source of inspiration or fear. Imaginings of how others will think of us are a broad field for wishful (or dreadful) thinking. The most famous use of the device is Shakespeare's.

> And Crispin Crispian shall ne'er go by,   *Henry V,* 4, 3
> From this day to the ending of the world,
> But we in it shall be remembered—
> We few, we happy few, we band of brothers....

That's the optimistic case. The device is often mixed with threats: you want to be remembered *this* way rather than *that* one, don't you?

> Your fate, and that of your posterity, depends on your present   *Cato* I
> conduct—do not give the latter reason to curse you, nor your-   (1787)
> selves cause of reprehension; as individuals you are ambitious
> of leaving behind you a good name, and it is the reflection,
> that you have done right in this life, that blunts the sharpness
> of death.

> Is this act, the nameless infamy of which no pencil has color-   Brinkerhoff, speech
> ing dark enough to paint, no language words strong enough   in the House of
> adequately to characterize—at which posterity will blush,   Representatives
> which Christianity must abhor—shall this be our act? ...   (1847)
> Other men's children will not have the curiosity to look into
> the acts and votes of a man so humble as myself: my own will.
> That page shall never meet their eye.

Compare:

> Future generations will not care to look back at our debates,   Labouchere, speech
> and I think that even if they do we ought not to minister to   in the House of
> their folly.   Commons (1887)

A popular form of this argument plays to the desire to be on the "right side of history." A study in that theme is found in the arguments made after Chamberlain tried to negotiate peace with Hitler in 1938. Those who liked the agreement they reached argued with those who didn't about what historians would think later. Their predictions naturally matched their other views: those who supported the agreement thought that later historians would, too. As often happens, the appeals to what history would think were a magnifier of whatever the speaker thought at the time—a current opinion passed through a fantasy about a future holder of it.

Burgin, speech in the House of Commons (1938)

Students of history will regard the Prime Minister's visit, in morning dress, travelling by a civilian passenger aeroplane as one of those great occasions when an unarmed individual has gone to the commander on the other side.... Within a few hours of his arrival the Prime Minister secured—and it is by no means the least valuable of his achievements—an assurance that the order to invade Czechoslovakia by armed German troops would not be given unless something catastrophic occurred in Czechoslovakia.

Amery, speech in the House of Commons (1938)

[Burgin] referred repeatedly to the future student of history. Can we be sure that that future student will say of this settlement that, underneath the minor adjustments and mutual civilities of Munich, it represents anything else than the triumph of sheer, naked force, exercised in the most blatant and brutal fashion? ... Will it figure in history as anything else than the greatest—and the cheapest—victory ever won by aggressive militarism?

↪ *Argumentum ad misericordiam* (appeal to pity). Making a pitch to the listener's feelings of pity, sympathy, or guilt. It's not an appeal to reason, but it need not be a fallacy if it's presented as just what it is.

Foster, speech in the House of Representatives (1910)

Imagine the awful suffering that must have taken place in that mine. Think of the widows and orphans left in the world as a result of that accident. Tell me that nothing should be done: why, Mr. Chairman, we have already waited too long.

Douglass, *My Bondage and My Freedom* (1855)

Cast one glance, if you please, upon that young mother, whose shoulders are bare to the scorching sun, her briny tears falling on the brow of the babe in her arms. See, too, that girl of thirteen, weeping, yes, weeping, as she thinks of the mother from whom she has been torn.... Suddenly you hear a quick snap, like the discharge of a rifle; the fetters clank, and the chain rattles simultaneously; your ears are saluted with a scream that seems to have torn its way to the center of your soul. The crack you heard was the sound of the slave whip;

the scream you heard was from the woman you saw with the
babe. Her speed had faltered under the weight of her child
and her chains; that gash on her shoulder tells her to move on.

Douglass wants his listeners to see in their minds what he has seen
himself. This isn't a fallacy because it isn't offered as a logical argument. He's trying to improve the information from which arguments
and conclusions will be drawn. Maybe the emotions stirred by such
words are appropriate and *should* influence what comes next.

The fallacy occurs, and is rightly attacked, when pity and sympathy
are passed off as arguments in themselves. Examples of warnings
against it:

> He appears to have reckoned upon finding in us a disposition
> to believe anything in behalf of the unfortunate, and to have
> thought that our imaginations could not harbor the idea of
> two parties cutting each other's throats, and neither of them
> in the right.

Mill, *Catiline's Conspiracy* (1826)

> It will not do always to assume that the weaker party is in
> the right, for little States, like little individuals, are often
> very quarrelsome, presuming on their weakness, and not
> unfrequently abusing the forbearance which their weakness
> procures them.

Cobden, speech in the House of Commons (1854)

7

Antidotes to Aggression
and Emotion

➻ *Antidotes to fear.* Sometimes you can beat back scare tactics just by pointing them out. As soon as anything is seen as an effort to manipulate, it's less effective and tends to seem offensive. You can add an appeal to the better instincts of the audience and confidence that they won't be taken in.

Smith, *Address to the People of New York* (1788)

The apprehension of danger is one of the most powerful incentives to human action, and is therefore generally excited on political questions: But still, a prudent man, though he foreseeth the evil and avoideth it, yet he will not be terrified by imaginary dangers.

Mill, *The British Constitution* 2 (1826)

I beg you to remark how many advantages these gentlemen have over me. We are always ready to believe what we fear. The orator who has the fears of his audience on his side, has only to awaken the emotion by a few frightful words, and persuasion follows of itself. Very different is the task of him who has the fears of his audience against him.

Duncan, speech in the House of Representatives (1830)

Panic! Panic! Panic! That's the string to pull.... The cry of "panic and desolation" is one of the standing modes of electioneering. The people understand it, and are no longer to be gulled by it, and they look with contempt upon those who make it.

One can further bring down the heat by reducing the debate to specific questions of fact.

Henry, speech at Virginia Ratifying Convention (1788)

I made some observations on some of those dangers which these gentlemen would fain persuade us hang over the citizens of this commonwealth, to induce us to change the government, and adopt the new plan. Unless there be great and awful dangers, the change is dangerous, and the experiment ought not to be made. In estimating the magnitude of these dangers, we are obliged to take a most serious view of them—to see them, to handle them, and to be familiar with them. It is not sufficient to feign mere imaginary dangers; there must be a dreadful reality. The great question between us is, Does that reality exist?

You can also fight fire with fire: whatever is frightening on one side should be balanced against a fair picture of what's frightening on the other. If X is scary, so is avoiding X.

It is true there may be danger in delay; but there is danger in adopting the system in its present form; and I see the danger in either case will arise principally from the conduct and views of two very unprincipled parties in the United States—two fires, between which the honest and substantial people have long found themselves situated.

Lee, *Letters from the Federal Farmer* V (1787)

Attempts have been made, and will be repeated, to alarm you with the fear of consequences; but reflect there are consequences on both sides, and none can be apprehended more dreadful, than entailing on ourselves and posterity a government which will raise a few to the height of human greatness and wealth, while it will depress the many to the extreme of poverty and wretchedness.

Smith, *Address to the People of New York* (1788)

Or fear and disgust are indeed in order, but should be directed at the authors of the inflammatory tactics.

Beware of those who wish to influence your passions, and to make you dupes to their resentments and little interests—personal invectives can never persuade, but they always fix prejudices which candor might have removed—those who deal in them have not your happiness at heart. Attach yourselves to measures, not to men.

Cato 1 (1787)

Fear, Sir, is a bad counsellor, and it is no great proof either of wisdom or of virtue to take counsel from nothing but fears

Mill, *The British Constitution* 2 (1826)

when any good is to be done. But the honourable gentleman seems to be one of those who are always apprehending evil to the many from the many, never from the few. Such a man appears to me to be an object of very rational fear.

↦ *Let them laugh.* Fears of laughter and humiliation can be set against the practical cost of worrying about them.

Burke, Speech on American Taxation (1774)

They tell you, Sir, that your dignity is tied to it. I know not how it happens, but this dignity of yours is a terrible incumbrance to you; for it has of late been ever at war with your interest, your equity, and every idea of your policy.

Grosvenor, speech in the House of Representatives (1813)

I am weary, weary of this perpetual and confused din about our national honor. Not a measure of more than ordinary mischief travels through this House unconnected with this topic of declamation.

Worry about laughter often amounts to a worry about status. You can drain that anxiety by addressing the status of the parties—elevating the listeners (they should be above worries about laughter) or diminishing whoever laughs (who cares what they think?).

Schurz, speech in Chicago (1899)

Nobody will laugh at us whose good opinion we have reason to cherish.

Churchill, speech at Manchester (1913)

No doubt there are many in both countries that will pour ridicule upon the proposal which I make. They will try to involve it in clouds of suspicion and suggest that there is some trick lurking behind what looks like a fair offer, and who will blame me in unstinted terms for having referred to such subjects at all. Let them mock.

↦ *Exposing stratagems.* You can take the force out of any stratagem by exposing it. Sometimes the exposure is real: something underhanded or fallacious has been tried. Sometimes the exposure is all or partly fictitious: whether or not any trick was tried, the other side's argument is described that way.

His Grace, like an able orator, as he is, begins with giving me a great deal of praise for talents which I do not possess. He does this to entitle himself, on the credit of this gratuitous kindness, to exaggerate my abuse of the parts which his bounty, and not that of nature, has bestowed upon me.

Burke, *Letter to William Elliot* (1795)

An incendiary narrator of what passed at Manchester affirms, perhaps, that "one hundred persons were slain." Suppose, indignant at this extravagant falsehood, I answer, "No, no, not a hundred, the number of sufferers was six only." "Six *only!*" is then the exclamation, "O barbarian! it is thus that you trifle with the sacrifice of human life!" This, Sir, is the common trick. It consists in first putting forth a monstrous exaggeration of calamity for the express purpose of inviting contradiction; and then holding up to public indignation the man who reduces the exaggeration to the reality, as if he were the unfeeling defender and approver of whatever part of the calamity he does not deny.

Canning, speech in the House of Commons (1819)

We are perpetually told that women are better than men, by those who are totally opposed to treating them as if they were as good; so that the saying has passed into a piece of tiresome cant, intended to put a complimentary face upon an injury, and resembling those celebrations of royal clemency which, according to Gulliver, the king of Lilliput always prefixed to his most sanguinary decrees.

Mill, *The Subjection of Women* (1869)

↠ *They always say that.* Putting a provocative or overblown claim into doubt by saying that it's not only wrong but trite. This impugns the imagination of the claim as well as the truth of it.

The dictum that truth always triumphs over persecution, is one of those pleasant falsehoods which men repeat after one another till they pass into commonplaces, but which all experience refutes.

Mill, *On Liberty* (1859)

When a gentleman goes out on a special Mission, we are always told that he is making noble sacrifices for his country. That, I am bound to say, is all claptrap. Gentlemen are glad

Labouchere, speech in the House of Commons (1888)

to go out on special Missions, and obtain some sort of political position by negotiating Treaties, spending the country's money, and enjoying themselves.

Nye, speech in
the House of
Representatives
(1912) We are always told that the way to have peace is to prepare for war. No long-standing proverb or saying has less sense or less logic. I assert that the way to prepare for peace is to be peaceful.

The point can be made more *ad hominem* in spirit: the makers of the grim claim always say such things because that's the sort of people they are.

Campbell-
Bannerman, speech
in the House of
Commons
(1895) There are plenty of pessimists about, croakers and detractors, who are always ready, either from sheer love of the art of denigration, in the interest and with a view to the adoption of some untried theory, to denounce existing arrangements, and who generally do so with that airy and summary judgment which we never find except in company with imperfect information and a total lack of responsibility.

↦ *The track record.* The theme just shown can be made empirical: you remind listeners of past claims by those who are making emotional appeals and predictions. They haven't just said it all before; they've been wrong before. This may again be an *ad hominem* point, since you're attacking the adversary rather than the argument. But that can be legitimate if a claim depends on the credibility of the person making it.

Ward, speech in
the House of
Representatives
(1866) The land groans under your despotism, they exclaim. These terrible assertions would alarm us did we not "consider the source." These same persons and their party said, when treason's grip was at the nation's throat, and its guns commanded this capital, and our Government was trembling in the balance, "Oh! you cannot coerce a State!"

Pickler, speech in
the House of Repre-
sentatives (1893) As "calamity howlers" they outstrip all other men, whenever the people want an expansion of the currency. When we had the Sherman bill under consideration they came forward and

in the same tone as now preached calamity. They said that the nation would go to destruction if we adopted any of those propositions. Yet the Bland-Allison Act became a law; the Sherman Act became a law; and this Government prospered under both those measures. Yet we still have the same argument presented here today.

And the claim need not be *ad hominem*. It can just be inductive: the prediction has been made before and is always wrong. It's probably wrong again.

> One very remarkable thing is the striking family likeness between all these acts of aggression and annexation. We are always told that they are undertaken for the benefit of the people of the countries annexed; that the great body of the inhabitants are passionately in our favor and eager for our coming. We are assured that there will be very little occasion for fighting; let us send a few regiments, or two or three ships of war, and the people would crowd to welcome us, and fall down and embrace our knees with transports of gratitude and loyalty. We were told that this would be the case in the Transvaal and in Zululand. But the very reverse has always happened.

Richard, speech in the House of Commons (1886)

> We are told on this floor that a large standing army is dangerous to our liberties and will revolutionize our form of government. Mr. Chairman, I am now 61 years old, and all my life I have been hearing or reading of the many dangers to our liberties and Government either hanging over us or just a little ahead. When I was younger I was alarmed at the awful predictions of the men who saw the ruin of the United States just ahead, but now that I am older I laugh at them. The ruin of our country has always been just ahead ever since we started.

Gibson, speech in the House of Representatives (1899)

↠ *Too many claims.* Your adversaries make so many claims that some of them will no doubt be right. Maybe they scatter some fair points among many that aren't. Flagging this lets you acknowledge the good ones while reducing their force.

Woomer, speech
in the House of
Representatives
(1894)

He said so many things and wandered about so much that I was reminded of the old man who had the shaking palsy, showing his little son how to shoot a bird in a large, bushy-topped tree. He killed the bird, but his little son said: "No wonder, papa; you held the gun all over the tree." Mr. Walker held his gun all over the tree, and of course made some good points.

People sometimes make lots of predictions so that they can claim success no matter what happens. You can note this to head off wrongful admiration.

Mann, speech in
the House of
Representatives
(1916)

There may have been those who actually foresaw what was then actually coming, though it is very easy to prophesy in advance upon either side of a question and then claim that you are right if one of your prophecies comes true.

Making this point before the future arrives prepares the audience to be unimpressed later.

Saulsbury, speech
in the Senate
(1913)

Suppose these dire disasters so glibly predicted by Republican Senators do not happen. One says they may not happen at once, may not come for years. Another says that mills are closing and soup kettles being hung over the fires of public wrath and disappointment. We may be sure that whenever business trouble shall come, whatever its cause, all of it, even from business incapacity, will be attributed to Democratic misdeeds.

↦ *The revealing insult.* The other side has insulted you. Instead of arguing or retaliating, you ask why they *need* insults. Maybe it shows that a reasoned argument wasn't available. Who bothers with insults when they could be winning on the merits?

Mellish, speech
in the House of
Representatives
(1874)

A debater who resorts to irony, ridicule, or denunciation does so because he cannot afford to allow the positions of his antagonist to remain unanswered, and does not feel competent to refute them.

We all well understand that when a subject under discussion
elicits from its opponents nothing but epithets, it is reasonably
safe in the domain of logic.

Allen, speech in
the Senate
(1893)

It's also possible, and tempting, to add some condescension. An insult
is usually a blow to the status of the recipient. You turn it into a blow
against the status of its author.

I hope the House and those denounced will forgive the gentleman for these uncourteous and unparliamentary words. In
the heat of debate they were prompted by a sense of inability
to respond to our arguments; by the rage of impotence they
serve to fill a line in the Record which should have contained
an argument.

Turner, speech
in the House of
Representatives
(1877)

➻ *Nothing personal.* Pushing individual identities and personal trust
out of the dispute lowers the flame. Thus suppose the other side makes
a bad proposal. It depends on the trustworthiness of the people who
will carry it out. Those people are (perhaps) fine, but the proposal is
dangerous anyway. You need to separate the risks it creates from the
specific people involved. You can do this by restating the question at
a level that doesn't depend on the people involved, or by saying (or
assuming) that the people involved are great but that the problem
remains.

With me, Sir, it is not a personal question. I am willing
to admit that ministers, and members of parliament are as
good as any other men. I will even grant that they are better
than most. All I contend for is, that good as they may be,
they are men: and would they have us believe that they are
angels?

Mill, speech on
parliamentary
reform
(1824)

Why give to the President the power, without any cause or
emergency or crisis or exigency being in sight, to double the
Army practically at his will? Senators say, "Oh, you can trust
the President." We have trusted him. Congress is ready to
trust him again. It is not a question of trust in the President.

Butler, speech
in the Senate
(1901)

That is begging the question. It is child's talk. It is a flippant answer when a great principle is involved. It is an attempt to turn from a principle and make the issue a personal one.

8

Ethos

➤➤ *The display of modesty.* Your ethos, for rhetorical purposes, is your character. An ethical appeal is typically an attempt to persuade others by appealing to your credibility. Ethos can also refer to the character of your speech: it has more power if it's imbued with the qualities of character you can claim for yourself. Your own ethos is typically fortified by showing yourself to be humble, trustworthy, seeking the best for your audience, having the same values that they do, etc. This chapter thus considers various ways to position oneself in relation to the audience.

We begin with modesty. An apology for your meager abilities invites the audience to root for you, tells them to expect little, and prepares them to be impressed by anything more.

> I regret, I extremely regret, that my ability is so humble, my strength so feeble, my recollection so imperfect, as to render it impossible for me to give adequate expression to the feelings which inspire me. It is my fate, and I must submit to it.

Brinkerhoff, speech in the House of Representatives (1847)

Perhaps you *have* to go forward despite your limitations because your message is compelling.

> I am old and weak and at present unable to say more; but my feelings and indignation were too strong to have said less.

Chatham, speech in the House of Lords (1777)

A famous example of this sort of appeal was George Washington's speech at Newburgh in 1783, where he addressed conspirators planning a mutiny over their pay. After starting to read a supporting document, Washington reached for his glasses and said, "You must pardon me, for I have not only grown gray but almost blind in service to my country." Witnesses said that those assembled were moved to tears.

➻ *I beg your pardon.* Preparing the audience for more disappointment, this time with the substance of what you have to say: it's boring and you wish it weren't. Perhaps the argument you're about
to make will seem bland because it's such a plain statement of the
truth.

Burke, *Speech on Conciliation with the Colonies* (1775)

My plan, therefore, being formed upon the most simple
grounds imaginable, may disappoint some people, when they
hear it. It has nothing to recommend it to the pruriency of
curious ears.

Douglass, speech at London (1846)

I will take it for granted that you know something about the
degrading influences of slavery, and that you will not expect
great things from me this evening, but simply such facts as I
may be able to advance immediately in connection with my
own experience of slavery.

Maybe the subject makes monotony hard to avoid.

Mill, speech on primogeniture (1826)

It is probable that some gentlemen may not relish this pounds,
shillings and pence mode of reasoning, this application of
the rules of arithmetic to the computing of human feelings.
They may think all such calculations very dull; I cannot help
it. They will readily believe me when I declare that I should
have been very glad if what I say had been at once amusing
and useful.

Naturally the point can be made after one speaks rather than before:
the fatigue the audience now feels shouldn't be charged to your account. You might have been compelled to go on at length because
you're the underdog.

Burke, *Speech on Conciliation with the Colonies* (1775)

I have, indeed, tired you by a long discourse; but this is
the misfortune of those to whose influence nothing will be
conceded, and who must win every inch of their ground by
argument.

The best excuse of all: you're forced to be tedious by the other side
(so the audience should blame *them* if they're bored).

I beg pardon for having detained you so long; but your Lord-ships will be so good as to observe that no business ever was covered with more folds of iniquitous artifice than this which is now brought before you.

Burke, speech in the impeachment of Warren Hastings (1789)

➳ *I can't compete.* Those last tactics can be comparative: don't expect things from me as impressive as what you've heard from the other side or will soon. Noting the advantages of the adversary helps inoculate the audience against their charms.

I should be afraid to express myself in this manner, especially in the face of such a formidable array of ability as is now drawn up before me, composed of the ancient household troops of that side of the House and the new recruits from this, if the matter were not clear and indisputable. Nothing but truth could give me this firmness; but plain truth and clear evidence can be beat down by no ability.

Burke, *Speech on American Taxation* (1774)

I feel that I labor under great disadvantages in following gentlemen whose eloquent and pathetic appeals have affected the feelings and commanded the attention of the Committee; whilst, on my part, I have nothing to offer them but the plain-est kind of argument.

Barbour, speech in the House of Representatives (1819)

You can make the irony more open by praising the fine style of your adversaries in contrast to the substance of what they say.

I think I can afford to let the speech I delivered yesterday and the speech delivered by my colleague to-day go side by side to the people without a single word in reply to what he has said. His speech was so eloquent, so argumentative, so fanciful, that it would be impossible for me to come up to the level of it. The eloquence I cannot match; the argument requires no refutation; and it would be a pity to disturb the fancy.

Schurz, speech in the Senate (1870)

➳ *Prepare to be offended.* Bracing the audience to be shocked or dis-pleased. (A Greek expression for this is *prodiorthosis.*) This can gain you some credit for candor in saying what nobody wants to hear. It can also produce suspense and interest: now everyone wants to know what candid or shocking thing is coming.

Churchill, speech in the House of Commons (1938) I will, therefore, begin by saying the most unpopular and most unwelcome thing. I will begin by saying what everybody would like to ignore or forget but which must nevertheless be stated, namely, that we have sustained a total and unmitigated defeat, and that France has suffered even more than we have.

A warning can preempt bad reactions. Shock depends on surprise (it's hard to have such a feeling when you're watching for it), and now the surprise is gone. It can also provoke defiance in the listeners—a desire to show that they *aren't* shocked.

Douglass, My Bondage and My Freedom (1855) I shall here make a profession of faith which may shock some, offend others, and be dissented from by all. It is this: Within the bounds of his just earnings, I hold that the slave is fully justified in helping himself to the gold and silver, and the best apparel of his master, or that of any other slaveholder; and that such taking is not stealing in any just sense of that word.

And a warning can also be a scare tactic against people who might be tempted to take offense: anyone offended will be part of a class to which nobody wants to belong.

Roebuck, speech in the House of Commons (1865) I have no doubt that what I am going to say will give great offence to certain parties in this House, because I am about to attack and to expose a great sham. I have often found that a great sham has very ardent supporters.

A warning may serve, finally, as a frame for the picture about to be shown. It can tell the audience how they *should* feel. *Prepare to be shocked*, in this usage, is a self-fulfilling prophecy: *I'm counting on you to be shocked.*

Douglass, speech at London (1846) Allow me to speak plainly. Although it is harrowing to your feelings, it is necessary that the facts of the case should be stated. We have in the United States slave-breeding states.

→► *Disclaimers of emotional appeals.* Telling the audience that you're only appealing to reason.

> It is not my view to rouse your passions, I only wish to excite you to, and assist you in, a cool and deliberate discussion of the subject, to urge you to behave like sensible freemen.

Cato II (1787)

> I appeal to reason alone. I will attempt no excitement; I will use no *ad captandum* topics; I will refer myself to no popular impressions. On facts, and on facts only I rely.

Buxton, speech in the House of Commons (1831)

He's referring to a type of argument known more fully as *ad captandum vulgus* (to ensnare the mob): an appeal to the emotions or similar cheap trick to capture the imagination of the masses.

Sometimes *I'm not appealing to emotion* is said right after, or right before, an appeal to emotion. The point isn't really to keep feeling out of the case. The point is to cover it up.

> I do not wish, Mr. Chairman, to address myself to the feelings of gentlemen; I do not wish to enlist their passions, or I might say more. I wish a verdict in favor of the officers of the Revolution and their descendants from their sound sense and deliberate judgment only. They ask no favors.

Muhlenberg, speech in the House of Representatives (1836)

→► *Identification with the audience.* It helps your relationship with the audience if you belong to the same tribe.

> I am a Northern man. I was born at the North, educated at the North, have lived all my days at the North. I know five hundred Northern men to one Southern man. My sympathies, all my sympathies, my love of liberty for all mankind, of every color, are the same as yours.

Webster, speech at Buffalo (1851)

> I am one of you. You can not be against me without being against yourself.

Nelson, speech in the House of Representatives (1918)

Of course you might *not* be one of them in a literal sense, and then need to rely on interests that you share.

Tallmadge, speech
in the House of
Representatives
(1809)

We all have the same end in view, the good of our common country; but we have different ways of pursuing it. We are all embarked on board the same national ship, and must swim or sink together.

Settle, speech in the
House of Represen-
tatives (1897)

Our interests are identical with your interests; our peace is bound up with your peace.

↣ *Flattery*. Saying that you have high expectations of the audience. Listeners like someone who has a good opinion of them. It also raises the chance that they will act in the generous way you expect.

Lee, *Letters from the
Federal Farmer* VI
(1787)

I leave you, in all cases, to decide by a careful examination of my works, upon the weight of my arguments, the propriety of my remarks, the uprightness of my intentions, and the extent of my candor—I presume I am writing to a man of candor and reflection, and not to an ardent, peevish, or impatient man.

Flattery can also prepare the way for a harsh assessment.

Douglass, letter
to Thomas Auld
(1848)

I know you to be a man of some intelligence, and can readily determine the precise estimate which I entertain of your character. I may therefore indulge in language which may seem to others indirect and ambiguous, and yet be quite well understood by yourself.

(Douglass was writing to his former owner.) Flattery can be used, too, to cover up deficiencies, such as a failure to explain.

Corrance, speech
in the House of
Commons
(1868)

The Solicitor General moved its rejection; but he assigned no reason for this, or, if he did, one of this class—I think I have heard such from counsel when a particularly stupid jury was addressed—"Gentlemen, you are so intelligent I needn't enlighten you."

↣ *Disclaiming an audience*. Saying that your claims *aren't* addressed to a certain set of people. You're asking the audience to settle in your camp.

If there are any men at the South who think as some of our Northern men thought in former days, that our country is "too big for union," and "that Federalism is founded in mistake," (the sentiments of Fisher Ames, published by his friends,) to them I have nothing to say, and of them I have nothing to hope.

Clay, speech in the Senate (1838)

You might mean just what you say: *if you think X, then you don't belong here*—where some people in the audience may well think X and are at risk of departure. You're pressuring them to get in line with your view by respectfully saying that they aren't welcome otherwise. This also shows a fine lack of interest in pleasing everyone.

If there be any man who does not believe that slavery is wrong in the three aspects which I have mentioned, or in any one of them, that man is misplaced, and ought to leave us; while on the other hand, if there be any man in the Republican party who is impatient over the necessity springing from its actual presence, and is impatient of the constitutional guarantees thrown around it, and would act in disregard of these, he too is misplaced, standing with us. He will find his place somewhere else; for we have a due regard, so far as we are capable of understanding them, for all these things.

Lincoln, debate with Stephen Douglas at Quincy (1858)

Or the people you excuse from the room can be the ones you regard *favorably*. Perhaps you're going to give a scolding but exempt those who don't deserve it. Or you single out individuals for specific pardon in a display of evenhandedness.

The House of Commons has pledged itself to a repeal of the duty on paper. An abstract Resolution on the subject, moved by my right hon. Friend the President of the Board of Trade, was passed, the only real opposition to it having been offered by my hon. Friend the Member for Norfolk, the only consistent man on his own side of the House. I have, therefore, nothing to say to him. He is a fine fossil remain.

Osborne, speech in the House of Commons (1861)

↠ *The high road.* You won't stoop to the methods of your adversaries. This puts you in a more appealing light and lets you take shots at them in passing.

Mill,
*The British
Constitution*
(1826)

I might, too, have followed the example of the honorable opener, and been the indiscriminate and unblushing eulogist of things as they are.... Practice renders men singularly perfect in these things, and after a twelvemonth's tuition under the honorable gentleman, I have little doubt that I should even have rivalled my master. But I leave these weapons to those who like them, or to those who can hope to be paid for them.

Bruen, speech
in the House
of Commons
(1836)

Sir, after several disappointments I eagerly seize the first opportunity of claiming from the House that indulgence which it usually grants to Members who have the misfortune to be placed in a situation similar to that in which I stand—if, indeed, any Member ever was the subject of such foul and false attacks—coarser epithets might be applied, but I refrain from following a vile example.

9

Humility

➤➤ *The chance of error.* We turn to humility—not so much the personal humility just shown (*please excuse my limited abilities …*), but displays of intellectual humility and requests for it. Our first theme is acknowledgment of the chance of error. Everyone is wrong often enough, and reminders about this can encourage second thoughts.

> So numerous indeed and so powerful are the causes which serve to give a false bias to the judgment, that we, upon many occasions, see wise and good men on the wrong as well as on the right side of questions of the first magnitude to society. This circumstance, if duly attended to, would furnish a lesson of moderation to those who are ever so much persuaded of their being in the right in any controversy.

Hamilton, *Federalist* 1 (1787)

> In 1847 there was a great Parliamentary duel between Macaulay and John Bright. Macaulay vainly endeavored to convince Mr. Bright that it was a good thing that the State should take some responsibility for the education of the people. Mr. Bright remained entirely unconvinced, and set his views forth in a memorable speech. Nobody holds those views now, and I only refer to the matter as a curious object lesson. When we remember that his were the opinions held by a vigorous section of a great Party within recent times, it should make us a little cautious as to what is colloquially called "cocksureness" about the permanent validity and weight of some political nostrum or some popular cry.

Davidson, speech in the House of Lords (1906)

Or you admit that *you* might be wrong. When you overcome your doubts in the end, or resolve them this way rather than that way, it encourages the audience to do the same.

Root, speech in
the Senate
(1913)

I realize, sir, that I may be wrong. I have often been wrong. I realize that the gentlemen who have taken a different view regarding the meaning of this treaty may be right. I do not think so. But their ability and fairness of mind would make it idle for me not to entertain the possibility.

⤳ *Great vs. small.* You can adjust the perspective of the audience by putting great things next to small ones. The usual great things are important values, mighty institutions, or whole generations of people. The little ones are us here and now. The difference can encourage generosity and other virtues.

Sheffield, speech
in the House of
Representatives
(1862)

It matters little whether you or I may die today or ten years hence; but it is a matter of consequence to the civilized world, not only to men of this generation, but to the men of all future times, that this Government should not be overthrown.

Reagan, speech
in the Senate
(1890)

However much importance we may attach to ourselves and to the parts we play in life, when we have joined our friends on the other shore the world will move on, and our own country will continue its march to the great destiny which awaits it, the same as if we had never lived, and we shall soon be re-membered no more. This is not a cheerful reflection, except for the promise beyond the grave for those who have done well in this life. But if such reflections shall teach us greater humility, cause us to be more just, make us more charitable to one another, and lead to a broader philanthropy, they are not without their uses.

As a reason to disregard insults and the people who offer them:

La Follette,
speech in
the Senate
(1909)

Great ideas thrust themselves into the arena; they are an-tagonistic; one is right and one is wrong; and as the contest goes on the men who are drawn into that contest are but the instruments in those great ideas of evolution in the progress of the race. Mr. President, does anybody suppose that I am to turn aside in this debate to answer some petty and contempt-ible attack upon me personally?

As a way to throw emphasis on the works and sacrifices of others, and on the obligations they create:

> The world will little note, nor long remember, what we say here, but it can never forget what they did here.

Lincoln, Gettysburg Address (1863)

↦ *Temporal humility*. Many arguments call for judgments about what was said and done long ago. The views of people in earlier times will often seem backward. The same will seem true of current times once they are past.

> Ages are no more infallible than individuals; every age having held many opinions which subsequent ages have deemed not only false but absurd; and it is as certain that many opinions, now general, will be rejected by future ages, as it is that many, once general, are rejected by the present.

Mill, *On Liberty* (1859)

Examples of sound cautions against the use of modern standards to judge people who lived earlier:

> As we would have our descendants judge us, so ought we to judge our fathers. In order to form a correct estimate of their merits, we ought to place ourselves in their situation, to put out of our minds, for a time, all that knowledge which they, however eager in the pursuit of truth, could not have, and which we, however negligent we may have been, could not help having. It was not merely difficult, but absolutely impossible, for the best and greatest of men, two hundred years ago, to be what a very commonplace person in our days may easily be, and indeed must necessarily be. But it is too much that the benefactors of mankind, after having been reviled by the dunces of their own generation for going too far, should be reviled by the dunces of the next generation for not going far enough.

Macaulay, *Mackintosh's History* (1835)

> Men must be judged by their own knowledge at the time they acted, not by ours; by the circumstances with which they were surrounded, and not by those which environ us. What may appear unfathomable problems to the wise men of one

Clark, speech in the House of Representatives (1899)

generation may be clear as crystal to even the dullest of the
succeeding generation.

→→*Mea culpa.* When we don't agree with other people, the natural assumption for any of us is that they're wrong. It's judicious to
think about the opposite possibility: *we're* wrong, or slow, or don't
understand. You can express this by asking the audience to consider
where the greater chance of error lies: on their side or on the side
of whoever or whatever they might be inclined to attack. That last
group can include people and institutions that have earned some
deference.

Burke, *An Appeal*
from the New to
the Old Whigs
(1791)

[Great critics] have taught us one essential rule.... It is this:
that, if ever we should find ourselves disposed not to admire
those writers or artists (Livy and Virgil, for instance, Raphael
or Michael Angelo) whom all the learned had admired, not
to follow our own fancies, but to study them, until we know
how and what we ought to admire; and if we cannot arrive
at this combination of admiration with knowledge, rather to
believe that we are dull than that the rest of the world has
been imposed on. It is as good a rule, at least, with regard to
this admired constitution.

The humility can also be made personal between the speaker and
listener.

Houston, speech in
the House of
Representatives
(1856)

I am very unfortunate in my efforts to make the gentleman
from Ohio understand me; but I am sure the fault must be
mine.

A (more) facetious version of this idea from Swift:

Swift, *Tatler* no.
59 (1709)

I hope, Sir, you will not take this amiss: I can assure you, I
have a profound respect for you; which makes me write this,
with the same disposition with which Longinus bids us read
Homer and Plato. When in reading, says he, any of those cel-
ebrated authors, we meet with a passage to which we cannot
well reconcile our reasons, we ought firmly to believe, that
were those great wits present to answer for themselves, we

should to our wonder be convinced, that we only are guilty
of the mistakes we before attributed to them.

↦ *Speaking for myself.* Saying that someone else's behavior isn't
something you would do yourself or that it would embarrass you.
This doesn't quite point the finger directly; you confine your claim
to your own comfort. Of course the implication is that your adversaries should feel as you do—or would, if their sensibilities weren't
so debauched—but that's formally left to inference.

> How does it comport with candor and honesty, to be con-
> tinually crying against the other party, for that which they
> themselves are most guilty of? Sir, were I to be guilty of such
> a course, I should blush to meet my constituents, or to appear
> before an intelligent American public.

Bynum, speech in the House of Representatives (1838)

> That is no explanation at all; or, at any rate, it is an explanation
> which I myself would be ashamed to be made the organ of in
> any assembly of gentlemen.

Reed, speech in the House of Commons (1887)

When using this idea, it's common to say that you aren't presuming
to judge. *They can do as they like, but for my part....*

> I will not call gentlemen traitors who vote contrary to what
> I do. I will not; it would be unparliamentary; it might be
> uncharitable and unjust; for I am always willing to make al-
> lowance for differences of sentiment. But this I may say, that
> were I to do it, I should regard myself as a traitor.

Brinkerhoff, speech in the House of Representatives (1847)

↦ *Let the experienced judge.* Saying that we shouldn't pass judgment
on others unless we've gone through the same things. The usual point
is that critics are underestimating someone else's suffering because
they're standing too far from it.

> But if you say, you can still pass the violations over, then I
> ask, Hath your house been burnt? Hath your property been
> destroyed before your face! Are your wife and children des-
> titute of a bed to lie on, or bread to live on? Have you lost a
> parent or a child by their hands, and yourself the ruined and

Paine, *Common Sense* (1776)

wretched survivor! If you have not, then are you not a judge of those who have.

Blanton, speech in the House of Representatives (191)

We members of Congress who are in full possession of our faculties, and who have never suffered physical injury, who have perfect our hands and arms, our feet and legs, our eyes to see, who can walk and run and jump as we will, are not in a position to see through the eyes of the cripple, destitute of funds and property, looking the cold world squarely in the face: without backing or assistance, and in competition with it must earn his daily bread.

In a sense these appeals are highly reasonable: if you haven't experienced X, perhaps you *don't* know what it's like. Maybe you should learn more before you make a callous judgment. On the other hand, policies routinely are made (as they must be) by people who haven't themselves gone through whatever the stakes involve. Disqualifying someone from debate in that circumstance should be done consistently if it's done at all, and few would do it consistently.

➤➤*Let the listener judge.* Leaving judgment about a point to the audience. The deference to them is flattering and sounds like fair play.

Lincoln, debate with Stephen Douglas at Quincy (1856)

I maintain that you may take Judge Douglas's quotations from my Chicago speech, and from my Charleston speech, and the Galesburg speech,—in his speech of today,—and compare them over, and I am willing to trust them with you upon his proposition that they show rascality or double-dealing. I deny that they do.

Jenckes, speech in the House of Representatives (1870)

The sophistry and its refutation go forth together. Either he misunderstands the meaning of the language I have used with much care, or I do. Let those who read judge.

Or you count on the listeners to reach the right conclusion because you can't bear to belabor it.

Cobbett, *Remarks on the Blunderbuss* (1796)

An accusation may be so completely absurd and impudent, that no one can attempt to refute it, without sinking, in some degree, towards a level with the accuser; and as I have no inclination to do this, I leave the present one to be answered by the indignation of the reader.

10

Magnanimity

↦ *Willing to lose.* You want to lose if you're wrong. Hoping that right will prevail earns good will from the audience and shows due modesty (since it acknowledges that you could be wrong; cf. p. 67) but also confidence (since you don't seem too worried about it).

Hamilton, speech at New York Ratifying Convention (1788)

However weak our country may be, I hope we never shall sacrifice our liberties. If, therefore, on a full and candid discussion, the proposed system shall appear to have that tendency, for God's sake, let us reject it! But let us not mistake words for things, nor accept doubtful surmises as the evidence of truth.

Venable, speech in the House of Representatives (1852)

When have the rights of the West not been respected by gentlemen from other portions of the Union? I ask the gentleman to answer my question, for I should loathe myself if I supposed myself capable of voting for or against a bill because it was to benefit any particular section of the country. I want to put the history of the country right. I want to be rebuked if I am wrong.

Stewart, speech in the House of Representatives (1884)

I am so sure that truth is on my side of this question that instead of being afraid I absolutely court an investigation of it. I am willing to know the truth about it. If my party cannot be sustained by the truth, then I for one say it ought not to be sustained.

↦ *The principle of charity.* Taking on the other side's case at its best, not its worst; addressing the problems that are hardest for you, not easiest. This is good intellectual etiquette. It shows fearlessness and satisfies onlookers. An example from Mill:

Mill, *On Liberty* (1859)

In order more fully to illustrate the mischief of denying a hearing to opinions because we, in our own judgment, have condemned them, it will be desirable to fix down the discussion to a concrete case; and I choose, by preference, the cases which are least favorable to me—in which the argument against freedom of opinion, both on the score of truth and on that of utility, is considered the strongest.

Mill went on to talk about the most basic moral beliefs; he said they were the best cases for his antagonist because "he will be sure to say (and many who have no desire to be unfair will say it internally), Are these the doctrines which you do not deem sufficiently certain to be taken under the protection of law?" An application from debates about slavery:

> Let us now take the most favorable case for the slaveholder— say that of our mortal enemy, taken in the very act of a malicious attempt upon our property, our liberty, or our life even. Surely, if we have Divine authority to enslave our fellow creature in any case, this would be that case. But no; not for a moment.

Wade, speech in the House of Representatives (1860)

Robert Southey once said that governments are made most secure by training the public in religious observance. Macaulay's reply:

> Let us take then the case of all others most favorable to Mr. Southey's argument. Let us take that form of religion which he holds to be the purest, the system of the Arminian part of the Church of England. Let us take the form of government which he most admires and regrets, the government of England in the time of Charles the First. Would he wish to see a closer connection between Church and State than then existed?

Macaulay, *Southey's Colloquies on Society* (1830)

Macaulay went on to observe that Charles the First was beheaded. (Southey might not have agreed that this was his best case.)

↠ *Half charity.* Taking a charitable view (or saying you are) sometimes makes things tougher for your adversary. It emphasizes how bad the facts really are; it makes a harsh judgment sound restrained.

> I am willing from a strain of candor to admit that this author speaks at random; that he is only slovenly and inaccurate, and not fallacious.

Burke, *The Present State of the Nation* (1769)

Mason, speech in the Senate (1803)

The gentlemen pant for war, and care not for what or with whom; they pursue war with a deplorable infatuation, and the most charitable construction that can be put upon their conduct is, that they know not what they do.

Or you show confidence in the other side's good intentions, but in a way that creates doubt and calls for watchfulness. You say *I'm sure they aren't ...* but imply *they'd better not be ...*

Hamilton, speech at New York Ratifying Convention (1788)

Sir, we hear constantly a great deal which is rather calculated to awake our passions, and create prejudices, than to conduct us to the truth, and teach us our real interests. I do not suppose this to be the design of the gentlemen. Why, then, are we told so often of an aristocracy?

Out of a similar instinct for half-charity, you can hope that something you heard wasn't really said—that you misunderstood it, or that it wasn't said by whoever seemed to say it.

Crawford, speech in the Senate (1811)

I hope I misunderstood the gentleman; if I am mistaken it will afford me great pleasure to be corrected, because the declaration made a very strong impression upon my mind, and excited the most unpleasant sensations.

Macaulay, *Sadler's Law of Population* (1830)

If these lines are not Mr. Sadler's, we heartily beg his pardon for our suspicion—a suspicion which, we acknowledge, ought not to be lightly entertained of any human being.

↠ *Passing over minutiae.* Putting aside criticism of the other side's minor failures. This calls attention to the major ones and makes them sound large.

Brutus I (1787)

There are many objections, of small moment, of which I shall take no notice—perfection is not to be expected in any thing that is the production of man—and if I did not in my conscience believe that this scheme was defective in the fundamental principles—in the foundation upon which a free and equal government must rest—I would hold my peace.

It is not my design to dwell upon every objection that has been started, either by Franklin or the town-meeting; I shall content myself with answering those only in which they discover an extraordinary degree of patriotic presumption or dishonesty.

Cobbett, *A Little Plain English* (1795)

I will not dwell upon his minor peccadilloes, but shall only allude to those by which he is continually offending.

Sheil, *Francis Blackburne* (c. 1827)

↠ *High expectations.* You expect the best of the other side (or of someone else), and use disappointment as a threat or punishment.

I bow humbly before the genius of Ulysses S. Grant. I recognize him as the greatest, broadest, wisest intellect of this generation. I cannot believe that he will degenerate into a puppet to be pulled by wires held in the hands of the gentleman from Illinois.

Donnelly, speech in the House of Representatives (1868)

Or you say: you're disappointing me; won't you stop? This can take the edge off a criticism by putting it in a flattering way.

The gentleman makes the argument *ad hominem* that if you do this for the citizens of New Mexico, why do you not make the same grant to other Territories? It is unworthy of the gentleman from Texas. It is unworthy of such an able lawyer as he is.

Elkins, speech in the House of Representatives (1876)

The difference between what you expected and what you got can also give a criticism more bite: your adversary has shown that your expectations weren't realistic.

Even the cultivated, scholarly, and talented member from Virginia used such demagogical claptrap in speaking of the manufacturers of quinine. I expected better things from him, and was, I confess, somewhat surprised; but I console myself with the philosophical reflection that we are all human, and nature crops out occasionally no matter how much we may have done to conceal it.

Neal, speech in the House of Representatives (1883)

⤞ *The appeal to common ends.* Recognizing that both sides want the same things in the end. (Cf. p. 64.) This can lower the temperature by suggesting that everyone means well and just differs on tactics. This often means stating the shared purpose at a high level of generality.

Kearns, speech in the House of Representatives (1916)

If I happen not to agree with you, you ought not charge me with all these political and mercenary crimes. If you do not agree with me, I should not charge you as being spineless to the degree that you would not, if need be, defend your homes against any and all invaders, and neither do I. The one is just as patriotic and loyal, just as courageous and brave as the other. We would all attain the same peaceful end, but by a different method.

This type of claim can also be used in a way less conciliatory. You establish or concede that both sides are starting from the same place, but use that point of departure to argue about the best means to the end. I like X as much as the next person, but—etc.

Mason, speech at Virginia Ratifying Convention (1788)

I solemnly declare that no man is a greater friend to a firm union of the American states than I am; but, sir, if this great end can be obtained without hazarding the rights of the people, why should we recur to such dangerous principles?

Stephen, *Liberty, Equality, Fraternity* (1873)

In a certain sense I am myself a utilitarian. That is to say, I think that from the nature of the case some external standard must always be supplied by which moral rules may be tested; and happiness is the most significant and least misleading word that can be employed for that purpose.... To say, however, that moral speculation or legislation presupposes on the part of the moralist or legislator a desire to promote equally the happiness of every person affected by his system or his law is, I think, incorrect.

⤞ *Looking forward.* You can change the tone of a debate by moving it into a different tense. Arguments about the past naturally focus on blame. Talking about the future makes agreement easier to find.

My right hon. Friend shakes his head, and says they are not responsible for the acts of a previous Administration. Sir, it is not so much with reference to who is to blame for the past, but to those who are responsible for the future, that I ask these questions. What are to be your future institutions?

Ellice, speech in the House of Commons (1845)

The question with us now is not one of ancestors and how we got here, but it is a question of vital importance and interest to determine where we are going and how we will get there.

Focht, speech in the House of Representatives (1916)

We have a condition confronting us, and the question is, How are we to remedy it? Not "Who is to blame?" Not "Why he or it is to blame?" But the blame being here, and the condition existing, the question is, "What is the best thing to do under the circumstances?"

Dewalt, speech in the House of Representatives (1918)

11

Empathy and Related Uses of Imagination

➤➤ *Distinguishing people from positions*. It's easy to resent people who get in one's way, and to regard people with contrary views as villains.

Hume, *A Treatise of Human Nature* (1740)

It seldom happens, that we do not think an enemy vicious, and can distinguish betwixt his opposition to our interest and real villainy or baseness.

Black, argument in *Ex parte Milligan* (1866)

Public officers of any Government, when they are engaged in a severe struggle to retain their places, become bitter and ferocious, and hate those who oppose them, even in the most legitimate way, with a rancor which they never exhibit toward actual crime.

Sometimes a kind use of the imagination can reduce the severity of this disease in human affairs. You're furious at the other side for using tactic X; so imagine your side using the same tactic, or something similar, and ask if you'd be as indignant. You can tactfully invite others to consider the same question.

Bayard, speech in the Senate (1880)

It may be adopted as a wise rule in arriving at an estimate of men and their careers, to precede a formation of judgment of an antagonist, by the inquiry, "How would we have regarded the action of our adversary, had his energies been exerted in favor of the party and policies with which we ourselves have been allied?" May it not well be, that seen thus through a medium of sympathetic *ends*, the *means* of attainment, would have appeared somewhat less objectionable?

➤➤ *Change of shoes*. It likewise helps to imagine being in the shoes of others (and to ask them to think about the reverse). Many little variations on this theme are possible, depending on whether it's used in the first, second, or third person, and which side is being invited to change places with the other. These experiments are especially nice when the shoes that get switched belong to someone in a position of power.

> In reply to the principle the Senator enunciates, that a man who lives in a city should have a larger salary than one who lives in the country, I do not think he would like it very well if the same rule were made applicable to members of Congress.

Logan, speech in the Senate (1886)

> We are informed that when a prisoner's beard is wrongfully cut off in a gaol it is only for the purpose of trimming. I would like to see the process applied to right hon. Gentlemen opposite and see how they would like it.

Healy, speech in the House of Commons (1889)

The mood of the point can turn from speculation to accusation: the people doing this or that would complain loudly if they were at the receiving end of the same.

> Ah, Sir, my hon. Friend would not have been caught napping if a Tory Government had proposed such extravagant measures as he now leaves for the salutary correction of the House of Lords. We should then have had no voting that black was white, but we should have had debate upon debate, and division upon division, and every clause would have been sifted, and every fraction of every charge contested, with unshrinking pertinacity, and the lists of majorities and minorities would have been circulated in red and black ink throughout every district in the empire.

Sinclair, speech in the House of Commons (1836)

A variation: we're just reacting as you would in our position. Thus Paine's comment to the British:

> The Congress have as much right to command the king and Parliament in London to desist from legislation, as they or you have to command the Congress. Only suppose how laughable such an edict would appear from us, and then, in that merry mood, do but turn the tables upon yourself, and you will see how your proclamation is received here.

Paine, *The American Crisis* (1783)

Lincoln's defense of a vote that he cast against the Mexican-American War:

Lincoln, letter to William Herndon (1848)

You fear that you and I disagree about the war. I regret this, not because of any fear we shall remain disagreed after you have read this letter, but because if you misunderstand I fear other good friends may also.... I will stake my life that if you had been in my place you would have voted just as I did.

Douglass's recollection of the wife of his owner:

Douglass, *My Bondage and My Freedom* (1855)

We were both victims to the same overshadowing evil—she, as mistress, I, as slave. I will not censure her harshly; she cannot censure me, for she knows I speak but the truth, and have acted in my opposition to slavery, just as she herself would have acted, in a reverse of circumstances.

Turning around the train of thought: we would feel as they do if we were in *their* shoes. This can be a salutary appeal to those on your own side—a way to call for cool heads to prevail.

Lincoln, debate with Stephen Douglas at Peoria (1854)

Before proceeding let me say that I think I have no prejudice against the Southern people. They are just what we would be in their situation. If slavery did not now exist among them, they would not introduce it. If it did now exist among us, we should not instantly give it up. This I believe of the masses North and South.

Bagehot, *The English Constitution* (1894)

He is sure to leave upon the colony the feeling that they have a ruler who only half knows them, and does not so much as half care for them. We hardly appreciate this common feeling in our colonies, because *we* appoint *their* sovereign; but we should understand it in an instant if, by a political metamorphosis, the choice were turned the other way—if *they* appointed *our* sovereign. We should then say at once, "How is it possible a man from New Zealand can understand England?"

↠ *Distributing virtue evenly.* Another step like the ones just shown: acknowledging that the people on your side aren't better than those on the other. You can use this gracious point to set up a claim about the other side that might be taken the wrong way. You start, in effect, by making clear that it's nothing personal.

> I do not intend, Mr. Speaker, to indulge in any bravado, or boasting, or threatening about what the North is going to do. I do not propose to draw any comparison between the prowess of the South and that of the North. There is bravery in both sections of the Union; chivalry in both sections; prowess in both sections. We are a brave people. It is not a question whether the North is to whip the South or the South to whip the North. I am not going to discuss that. I have no taste for that sort of discussion.

Farnsworth, speech in the House of Representatives (1861)

(He was arguing that secession would be suicide for the southern states.)

> I am not so narrow as to suppose that all the political virtue is on one side and all the political vice on the other. Indeed, I see some men who are so brilliant and attractive that I would like to bring them into the Democratic party. I think they would improve any organization. And we have some who, bad as it is, could still make the Republican party a little worse.

Bailey, speech in the Senate (1902)

(He was about to say that the Republican party was doing a bad thing.)

> I have no sort of sympathy for any man who thinks for one moment that a man who is a citizen of the United States is for that reason any wiser intellectually, any better morally, any stronger physically than a subject of the Kaiser or the Czar or the King of Great Britain, or per se than even a subject of the Sultan of Turkey.

Williams, speech in the Senate (1914)

(He was arguing to restrict immigration.)

You can use this pattern to criticize others who *do* imagine that their side consists of finer people than the other side. It probably isn't true.

Hamilton,
Objections and
Answers Respecting
the Administration
(1792)

They assume to themselves, and to those who think with them, infallibility. Take their words for it, they are the only honest men in the community. But compare the tenor of men's lives, and at least as large a portion of virtuous and independent characters will be found among those whom they malign as among themselves.

Mann, speech in the
House of Represen-
tatives (1914)

I suspect the motives of any gentleman when he construes a contract, holding up his hands in holy horror and saying, "Watch me, I am honorable, other men are dishonorable."

↠ *Consider the circumstances.* Another related idea. When people do bad things (or good ones), we easily think it was because of their personal qualities—they have bad character, etc. It can be a useful corrective to point out the force of circumstances in producing such results.

Williams,
speech in the
Senate
(1916)

Whenever any people anywhere begin to inquire into fundamentals—whenever people begin to question what has traditionally been held to be fundamental in human, political, or social conduct—those people are apt to go to extremes; and if you flatter yourselves that they do it because they are French or because they are Mexicans or because they are something else, you flatter yourself with little cause. You, yourself, under the same circumstances would probably or might possibly do the same thing. Your so-called civilization is about skin deep.

When Jewish people weren't allowed to hold various political offices in England, the rules were defended on the ground that Jews were less loyal to the country than Christians. Macaulay rejected the premise, but also used our current theme; he said that Jewish people had the same attitude you would expect of anyone who was treated the same way.

Macaulay, *Civil*
Disabilities of the
Jews (1831)

They are precisely what any sect, what any class of men, treated as they have been treated, would have been. If all the red-haired people in Europe had, during centuries, been outraged and oppressed, banished from this place, imprisoned in that, deprived of their money, deprived of their teeth, convicted of the most improbable crimes on the feeblest evidence, dragged at horses' tails, hanged, tortured, burned alive, if, when manners became milder, they had still been subject to debasing restrictions and exposed to vulgar insults, locked up in particular streets in some countries, pelted and ducked by the rabble in others, excluded every where from magistracies and honors, what would be the patriotism of gentlemen with red hair?

↦ *Blame yourself.* The opposite mistake is also possible, and is common when looking at ourselves: excusing bad acts by thinking that we just did what anyone would have done under the circumstances. We're always the most sympathetic characters in our own stories. Misjudgments made under this heading or the previous one are instances of what cognitive psychologists would now call attribution error.

No man ever answered in his own mind (except in the agonies of conscience or of repentance, in which latter case he throws the imputation from himself in another way) to the abstract idea of a *murderer*. He may have killed a man in self-defense, or "in the trade of war," or to save himself from starving, or in revenge for an injury, but always "so as with a difference," or from mixed and questionable motives. The individual, in reckoning with himself, always takes into the account the considerations of time, place, and circumstance, and never makes out a case of unmitigated, unprovoked villainy, of "pure defecated evil" against himself.

Hazlitt,
*On the Knowledge
of Character*
(1821)

Self-serving errors like these can also be made collectively.

This would have left a rankling wound in the hearts of the people, who knew they had failed in the accomplishment of their wishes, but who, like the rest of mankind in all ages, would impute the blame to anything rather than to their own proceedings.

Burke, *Letter
to a Noble Lord*
(1796)

II

Inference and Fallacy

WE TURN to logic and kindred topics. The chapters to come will consider inferences—how they're formed, and fallacies and other mistakes that can make them unsound. This section also looks at additional ways to test the soundness of a principle: how it responds under stress and whether it leads to mischief practically or conceptually. And finally we'll see arguments about whether a principle and its maker are consistent, and whether they need to be.

12

Deduction and Induction

➤➤ *Syllogisms.* A syllogism is a form of deductive reasoning with three parts: a major premise, a minor premise, and a conclusion. The major premise is a general statement; the minor premise is a specific one. Together they produce a conclusion. To borrow the stock example introduced in these words by Mill:

> All men are mortal.
> Socrates is a man.
> Socrates is mortal.

That example doesn't illustrate well why anyone might care about syllogisms, but it shows roughly how they work. The first part—the major premise—states a rule, principle, or generalization. It contains two terms and relates them to each other. Then the minor premise locates a particular subject within the rule; it also contains two terms. In this way a third claim is produced—a conclusion, which might be something not previously understood and appears to be a new piece of knowledge. In fact deductive reasoning can't quite deliver new knowledge; it unfolds the knowledge already contained in the premises, but latent.

To note some other terminology for those who wish it: *Socrates* is the subject of the syllogism—the thing under discussion. *Mortal* is the predicate—the property ascribed to the subject, or the thing being said about it. The subject and predicate each appear in one of the premises. There there's the *middle term* of the syllogism, which appears in both premises but not in the conclusion: in this case, *man* (or *men*). You can see the formal fit of the example to Aristotle's definition of a syllogism: an "argument in which, after certain propositions have been assumed, there necessarily results a proposition other than the assumptions because of the assumptions." (*Topics* I 1, 100a25)

Many variations on the pattern just shown are also possible in which one of the premises is negative or partial (*no men* or *some men* instead of *all men* in the major premise, with other changes in the minor premise, etc.), and many other distinctions can be drawn between syllogisms of different types. Those variations are all worth close study for the aficionado of argument. But for many practical purposes—and to understand the customs of argument in the times and places at issue in this book—it's enough just to grasp the use and abuse of the basic syllogistic *structure* of deductive reasoning: the general proposition followed (or sometimes preceded) by the particular case said to fit within it.

A valid syllogism creates a result that sounds airtight and *is* airtight if the premises are true. While few people use syllogisms expressly, many arguments have this structure once you unpack them. An example where it's near the surface:

Fowler, speech in the House of Commons (1883)

I am not going to weary the House with a long speech on this question; I want to put the syllogism, so to speak, as shortly and as concisely as I can. Taxation and representation go together; women are taxed; women ought to be represented.

Mill, who wrote a treatise on formal logic, was naturally attracted to the syllogistic form of argument in debate.

Mill, speech on parliamentary reform (1824)

What I understand by the Constitution is, the securities which are taken for the good conduct of public functionaries. When those securities are insufficient, the Constitution is bad. In England, the Honourable Gentleman had acknowledged that the securities are insufficient, for he has acknowledged that public functionaries do misconduct themselves. This is to admit every thing that I require. It is to admit that the Constitution is inadequate to its end.

Mill, speech on parliamentary reform (1824)

It being proved that our own government is a government of two hundred families: and it being evident that according to the laws of human nature, a government of two hundred families cannot be otherwise than a bad one: any one may supply the conclusion.

→→ *Enthymemes.* An enthymeme is a fancy word for a simple idea: a syllogism in which one of the premises isn't stated. ("Enthymeme" means "in the mind"; the missing part of the logic is filled in by the mind of the reader.) Everyday debates tend to work this way. One premise is said out loud; the other is left in the background. Spotting this will help you understand why many arguments seem so maddening. They take a premise for granted when it needs to be clarified and supported. Debaters sometimes avoid making a premise explicit just so they won't have to defend it.

We just saw this syllogism:

Taxation and representation go together; women are taxed; women ought to be represented.

These would be enthymemes based on the same reasoning:

Women are taxed, so women ought to be represented.
Taxation and representation go together, so women ought to be represented.

Each of those examples drops one of the premises from the original syllogism and leaves it to be understood. In the first, the major premise is missing. That is the most common kind of enthymeme. The audience is expected to know, or infer, that taxation and representation go together. In the second example, the reader is expected to fill in the minor premise—i.e., that women are taxed.

He would not take the crown;   *Julius Caesar* 3, 2
Therefore 'tis certain he was not ambitious.

That's an enthymeme with an implied major premise: the ambitious all seek the crown.

The gentleman from New Hampshire has defined a republican government to be that in which all the men participate in its power and privileges; from whence it follows that where there are slaves, it can have no existence.
Pinkney, speech in the Senate (1820)

That's an enthymeme with an implied minor premise: slaves don't participate in the power and privileges of government. (Pinkney

thought the major premise was wrong. The paradigmatic republic
in those days was the Roman one, which had slaves.)

Kingsley, *The*   Gibbon, as *advocatus diaboli*, of course gives the doubt against
Roman and the   Dietrich, by his usual enthymeme—All men are likely to be
Teuton (1864)   rogues, ergo, Dietrich was one.

Gibbon's enthymeme is missing a minor premise: Dietrich is a man.
(But the enthymeme is defective because the major premise only
speaks of likelihood.)

As that last example shows, sometimes the missing premise in an
enthymeme is trivial and can be omitted without risk of controversy.
But a missing premise may be wrong or questionable and yet do much
of the work in an argument; it needs to be smoked out and examined.
An example of an effort to clarify and then attack an enthymeme by
filling in the unspoken premise:

Horne,   Let us see how this argument runs. "Unemployment is rife in
speech in   Scotland. Therefore, there should be a Scottish Parliament."
the House of   It is perfectly obvious that there is some missing premiss in
Commons   that syllogism. How does it require to be stated? "Unem-
(1946)   ployment is rife in Scotland; Parliaments are the cure for
                 unemployment; therefore, there should be a Parliament in
                 Scotland." You have only to state the proposition in that way
                 to see how false the whole assumption is. Are Parliaments
                 the cure for unemployment? What has this Parliament been
                 doing ever since the War and how much has it achieved to
                 cure unemployment?

➤➤ *The sorites* (accumulation of arguments). A *sorites* is a series of
propositions in which the predicate (last part) of each becomes the
subject (first part) of the next. So the propositions are linked, and
they pile up until they reach a conclusion far from where they started.
(*Sorites* is Greek, and is pronounced sor-*eye*-teez; it means "pile" or
"heap.") An ancient example:

Caracalla (emper-   It is clear that if you make me no requests, you do not trust
or *c.* 200 AD), in   me; if you do not trust me, you suspect me; if you suspect
Gibbon, *Decline and*   me, you fear me; if you fear me, you hate me.
Fall of the Roman
Empire (1776)
(H. Milman note)

Notice that the elements of the chain can be broken out into implied syllogisms. Someone who makes no requests of others doesn't trust them; you made no requests of me; therefore you don't trust me; etc. (You can view a sorites as a series of enthymemes.) In this case, as with other deductions, the logic may be valid but the conclusion still false because the premises aren't true. As that example also shows, the sorites goes naturally with the rhetorical device known as *anadiplosis*, in which the last words of one clause become the first words of the next. The persuasive power of the sorites is drawn partly from these verbal connections between the elements of it.

Some say that the end of a good sorites should point back to the beginning and create a loop, as in these cases:

> Man is born a predestined idealist, for he is born to act. To act is to affirm the worth of an end, and to persist in affirming the worth of an end is to make an ideal.

Holmes, speech at Harvard University (1911)

> *Ernest.* Surely you would admit that the great poems of the early world, the primitive, anonymous collective poems, were the result of the imagination of races, rather than the imagination of individuals?
>
> *Gilbert.* ... Not when they received a beautiful form. For there is no art where there is no style, and no style where there is no unity, and unity is of the individual.

Wilde, *The Critic as Artist* (1891)

The sorites can produce valid reasoning, but all the links can make an audience nervous or give an adversary an opening for skepticism.

> The hon. and learned Member for Brighton constructed a climax of which the descending steps were—an enlarged constituency will result in a deteriorated House of Commons; a deteriorated House of Commons will surrender its guidance and its liberties to an arbitrary Minister; an arbitrary Minister will select an unprincipled Speaker; and thus, Sir, the extension of the franchise effected by the Conservative Reform Act of 1867 is to find its consummation in the degradation of the Chair. This very much reminds me of the schoolboy

Fowler, speech in the House of Commons (1882)

syllogism—Greece was ruled by Themistocles, he was ruled by his wife, she was ruled by her little boy—ergo, the little boy ruled Greece.

The type of sorites just discussed is distinct from the sorites *paradox*, which is the subject of a separate entry (see chapter 17).

➤➤ *Induction vs. deduction.* Deduction and indication are two ways of drawing inferences. Deduction, as we've seen, starts with general premises and moves to specific conclusions. A valid piece of deductive reasoning produces certain knowledge: if the premises of the syllogism are true, the conclusion is also true. Induction works the other way around; it moves from specific observations to general conclusions. When you collect facts and draw conclusions about what they suggest, that's induction. When you generalize from the results of experiments, that's induction. Inductive reasoning doesn't produce certainty. It creates probabilities, but sometimes very great ones. You believe the sun will rise tomorrow because it has risen consistently in the past. That doesn't make it logically necessary that the sun will rise tomorrow, but we can call it highly probable.

Some cases where the use of induction in argument is conspicuous:

Macaulay, *Utilitarian Theory of Government* (1829)

We ought to examine the constitution of all those communities in which, under whatever form, the blessings of good government are enjoyed; and to discover, if possible, in what they resemble each other, and in what they all differ from those societies in which the object of government is not attained. By proceeding thus we shall arrive, not indeed at a perfect theory of government, but at a theory which will be of great practical use, and which the experience of every successive generation will probably bring nearer and nearer to perfection.

Calhoun, speech in the Senate (1848)

Ireland has been held in subjection by England for many centuries, and yet remains hostile, although her people are of a kindred race with the conquerors. The French colony in Canada still entertain hostile feelings towards their conquerors, although living in the midst of them for nearly one hundred years. If we may judge from these examples, it would not be unsafe to conclude that the Mexicans never will be heartily reconciled to our authority.

Compare this case:

> I need only point this thinking company, for you are all men of thought and judgment, to the facts of history, and ask you to say whether they do not prove that an army conscripted, as you call it, can be as brave as lions and conquering as heroes. Think of Germany through the unification of her army and the selection of her men after the lesson of Jena, humbling proud Austria in 1866, in a period of about seven weeks. Think of Prussia humbling the proud Frank and capturing Napoleon the Third and his army at Sedan in 1870-71 in a period of seven weeks. Gentlemen, those were what you call conscripts, and selected conscripts, too. Were they lacking in valor and vigor? No.

Graham, speech in the House of Representatives (1917)

This looks similar to the previous instances of induction because it moves from examples to a conclusion. But then counterexamples could quickly be given in which conscription has failed. So the examples that Graham offers don't quite support a general conclusion, at least not a strong one. They just disprove a false generalization.

Inductive and deductive reasoning are routinely used together. Induction (evidence and examples) will produce a conclusion. The conclusion is then used as a major premise to produce a deduction. The major premise seen earlier—*all men are mortal*—is an example. Where does that idea come from? Inductive reasoning: it's been true of everyone seen so far. But when that conclusion is turned into a premise, it gives us new conclusions (*Socrates is mortal*) without more evidence. This is all commonplace. You put Tabasco sauce on your food a few times and don't like it. You decide that you don't like Tabasco sauce on your food in general because it's too hot (a conclusion reached by induction); you refuse it next time because you say it will ruin your food (a deduction, using the earlier conclusion as a major premise).

In some settings one might *prefer* an inductive approach to a deductive one; deductive reasoning can even be made the subject of sneers. When people express that view, their problem isn't with deduction as such (nobody can do without it). It's with certain ways in which people get their major premises. If a major premise is based tightly on observed facts, everybody likes the deductive reasoning that follows from it. But a major premise can be drawn more or less *a priori*—that is, not directly from experience but from a theory that may have a loose relation to the evidence we can see. The problems arise, in effect, when advocates don't just talk about their experience with Tabasco sauce but theorize generally about condiments. Lovers of induction don't like this. They want conclusions—which get turned into major premises—that cover only the facts they're drawn from. Some expressions of this taste in practice:

Bayne, speech in the House of Representatives (1886)

He will not deign to apply inductive methods, the methods universally acknowledged by modern scientists as the true ones, by considering the causes and effects of the monetary system of any one nation. Not he; that would be too small a subject for so great a man. He prefers to construct a magnificent pyramid of theory which will embrace all the people of the world and all the money of the world.

Loud, speech in the House of Representatives (1892)

Free traders have such a contempt for facts, experience, and the opinions of manufacturers that they protest against the inductive method and declare only the deductive is of any value. That is to say, facts are of no value. Suppositions thus rule in their science, not truth. What Yale, Harvard, Prof. Sumner, and Prof. Perry think is of more value than what any manufacturer knows.

Preferring induction can also mean something more specific: you like experiments better than speculation. The point may be forward-looking—i.e., let's try things rather than arguing in the abstract.

Williams, speech in the Senate (1869)

Whether or not female suffrage in the United States will be of advantage to women does not depend on any speculation of man, but upon practical experiment, and if it should be tried in one State, as it might be under the amendment I propose, and found to be a success and satisfactory to all concerned, then by an act of Congress it might be extended to all the States.

Or the point can refer to the present: why argue about what might happen when we can look what *has* happened?

It may however be thought that in studying the classics even as they are studied at our Universities, it is difficult not to imbibe some liberality of sentiment and some valuable information. So one would think, and if our Universities had not existed it would probably to this day have remained a problem whether it was possible for great bodies of young men to study the classics in such a manner as not to derive one particle of advantage from them. Our Universities however have so nearly succeeded in this attempt that the possibility of the thing is now placed beyond the reach of doubt.

Mill, *The Universities* (1826)

The portrayal of the evils to flow from woman suffrage such as we have heard pictured today by the Senator from Georgia, the loss of harmony between husband and wife, and the consequent instability of the marriage relation, the neglect of husband and children by wives and mothers for the performance of their political duties, in short the incapacitating of women for wives and mothers and companions, will not much longer serve to frighten the timid. Proof is better than theory. The experiment has been tried and the predicted evils to flow from it have not followed.

Dolph, speech in the Senate (1887)

13

Circularity

A fallacy is an error of logic or other specimen of faulty reasoning. Formal fallacies are errors in the form of a deductive argument. Informal fallacies are simply bad reasoning; they're typically arguments based on premises that don't hold up or that don't prove what they're said to prove. Informal fallacies are much more common in everyday argument. They will be our focus here. This chapter and the next two discuss some common fallacies, most of them informal. This one starts with circularity and some related problems.

↠ *Circular arguments.* A circular argument is one where a premise depends on the conclusion instead of proving it. Stated more practically: you give a reason for X, but the reason is only convincing if X is already true. Claims of circularity are common both ways in arguments about religion.

Huxley, *Controverted Questions* (1892)

The infallibility of the Bible is testified by the infallible Church, whose infallibility is testified by the infallible Bible.

Chesterton, *Orthodoxy* (1908)

If I say, "Medieval documents attest certain miracles as much as they attest certain battles," they answer, "But medievals were superstitious"; if I want to know in what they were superstitious, the only ultimate answer is that they believed in the miracles.

An example from moral philosophy:

Hume, *A Treatise of Human Nature* (1740)

I would fain ask any one, why incest in the human species is criminal, and why the very same action, and the same relations in animals have not the smallest moral turpitude and deformity? If it be answered, that this action is innocent in animals, because they have not reason sufficient to discover its turpitude; but that man, being endowed with that faculty which ought to restrain him to his duty, the same action instantly becomes criminal to him; should this be said, I would reply, that this is evidently arguing in a circle. For before reason can perceive this turpitude, the turpitude must exist.

The claim in simpler form: "Incest is immoral in people but not in animals." Why? "Because humans have reason, which allows them to understand the immorality of it." That reason is convincing if the belief behind the original claim of immorality is already true; otherwise not.

↦ *Begging the question.* This phrase can simply refer to circularity: supporting a conclusion with a premise that takes the truth of the conclusion for granted. It can also refer, less formally, to the implicit circularity of stating a conclusion as if it were proven when it *needs* proof. Such a claim can be described as fallacious because a proposition can't prove itself.

This pattern appears often in politics, as when someone puts a label onto an enemy without good evidence that the label fits. The same thing can be done with words of praise. The controversial is treated as uncontroversial.

> The two sides of the Spanish Civil War had between them nine or ten names expressing different degrees of love and hatred. Some of these names (e.g. "Patriots" for Franco-supporters, or "Loyalists" for Government-supporters) were frankly question-begging, and there was no single one of them which the two rival factions could have agreed to use.
>
> Orwell, *Notes on Nationalism* (1945)

He means: someone is being called a "loyalist" as if it were a fact; actually it's a disputable claim, and its maker is pretending the dispute doesn't exist. You should *argue* that someone ought to be called a loyalist, not talk as though everyone agrees about it. Question-begging like this often lies behind the use of other labels that express judgments.

> MR. FARNSWORTH. If Congress should pass a useless statute costing the Government one hundred thousand dollars a year, would the gentleman be in favor of keeping that law upon the statute-book?
>
> Exchange in the House of Representatives (1871)

MR. COBURN. I suppose not. The gentleman begs the question when he says this is a useless statute. It may save the Government.

Stephen, *Liberty, Equality, Fraternity* (1873) Even if our moral intuitions told us that it is wrong to commit murder, they would be of no use unless they also told us what no moral intuition ever yet told anyone—namely, what was the meaning of the word "murder," and how the killings which do amount to murder are to be distinguished from those which do not.

Burroughs, speech in the House of Representatives (1919) Neither is it very satisfying to my mind to have the committee tell us, as they do tell us in their report, that we should have an "adequate" Navy. That is simply begging the whole question. We all want an adequate Navy. But what is an adequate Navy?

In each case someone has used a word—*useless* or *murder* or *adequate*—to describe something. The word is put forward as if it had a clear meaning and was obviously a good fit. The objection is: you're assuming too much by using that word. The question is *whether* the thing at issue is useless or murder or adequate.

Nowadays some people use "begging the question" to mean something else: that a statement *raises* a question. "I hated that book." "That begs the question what books you do like." Friends of literacy avoid this usage.

↦ *Tautology*. A tautology is a claim that's always true because it's true by definition, and therefore trivial. (This at least is its meaning in ordinary criticisms of an argument; more technical definitions are possible, but we'll leave them aside for our practical purposes.) A tautology typically involves a repetition of elements. *What's done is done* can be considered a tautology (though its meaning isn't always trivial). In the more interesting cases the repetition isn't so open. Saying that others commit a tautology usually means they've made a claim that *sounds* like an argument but unwittingly says the same thing twice in different words.

> It is therefore a truism, almost a tautology, to say that all magic is necessarily false and barren; for were it ever to become true and fruitful, it would no longer be magic but science.

Frazer, The Golden Bough (1922)

A tautology can take longer to trace. Someone says that X will be accomplished by doing Y. But then Y is defined in a way that sounds the same as X, so maybe the advice isn't of much use. This was Macaulay's view of utilitarianism.

> The principle of Mr. Bentham, if we understand it, is this, that mankind ought to act so as to produce their greatest happiness. The word *ought*, he tells us, has no meaning, unless it be used with reference to some interest. But the interest of a man is synonymous with his greatest happiness:—and therefore to say that a man ought to do a thing, is to say that it is for his greatest happiness to do it. And to say that mankind *ought* to act so as to produce their greatest happiness, is to say that the greatest happiness is the greatest happiness—and this is all!

Macaulay, Westminster Reviewer's Defence of Mill (1829)

In other words, telling people that it's in their best interests to pursue their greatest happiness is like telling them it's in their best interests to pursue their best interests. It's telling them nothing.

Tautologies also are common when someone says it's *wrong* to do X, where X is a loaded term that hasn't been defined well enough. It may turn out that X is just another way of saying "wrong." The example a moment ago from Stephen might be viewed as an instance of this: "it's wrong to commit murder" can be read as meaning "it's wrong to kill wrongfully," which doesn't tell us anything we didn't know; it may be true, but it doesn't advance our understanding. A similar case:

> All admit that any authority ought to be disobeyed which commands immoral acts; but this is one of those tautological propositions, so common in popular morality, which convey no real information; the question is, what acts there are which do not cease to be immoral when they have been commanded by a rightful authority.

Sidgwick, Methods of Ethics (1874)

↦ *Regress.* A problem similar to circularity: the argument doesn't solve the problem at issue; it just pushes the problem back or elsewhere, like a bump in a rug. The explanation requires an explanation, for example, and the second explanation requires a third one, etc. The regress is expressed in Juvenal's famous saying *quis custodiet ipsos custodes?* (Who will guard the guards themselves?) The maxim in modern times often leaves out the *ipsos.*

Tucker, speech in the House of Representatives (1879)

But it is said, Why should the Army not keep peace at the polls? Is not peace desirable there? I do not deny this; but who shall do it, is the question. *Quis custodiet custodes?* Who shall keep the keepers? I venture to apply the story of the old Virginian who offered to bet upon the race between Henry and Eclipse. The bet was taken. "Who'll hold the stakes?" he said. "Squire Jones," was the reply. "But who'll hold Squire Jones?"

John Stuart Mill's father was criticized for making proposals with this kind of defect. He said that public officials always act against the interests of their communities. They need to be checked by others; bad behavior in the legislature, Mill said, should be reined in by a convention that would have the legislature at its mercy. But then what about bad behavior in the convention?

Macaulay, *Mill on Government* (1829)

As soon as they are a convention, as soon as they are separated from the people, as soon as the supreme power is put into their hands, commences that interest opposite to the interest of the community which must, according to Mr. Mill, produce measures opposite to the interests of the community. We must find some other means, therefore, of checking this check upon a check; some other prop to carry the tortoise, that carries the elephant, that carries the world.

Macaulay refers to the Hindu myth in which the world is carried by elephants that stand on a turtle. Explaining the turtle's source of support is a standard example of infinite regress—as in the anecdote about the child who, when asked what the last elephant stands on, says *a turtle*; and what does that turtle stand on? —*another turtle*. And that one? —*it's turtles all the way down.*

This theme comes up often when a judgment depends on subjective or disputable criteria. Someone will try to solve the problem by classifying the judgment in a new way, but this only moves the problem around; for who will decide whether the classification fits, or how it works?

> He had heard it avowed, that the religion which ought to be established in a state, was not that which the majority said they believed, but that the doctrines of which were true.... It was difficult to argue with anybody entertaining such an opinion; for where was the test by which such an argument could be tried?

Ricardo, speech in the House of Commons (1823)

> To say that society ought to be governed by the opinion of the wisest and best, though true, is useless. Whose opinion is to decide who are the wisest and best?

Macaulay, *Southey's Colloquies on Society* (1830)

14

Ad Hominem Arguments

↣ *Argumentum ad hominem* (argument to the person). This expression has multiple meanings. First and most commonly now, it refers to a fallacy: attacking (or praising) the maker of a claim rather than the merits of it. That's a fallacy because the attack doesn't touch the logic of whatever point is in dispute.

The most brute form of *ad hominem* attack is simply abusive. Instead of replying to a proposal or argument with a counterargument, one replies by characterizing the maker of it.

Boswell, *Life of Johnson* (1791)

SIR ADAM. "But, Sir, in the British constitution it is surely of importance to keep up a spirit in the people, so as to preserve a balance against the crown."

JOHNSON. "Sir, I perceive you are a vile Whig."

Lowe, speech in the House of Commons (1872)

The hon. Baronet the Member for West Essex, as I understand, does not allege that he has anything to say against my Motion, but he proposes to supersede it by a Committee. He is one of those persons who would burn down my house in order to roast his own pig.

Or the adversary isn't decried directly but is nevertheless made the issue.

Gerry, *On the New Constitution* (1788)

Where then were the class who now come forth importunately urging that our political salvation depends on the adoption of a system at which freedom spurns?—Were not some of them hidden in the corners of obscurity, and others wrapping themselves in the bosom of our enemies for safety?

The *ad hominem* appeal is also seen whenever a point is attacked because it came from so-and-so and we all know what *that* means. Or when those who resist an argument are said to be ethically backwards or out of step with the right way of thinking. *Ad hominem* arguments of that general kind are greatly in fashion at this writing (but then they never really go out of style). Criticizing or praising the maker of an argument is usually easier than taking the argument seriously and may be more effective.

> The Honorable Gentleman's auxiliary syllogism is a very short one and it amounts to this. My argument is conclusive: why? Because all who dispute it are radicals and cut throat thieves, which is a very pretty way of arguing and a short cut to infallibility.

Mill, speech on parliamentary reform (1824)

There are more specific and less abusive forms of *ad hominem* appeal, such as the circumstantial kind: saying that a claim is infected by a bias on account of the speaker's position. This may be true and important if the speaker's credibility matters. But it's not relevant to the *logical* force of a claim.

> The gentleman from Kansas says these questions are mostly settled. Ah, Mr. Chairman, he would not say that if he lived in an irrigation State.

Shafroth, speech in the House of Representatives (1903)

> A convention of dairymen has been heard upon this subject; let us now have a convention on the other side of the question. As to the dairymen, of course they have consulted their own interests. That is inevitable. It is an infirmity of humanity. We are all selfish, and the dairymen, notwithstanding the simplicity of their pastoral life, are not exempt from the common weakness.

Curtin, speech in the House of Representatives (1886)

These last two arguments are *ad hominem* because they seek to undermine claims by pointing to the positions of the people who made them. The arguments might be salvaged from fallacy if they're followed by reasons why the positions that those bad perspectives produce are wrong in substance.

The *ad hominem* argument isn't always used in a negative way. The *ipse dixit* (see below) can be considered a positive form of the pattern. And more generally the identity of the person who makes a claim can be treated as a point in favor of it—and this, too, can provoke objection.

Smith, *Address to the People of New York* (1788)

Let the constitution stand on its own merits. If it be good, it stands not in need of great men's names to support it. If it be bad, their names ought not to sanction it.

Labouchere, speech in the House of Commons (1889)

The Attorney General thinks he has answered my right hon. Friend when he says, "I am the author of the apology." The rapturous cheers which burst from hon. Gentlemen opposite at this extraordinary *argumentum ad hominem* were perfectly astounding. I do not care whether the Attorney General, or Mr. Soames, or the *Times*, or Mr. Walter did it. I say that the apology was a most disgraceful and sneaking apology.

An *ad hominem* argument can also be a somewhat different thing: an argument that someone is being inconsistent. Plato displays Socrates making many arguments like this; he shows that his partners contradict themselves. This kind of argument isn't a fallacy if it's used in the right way. Its force is just limited. It amounts to showing that your own beliefs require a conclusion contrary to what you're saying or doing. The argument is *ad hominem* because it's only working with (and treating as givens) the claims and assumptions of the person who is the subject of it.

Stephen, *Note on Utilitarianism* (1869)

The expression, "You, as Christians, ought to love one another," is an argument *ad hominem*. You acknowledge principles which, if applied to practice, would make you love one another.

If an *ad hominem* inquiry exposes an inconsistency in your thinking, it doesn't prove that either half of the inconsistency is right or wrong. It just shows that you're contradicting yourself, and perhaps that you don't really understand what you're talking about. Your beliefs might all be wrong, in which case their inconsistency is an embarrassment to you but needn't be important to anyone else.

Your inconsistency may sometimes be relevant to others after all for a reason noted above: you're proposing to speak as an authority on a topic. But suppose the issue is simply the merit of a proposal. In that case it can be important not to dwell too much on whether the people arguing about it are consistent. Other people's welfare might depend on the outcome of the debate; why should they suffer because the advocates on either side are hypocrites?

It might be said, how could those who had voted against an impeachment, now vote for it? This, as an argument *ad hominem* might be attended to: if the party accused was only to be considered, there might be some ground for such an argument; but there was a third party whose interests were concerned—the public, and the whole body of the peerage.

Leycester, speech in the House of Commons (1805)

↦ *Tu quoque* (you also). Replying to a criticism by saying that its maker is also subject to it. This is usually considered a variety of *ad hominem* argument because it goes after the hypocrisy of the critic, not the accuracy of the criticism. Many types of *tu quoque* are familiar from equivalent English expressions. It can amount to saying *who are you to point fingers?*

He will, however, pardon me for suggesting to him, that, if I did assail him with far more acrimony than I am disposed to do, he is the last man in this house who ought to complain. Who is there that shows less mercy to a political adversary? Who is so relentless in the infliction of his sarcasms, even on his old friends and associates?

Sheil, speech in the House of Commons (1837)

Or the *tu quoque* can be like replying *you ought to know.*

MR. DILLON. He is a traitor.

MR. CHAMBERLAIN. Ah! The hon. Gentleman is a good judge of traitors.

Exchange in the House of Commons (1902)

(Dillon complained that this reply was unparliamentary; the Speaker said that he deprecated both sides of the exchange.) Or the *tu quoque* can be like saying *you're worse than I am.*

MR. WILLIAMS. Every Senator had a duty to be present if he had an amendment to offer, and if the Senator from Wisconsin

Exchange in the Senate (1920)

was not present it was his own fault. If I were not present, it would be my own fault.

MR. LENROOT. The Senator from Wisconsin will say to the Senator from Mississippi that he has been much more regular in attendance of the sessions of the Senate than the Senator from Mississippi.

MR. WILLIAMS. Mr. President, that is a mere *ad hominem* observation, which carries no weight and no influence with it.

The *tu quoque* is typically regarded as a fallacy for familiar reasons: a bad deed isn't made better because the critic has done it as well.

Morley, speech in the House of Commons (1888)

The only argument, therefore, which was left to the Government was the miserable *tu quoque* that the Liberal Governments in the past had done the same. But if Liberal Governments had done wrong in times past, that was no reason for the Conservatives to do wrong now.

But the *tu quoque*, like other *ad hominem* appeals, has some fair applications. It can call the motive of an attack or the credibility of the attacker into question in cases where those points are germane to the debate.

Balfour, speech in the House of Commons (1888)

The *tu quoque* argument, though it is, I admit, no justification whatever for the course of the present Government, has a most important bearing upon current controversies; for, after all, it enables the country to put a tolerably accurate estimate upon the value of the opinions of the gentlemen who chiefly occupy themselves with criticizing us.

Goschen, speech in the House of Commons (1888)

Tu quoque means not only a desire to recriminate; we have a deeper and a more valuable meaning, one we are free to press home…. The object is to show that there is obvious hollowness and insincerity in the charges made, that they are made at the spur of political necessity and with a particular political object, and that they are not believed in even by those who make them.

➤➤ *Projection.* A cousin of the *tu quoque*: a criticism fits the critic who makes it but *doesn't* fit the party being criticized. Instead of *you also*, the claim is *you rather*.

> The men who strive to bring back the Government to its original policy, when Freedom and not Slavery was national while Slavery and not Freedom was sectional, he arraigns as sectional. This will not do. It involves too great a perversion of terms. I tell that Senator, that it is to himself, and to the "organization" of which he is the committed advocate, that this epithet belongs. I now fasten it upon them.

Sumner, speech in the Senate (1856)

The reversal can be gentler: are you sure you aren't talking about yourself?

> The gentleman tells us, sir, that "one hour is long enough for a man of sense to speak, and a great deal too long for a fool." Whether the gentleman intends to make any application of his remark to the members of this House, I do not presume to know; I certainly shall make no such application, neither will I contend with the gentleman in deciding which part of his proposition is most applicable to himself.

Eastman, speech in the House of Representatives (1842)

This kind of claim can involve some psychological speculation: perhaps the critics attack faults they find uncomfortable in themselves. They're engaged in projection.

> The President seems to be in the situation of a man who, unconscious of his own inebriation, regards every other person whom he meets as having imbibed too freely.

Wortendyke, speech in the House of Representatives (1858)

➤➤ *Ipse dixit.* An *ipse dixit* is a statement with no more support than the fact that it was said and by whom. It's offered as if *saying* it should be enough to satisfy everyone that it's true. When first used in classical times, the expression referred to claims based on the words of a master such as Pythagoras: literally "he himself said it" (whatever *it* was), so it must be so.

The easy reply to an *ipse dixit* is just to say that there's no reason to believe it's right.

Mill, speech on population (1825)

No one can be required to argue against a bare assertion: if I shew that it is a bare assertion, I have surely done all that can be required.

Mockery may be in order.

Randolph, speech in the House of Representatives (1808)

You are told, sir, with a most imposing solemnity of voice and countenance, that this bill does not enlarge the powers of courts martial. Do you want proof? *Ipse dixit*—that gentleman says so; and surely you will not be so unreasonable as to doubt his word.

That last example suggests a more colloquial way to speak of an *ipse dixit*: it's a point made on the speaker's say-so. Sometimes the words "say-so" can be substituted with no change in meaning.

Clancy, speech in the House of Commons (1887)

One would have thought that the Chief Secretary, in the course of his speech, would have condescended to use some arguments in support of his case. He did not, however, attempt anything of the kind; he relies upon his own *ipse dixit*, which seems, in his mind, to settle everything.

And indeed, one can't be too careful about phrasing.

Exchange in the House of Representatives (1878)

MR. PATTERSON. His *ipse dixit* is hardly sufficient to set aside a well-settled practice of the House.

MR. ATKINS. I have offered no *ipse dixit*. The gentleman is very gratuitous in his remarks; he had better be more careful.

MR. PATTERSON. I did not mean it in any offensive sense at all.

MR. ATKINS. It is offensive.

The charge that you've made an *ipse dixit* can be refuted by separating the claim from the evidence for it.

Lincoln, debate with Stephen Douglas at Freeport (1858)

Judge Douglas recurs again, as he did upon one or two other occasions, to the enormity of Lincoln, an insignificant individual like Lincoln,—upon his *ipse dixit* charging a conspiracy upon a large number of members of Congress, the Supreme Court, and two Presidents, to nationalize slavery. I want to say that, in the first place, I have made no charge of this sort upon my *ipse dixit*. I have only arrayed the evidence tending to prove it, and presented it to the understanding of others, saying what I think it proves, but giving you the means of judging whether it proves it or not.

15

More Fallacies

↣ *Affirming the consequent.* This is a formal fallacy: a defect in the structure of a syllogism. In an "if … then" claim, the "if" part is known as the *antecedent.* The "then" part is the *consequent.* The fallacy lies in reversing those elements: you say that the *then* part is true ("affirming" the consequent), and conclude that the *if* part must therefore be true. Often it isn't. "If it rained, then the sidewalk will be wet," as a stock example goes. You can't (on that account) be sure that if the sidewalk is wet, it rained. (Someone may have just washed it.) Formally speaking, you'd be assuming that the converse of a conditional (if-then) statement is true. It might not be. Compare the *contrapositive* of an if-then statement, which necessarily *is* true (or rather it's just as true as the statement in its original form). You form the contrapositive by reversing the elements and negating both: if the sidewalk isn't wet, it didn't rain.

When someone affirms the consequent, it doesn't usually look quite as simple as it did in that little example. It might look like this:

Maclean, speech in the House of Commons (1891) I consider that if the old Whig maxim were true that taxation without representation is tyranny, then the converse is also true that representation without taxation is also tyranny.

(He was arguing that the Irish were overrepresented in the House.) To more easily see the fallacy in a statement like that, convert it to if-then form. The first claim comes to this: *if you are taxed, then you must be represented.* Assume that's true. Now the speaker wants to infer the converse: *if you're represented, you must be taxed.* This amounts to affirming the consequent of the first statement. It's bad reasoning. Of course that doesn't mean the second claim is wrong. It just doesn't *follow* from the first claim.

You can point out the risk of this fallacy when you mean to avoid it or want the audience to do so. An example from a bleak time:

Democrats may deny that they are responsible for these out-
rages; yet Democrats alone palliate and excuse them. Democrats alone secure the blood-stained benefits arising from the
kukluxing of Republicans…. While every Democrat is not a
Ku Klux yet every Ku Klux is a Democrat.

McKee, speech
in the House of
Representatives
(1871)

Again, you can see the risk of fallacy by turning the argument into
an if-then claim. If someone is a Ku Klux, then he's a Democrat;
but it doesn't follow that if someone is a Democrat, he's a Ku Klux.
Disclaiming that last idea (*disaffirming* the consequent, in effect) is
more than a display of precision. It preempts an objection that might
otherwise interfere with the main point: wait, I'm a Democrat and
I'm not a Ku Klux, etc. (To which the speaker can reply: we never
said all Democrats *were*; we said many of them *weren't*. But …)
Another example:

Not all novelties are improvements, but all improvements are
novel, and you can only, therefore, be sure of improvements
by giving eccentricity a fair hearing, and free room for as
much active manifestation as does no near, positive, recog-
nizable, harm to other people.

Morley, *Mr. Mill's
Doctrine of Liberty*
(1873)

As before, the logical relationships are clarified by converting the
statements to if-then form. If something is an improvement, then
it's novel; but it doesn't follow that if something is novel, it's an improvement. He assures the audience that he's not affirming the consequent.

↦ *The undistributed middle.* Affirming the consequent is sometimes
viewed as an instance of a larger problem: the *fallacy of the undistributed middle.* This happens when neither premise in a syllogism covers
everyone in the class that both of the premises mention. In effect you
wrongly assume that because two things have something in common,
they're also the same in other ways. All dogs have four legs; all cats
have four legs; but it doesn't follow that dogs are cats. The problem is
that there's a term—four legs—appearing in both premises, but never
any claim made about *all* things with that property. So the premises
don't add up to a valid conclusion.

To go through the point more formally: the "middle" term of a syllogism is one that appears in both premises but not the conclusion. To revise the famous dull example into a form that's cleaner:

> All people are mortal.
> All Greeks are people.
> All Greeks are mortal.

That syllogism works. The middle term is *people*. A term is "distributed" when it covers all members of the class it describes. Since the word *all* appears before *people* in the first line, the term *people* is distributed. The term *people* isn't distributed in the second line (it doesn't mean "every person"—i.e., that *all Greeks* and *all people* are the same group). But as long as that middle term is distributed in one of the two premises, you can produce a valid conclusion.

The usual presentation of our current fallacy puts the middle term at the end of both premises:

> Mortals are people.
> Greeks are people.
> Greeks are mortal.

The conclusion doesn't follow. Greeks and mortals might be *different* people. To seal off the problem, you need to distribute the word "people" by changing it to "all people"—so you're saying "all people are mortal" or "all people are Greeks." Those changes would lead to different conclusions, but at least to conclusions that are valid.

A literary example:

Poe, *The Purloined Letter* (1844)

This functionary, however, has been thoroughly mystified; and the remote source of his defeat lies in the supposition that the Minister is a fool because he has acquired renown as a poet. All fools are poets; this the Prefect feels, and he is merely guilty of a *non distributio medii* in thence inferring that all poets are fools.

The bad implied syllogism of the Prefect goes:

> All fools are poets.
> He's a poet.
> He must be a fool.

The word *poet* is the middle term and isn't distributed; we never hear anything about *all* poets. As you can see, this is indeed another route to affirming the consequent. *If he's a fool, he's a poet.* Fine—but you can't turn it around and say *if he's a poet, he's a fool.* The difference just lies in whether the idea is presented as a conditional statement or as a syllogism about membership in a set. Many claims can be expressed either way.

→→ *Equivocation; ambiguity.* The term *equivocation* can refer casually to the use of evasive language, but it's also a particular fallacy: using an ambiguity to make an argument seem more convincing than it is, as when someone uses the same word in two ways without giving notice (perhaps one way in the major premise of a syllogism and then differently in the minor premise). Macaulay accuses Mill (Sr.) of this in the example below. Mill had been trying to explain what people want and what we should expect them to do as a result; Macaulay thought that Mill was doing slippery things with the word "desire."

> The whole art of Mr. Mill's essay consists in one simple trick of legerdemain. It consists in using words of the sort which we have been describing first in one sense and then in another. Men will take the objects of their desire if they can. Unquestionably:—but this is an identical proposition: for an object of desire means merely a thing which a man will procure if he can.... The general proposition, however, having been admitted, Mr. Mill proceeds to reason as if men had no desires but those which can be gratified only by spoliation and oppression. It then becomes easy to deduce doctrines of vast importance from the original axiom. The only misfortune is, that by thus narrowing the meaning of the word desire the axiom becomes false, and all the doctrines consequent upon it are false likewise.

Macaulay, *Mill on Government* (1829)

Macaulay claims, in effect, that Mill made a syllogism with the middle term *desire*—but *desire* refers to different things in each premise. In Mill's major premise (according to Macaulay), "to desire" means "to wish to obtain anything." In the minor premise, it means "to wish to obtain what only coercion can deliver."

We can usefully note some related traps that involve the strategic use of ambiguity. The first occurs when a speaker uses a word that the audience will interpret in a certain way but that's only accurate when interpreted differently. From Mill (Jr.):

Mill,
*The British
Constitution*
(1826)

> That the House of Commons represents all interests, is in one sense true: but as it is not true in the sense in which it is meant to be understood; whenever this argument is used an imposture is practiced by the common instrument of imposture, an ambiguous term. They tell us and truly that interests are represented, but they do not tell us which interests.

Mill's idea was that people have two kinds of interests: an interest in the general good, which they share with everyone; and then private interests in making themselves better off at the expense of others. He was saying that the House represented the second set of interests rather than the first.

A speaker can use the same word in a way that will mean different things to different people. Then everyone may think they agree with the speaker (or with everyone else) when they don't.

Flanagan,
speech in
the Senate
(1872)

> A friend of General Jackson wrote him a letter asking him his views upon the subject of the tariff. General Jackson replied, "I am for a judicious tariff." That was a happy word. He could not have done better if he had had Aladdin's lamp and rubbed it and the genii of the world had responded. It was just as successful, because in the North a man could say, "My dear friend, General Jackson is in favor of a high tariff;" here in the South "a low tariff," thus pleasing all.

A similar problem can arise less nefariously when the same word is used differently by two opponents. Neither side may be trying to gain from the word's ambiguity. They just have different things in

mind and so are confusing each other or the audience. You can make
headway by exposing the problem.

> We all declare for liberty; but in using the same word we do
> not all mean the same thing. With some the word liberty may
> mean for each man to do as he pleases with himself, and the
> product of his labor; while with others the same word may
> mean for some men to do as they please with other men, and
> the product of other men's labor. Here are two, not only
> different, but incompatible things, called by the same name,
> liberty.

Lincoln, speech at Baltimore (1864)

➤➤ *Fallacies of composition and division.* You commit the fallacy
of composition if you assume that things true about the parts of
something must also be true of the whole that they create together.
Sometimes this expression just refers to generalizations made too
quickly: you assume the whole book is good (or bad) because part
of it is. But the more interesting and exact applications occur when
a property may be held by every member of the group and yet still
not be a property of the whole. For instance, suppose every member
of a group makes rational choices for themselves; yet because those
choices are self-interested, the result can't be assumed rational for
the group (maybe the group is now doomed).

Mill (Jr.) has been accused of committing this fallacy in his defense
of utilitarianism. He wanted to show that producing the greatest
amount of happiness altogether (for all people) is a moral good, and
that acts should be judged by whether they tend to have that effect.
He made this argument:

> No reason can be given why the general happiness is desir-
> able, except that each person, so far as he believes it to be
> attainable, desires his own happiness. This, however, being
> a fact, we have not only all the proof which the case admits
> of, but all which it is possible to require, that happiness is a
> good: that each person's happiness is a good to that person,
> and the general happiness, therefore, a good to the aggregate
> of all persons.

Mill, *Utilitarianism* (1863)

Mill assumes that since individuals each want happiness for themselves, it follows that the good of the *group* is also found in the total happiness of its members. But maybe not. People who want happiness for themselves might not want it for others; and the good of the group might be advanced in ways other than individuals each getting what they want.

Here's a practical example of the fallacy being dispelled; Hamilton argues that groups of people have lower standards of behavior than their members do when they act individually.

Hamilton,
Federalist 15
(1787)

Has it been found that bodies of men act with more rectitude or greater disinterestedness than individuals? The contrary of this has been inferred by all accurate observers of the conduct of mankind; and the inference is founded upon obvious reasons. Regard to reputation has a less active influence, when the infamy of a bad action is to be divided among a number than when it is to fall singly upon one. A spirit of faction, which is apt to mingle its poison in the deliberations of all bodies of men, will often hurry the persons of whom they are composed into improprieties and excesses, for which they would blush in a private capacity.

In other words, a group composed of good men may not be a good group, because people act differently when they band together.

The fallacy of division is the reverse problem: assuming that things true of a group are also true of each member of it. Since the book is good, each chapter must be good; a characteristic of a class of people belongs to each of them; etc. In Hamilton's example just shown, you'd commit this fallacy by assuming that if a group acts badly, each of its members must be bad. What's true of the whole may not be true for every case of which the whole is composed. Maybe it's best for the group if its members in general do X more than Y; but that doesn't mean it's best for *each* of them to act that way—as Macaulay once said.

Macaulay,
*Gladstone on Church
and State* (1839)

It is of very much more importance that men should have food than that they should have pianofortes. Yet it by no means follows that every pianoforte maker ought to add the business of a baker to his own; for, if he did so, we should have both much worse music and much worse bread.

-→ *Bait and switch; motte and bailey.* This pattern isn't always a fallacy, but it's a type of misbehavior in argument that is best treated here because it sometimes involves equivocation. You take provocative position X. Then when the position is challenged, you say that you merely meant Y—something less controversial than X and easier to defend. (Perhaps later you go back to saying X.) The effect is to rile people up with an unsound claim while avoiding accountability for it.

One form of this annoying practice has been described by the philosopher Nicholas Shackel as a motte-and-bailey maneuver. That label is a reference to motte-and-bailey castles, which have two parts: the bailey, which is the nice area (flat and surrounded by a fence or ditch) where the inhabitants prefer to be; and the motte, which is a tower on a hill to which everyone retreats when the bailey is attacked. In argument, the bailey is the exciting and provocative claim that a speaker makes. The motte is the safe and boring claim to which the speaker retreats when the exciting claim is challenged.

Shackel's definition of a motte-and-bailey doctrine is precise and is based on recent cases, so it's not easy to find perfect examples of his pattern from the time and place this book examines. But it's part of an old family of tactics: the bait and switch, perhaps with a bit of equivocation added. The equivocation occurs when the same words are used (and heard) in one way at first but then are interpreted differently when defended later by their author.

Here's an example. After the Civil War, the Ku Klux Klan engaged in racist violence in the southern states. Congress passed the Ku Klux Klan Act, which allowed the president to have Klan members arrested and prosecuted. In the election season of 1872, one platform for the Liberal Republican party called for no more "resort to unconstitutional laws to cure Ku Klux disorders." When that resolution was attacked in the Senate by Oliver Morton, another senator (Lyman Trumbull) defended it; Trumbull said that the resolution just meant all laws should be kept constitutional:

> Let me ask the Senator if he is in favor of an unconstitutional law for the purpose of suppressing Ku Klux disorders?

Morton replied:

> He says he is opposed to unconstitutional laws, and wants to know if I am not. Certainly I am. And he would have this country to believe that that was all this resolution meant!

Morton thought it clear that the authors of the platform meant to say that the Ku Klux Klan law should be repealed.

> That was a reference to the Ku Klux law, a reference to all the laws we have passed for the purpose of suppressing disorder in the South, a declaration that they are unconstitutional. That is the understanding we all have of what that platform meant. But the Senator says it only means that they are opposed to laws that are unconstitutional, without pointing out or without intimating that those already passed are unconstitutional.... I will not call that pettifogging; that is a word not proper for the Senate; but I will say that when my friend attempts to give a gloss and a construction like that to this platform he is doing violence to his own character, and is insulting the intelligence of those who are listening to him.

The same family of trick can be used by one person in a single argument; it doesn't require an adversary. The speaker says provocative things that attract attention but then qualifies them in ways that are less aggressive and less interesting. The listener comes away remembering the provocative parts and not the qualifications. Or the speaker keeps claiming to have intentions that are agreeable or at least moderate, but then makes points that have a very different effect on the audience. The innocuous general claim provides cover for ideas that are damaging and less defensible. This was more or less the complaint that Timothy Pickering made about a critic of the proposed federal constitution:

Pickering, *Refutation of the Federal Farmer* (1787)

> He, like the other anti-federal writers, is perpetually conceding and retracting. They all know that the people of these states feel the necessity of an efficient federal government; and

therefore they affect to desire the same thing: but in order to defeat the measure not only object to every material part of the system, but artfully start vain objects of fear and throw in here and there a sentence importing that such an efficient general government consistent with the liberties of the people is in the nature of things impracticable.

➤➤ *Ignoratio elenchi* (ignorance of refutation). The name of this fallacy means to describe a particular kind of mistake. You're trying to refute an argument but aren't showing that its premises are false or that its logic fails. Instead you're making a claim that may be true but is beside the point. They say the defendant is innocent; you reply that the crime was terrible. They say an idea is defective; you say it was offered in good faith. They say X is false; you reply that X is important. In each case you're saying something irrelevant, and thus showing an ignorance of how refutation works.

> The Senator from Kentucky has wholly missed the point in the case. He has occupied himself with the southern line, and has shown us the northern boundary, and the southern boundary of Chihuahua down to Durango, but has never said a single word about the eastern boundary, which is, after all, the only question which we have here.

Benton, speech in the Senate (1850)

A famous instance of this fallacy is attributed to Samuel Johnson.

> After we came out of the church, we stood talking for some time together of Bishop Berkeley's ingenious sophistry to prove the non-existence of matter, and that every thing in the universe is merely ideal. I observed, that though we are satisfied his doctrine is not true, it is impossible to refute it. I never shall forget the alacrity with which Johnson answered, striking his foot with mighty force against a large stone, till he rebounded from it, "I refute it *thus*."

Boswell, *Life of Johnson* (1791)

Mill was not impressed:

> This short and easy confutation overlooks the fact, that in denying matter, Berkeley did not deny any thing to which

Mill, *A System of Logic* (1843)

our senses bear witness, and therefore can not be answered by any appeal to them. His skepticism related to the supposed substratum, or hidden cause of the appearances perceived by our senses; the evidence of which, whatever may be thought of its conclusiveness, is certainly not the evidence of sense.

↦ *The straw man.* The fallacy of inventing arguments that are easy to beat rather than addressing the harder real ones. This is sometimes considered a particular case of the *ignoratio elenchi* fallacy discussed above. The "straw man" expression evidently refers to the creation of a scarecrow that can be torn apart in a fight.

Mondell, speech in the House of Representatives (1916)

I want to pay a little attention to the artistic straw man skillfully constructed and decorated by the gentleman from Wisconsin, after which he proceeded very adroitly to spar with the straw man and pierce him through. His straw man was his assumption that the people of the West believe that they own the lands within the borders of their States, or have a superior claim upon them. I have lived in the West a long time and I have never heard any such claim asserted by anybody.

You can reply by identifying the arguments that your side never made, as shown in the example above and here:

Morley, *Mr. Mill's Doctrine of Liberty* (1873)

Mr. Stephen labors certain propositions which Mr. Mill never denied, such as that society ought to have a moral standard and ought to act upon it. He proves the contradictory of assertions which his adversary never made, as when he cites judicial instances which imply the recognition of morality by the law.

Or, perhaps better, precisely distinguish the straw man from your actual position.

Macaulay, *Civil Disabilities of the Jews* (1831)

It would be monstrous, say the persecutors, that Jews should legislate for a Christian community. This is a palpable misrepresentation. What is proposed is, not that the Jews should legislate for a Christian community, but that a legislature composed of Christians and Jews should legislate for a community composed of Christians and Jews.

A straw-man argument is often signaled by the use of unattributed arguments: *people are saying X*; *I've heard it said that* ... etc. A good response is to ask for particulars.

> No one has yet appeared in this Society to deny that we ought to judge of the future from the past. This remark is perhaps required, because several of the defenders of history appeared to be of opinion that their opponents were chargeable with some such doctrine.... If honorable gentlemen will point out in the whole world a single individual who believes a theory for any reason except because he considers it to be founded upon experience, the justness of this classification may be admitted. No such theorist however can be pointed out, because none such exists.

Mill,
The Use of History
(1827)

The use of motte-and-bailey doctrines (discussed earlier in this chapter) has been fruitfully compared to the straw man arguments we're considering here. A straw man argument attacks a position that the other side didn't really take. A "weak man" argument is a mild variation on the straw man: someone attacks a position in its weakest or most ridiculous form rather than taking it at its best (or just in its most representative form; compare p. 74). A motte-and-bailey doctrine can be viewed as a roughly opposite move: someone seems to defend a claim that's under attack, but actually defends a more modest and plausible view into which the defective one has been temporarily changed. The tactics are similar because they both distort a position. The straw man distorts a position to make it easier to attack; the motte-and-bailey maneuver distorts a position to make it easier to defend.

16

Reductio ad Absurdum

➤➤ *Reductio ad absurdum generally.* Formally: proving a claim by showing that the denial of it leads to a contradiction. Less formally: refuting a principle by showing that its implications lead to a result that's absurd or unwanted. This device is prominent in the dialogues of Plato, and Euclid used it to prove many mathematical claims. It was the basis, for example, of his proof that there must be an infinity of prime numbers.

Burke used the *reductio ad absurdum* to criticize attacks on the clergy by French revolutionaries. Some people justified those attacks by pointing to what former members of the clergy had done. Burke suggested to his French correspondent where this principle led.

Burke, *Reflections on the Revolution in France* (1790)

As well might we in England think of waging inexpiable war upon all Frenchmen for the evils which they have brought upon us in the several periods of our mutual hostilities. You might, on your part, think yourselves justified in falling upon all Englishmen on account of the unparalleled calamities brought upon the people of France by the unjust invasions of our Henries and our Edwards. Indeed, we should be mutually justified in this exterminatory war upon each other, full as much as you are in the unprovoked persecution of your present countrymen, on account of the conduct of men of the same name in other times.

A use of the theme to argue against England's intervention after Hitler invaded Czechoslovakia:

Nicholson, speech in the House of Commons (1939)

We cannot be expected to indulge in war on behalf of a country in Central Europe. It is all very well to say that we should have been fighting, not for the country which provided the *casus belli*, but for the great principles of liberty and justice for which we stand, but one cannot altogether dissociate oneself from the *casus belli* in that sort of battle. Let us, as in geometry, reduce the matter to an absurdity. Imagine that there is a small republic in Central Siberia which is being oppressed by the surrounding Powers. Is it to be said that one would be justified in plunging the world into war on behalf of the principles of liberty if the *casus belli* is at such a distance that one cannot bring help or assistance?

That example illustrates the pattern and its limits. The *reductio ad absurdum* is a good way to show that nobody goes to war just for the sake of general principles; there are always more immediate reasons. But it doesn't say how to balance those things, or whether *these* reasons are good ones. Those are matters of calculation and degree more than principle and logic. In this and other ways, a *reductio ad absurdum* can amount to a snare. You make a claim, and others say it leads straight to a crazy extension; but there might be a more modest way to put the principle behind what you've said. And whatever the principle might be, you may want to contest whether the extreme case really follows from it. The point is general: a bad use of *reductio ad absurdum*, like any bad argument, often hides its premises. You can make progress by dragging them into the light.

A *reductio ad absurdum* can be carried out by focusing on the destructive force of an argument: it takes out the target, but then too much more.

> We are told that extent of territory, variety of climates, productions and commerce, difference of extent, and number of inhabitants, dissimilitude of interests, morals and politics, will render this consolidated Republican form of Government impracticable. But what is the drift and tendency of this mode of argumentation? It evidently militates with equal force against every species of general Government—call it by what name you will, whether Consolidation or Confederation, it matters not, all must be equally impracticable.

Stevens,
Americanus IV
(1787)

Stephen, *Liberty,*
Equality, Fraternity
(1873)
Mr. Mill says that if grown-up people are grossly vicious it is the fault of society, which therefore ought not to punish them. This argument proves too much, for the same may be said with even greater force of gross crimes, and it is admitted that they may be punished.

↠ *Where it would have led.* A variation on the *reductio ad absurdum*: a principle would have led to absurd results in the past. When some people complained that the proposed constitution had too many provisions that were new, Madison said:

Madison,
Federalist 14
(1787)
Had no important step been taken by the leaders of the Revolution for which a precedent could not be discovered, no government established of which an exact model did not present itself, the people of the United States might, at this moment, have been numbered among the melancholy victims of misguided councils, must at best have been laboring under the weight of some of those forms which have crushed the liberties of the rest of mankind. Happily for America, happily, we trust, for the whole human race, they pursued a new and more noble course.

Others said the constitution should be rejected because it created too many chances for abuse. John Dickinson came back with a point like Madison's.

Dickinson,
Letters of Fabius
IV (1787)
It seems highly probable, that those who would reject this labor of public love, would also have rejected the Heaven-taught institution of trial by jury, had they been consulted upon its establishment. Would they not have cried out.... "What! Can freedom be preserved by imprisoning its guardians? Can freedom be preserved, by keeping twelve men closely confined without meat, drink, fire, or candle, until they unanimously agree, and this to be innumerably repeated?" ... Happily for us, our ancestors thought otherwise. They were not so over-nice and curious as to refuse blessings because they might possibly be abused.

Notice a hazard in this sort of argument. No doubt it's true that too much fear of abuse would have caused harm in the past. But too *little* of it has caused plenty of bad things, too. It isn't fair to just point to the harm that a principle would have done. You need to compare it to the good the principle has done (or would have done elsewhere), and the bad things caused by too little of it. The right question isn't just where a principle would have led if used earlier, but how it compares on the whole to where the *alternative* would have led if used earlier.

➤➤ *The significance of extreme cases.* When can a proposition fairly be tested by taking it to an extreme? If it's a claim of principle, a failure to work in all settings may show that it's unsound in any of them.

> If they said, "We do not carry the principle to the extreme," then he would ask why they stopped short, and did not pursue their theory to its end? There could be only one reason, and that reason was, because they could not carry it to its consequences without exposing its folly—because the whole scheme was easily exposed as a gross and revolting absurdity.... They might as well allow a man, whose reasoning they had shown to be false, by showing the absurd consequences to which it led, to say, "Oh, I did not mean to arrive at that conclusion. I did not intend to go the length of asserting that two and two make five." No—very likely you did not; but you said that which by logical deduction from it led to the consequence that two and two are equal to five, and therefore you are proved to have said that which cannot be true.

Brougham, speech in the House of Lords (1842)

The contrary view: extreme applications aren't a good test; few principles can survive that kind of stretching. Of course it depends on the kind of principle at issue. But many moral and political arguments involve tradeoffs that make it hard to say, about anything that matters, *always* or *never*.

> There is hardly any theoretic hypothesis which, carried to a certain extreme, does not become practically false.

Hamilton, *Examination of the President's Message* (1802)

Russell, speech in
the House of Com-
mons (1891)

Nobody who has lived for 50 years ever dreams of carrying out anything to its logical conclusion.

Burke had a distinct objection to taking arguments to extremes: it's a habit that discourages people from pursuing reforms at all.

Burke, *An Appeal from the New to the Old Whigs* (1791)

This mode of arguing from your having done any thing in a certain line to the necessity of doing every thing has political consequences of other moment than those of a logical fallacy. If no man can propose any diminution or modification of an invidious or dangerous power or influence in government, without entitling friends turned into adversaries to argue him into the destruction of all prerogative, and to a spoliation of the whole patronage of royalty, I do not know what can more effectually deter persons of sober minds from engaging in any reform.

So it's hard to make general claims about when a principle should be tested by extreme cases. It's best settled by examining the principle itself. Does it *claim* to cover all cases? If so, you can ask whether it does; if not, you can ask whether it should. Some rules and principles are meant to apply to extreme cases; that's their point. A constitution, for example, is supposed to provide answers for hard questions and serious problems, not just easy ones.

Tucker, speech
in the House of
Representatives
(1820)

It is no answer to this argument to say that such an exertion of power as I have supposed is highly improbable. In expounding a Constitution, it is perfectly fair to test the correctness of a principle by extreme cases.

Mill,
On Liberty
(1859)

Strange it is, that men should admit the validity of the arguments for free discussion, but object to their being "pushed to an extreme;" not seeing that unless the reasons are good for an extreme case, they are not good for any case.

When arguing about whether a proposal will *work*, pointing to an extreme case has a different significance. The proposal might work fine if X or Y happens, but not if extreme case Z happens—raising questions about whether Z is likely enough to matter. A rule that is good most of the time might be enough. We can handle the unusual cases separately.

> When I declare that [agreement to be] a wise treaty, in which one party cannot make peace without the consent of the other, I am not to have extreme cases put for the purpose of shewing that inconveniencies may arise from such a stipulation. My answer to such an argument is short—that extreme cases ought not to be put. Extreme cases cannot be included in, nor ought they to be an objection to, a general rule; they must be met and provided for on their own specific grounds.

Grenville, speech in the House of Lords (1807)

17

Slippery Slopes

➔ *Slippery slopes.* Someone makes a proposal that seems harmless in itself. It's attacked because taking the good step now will lead to bad ones later. This pattern is often known now as a slippery slope, but it has been the subject of other metaphors as well.

Platt, speech in the Senate (1882)
> It will be useless to attempt to consider the features of a bill after we have committed ourselves to the principle as we are asked today to commit ourselves. It is the old story of the camel putting his nose within the tent, and then his shoulders, and finally the whole body of the animal.

A slope can be slippery when the logic of a principle is hard to contain.

Cecil, speech in the House of Lords (1871)
> We are always told that it is unnecessary to look beyond the Bill before us; that the actual proposition of the moment is the utmost limit which the Government intend to go, and that we need not trouble ourselves about the future or pursue the theoretical consequences of a principle which it is not intended to carry further. When, however, we have yielded to that reasoning and a few years have passed, we are told by the same persons that we have admitted a principle which must be carried to its extreme conclusions, and that we are precluded by our former concessions from opposing its logical consequence.

Senators once argued about whether the president's inauguration ball should be allowed to happen under the dome of the Capitol building. Said Charles Sumner:

Sumner, speech in the Senate (1869)
> Do not expect that the precedent is to be restrained to inauguration day. There will be other occasions. People will wish to dance on other days than inauguration day, in honor of some

victory, some other incident of life; and you must be prepared then either to vote that they shall, or to deny it, and, if you deny it, to make a distinction between the two cases. There was an old patriotic saying which our fathers borrowed from their English ancestors; and it was "oppose beginnings," *obsta principiis*; and I incline to think that on this occasion it may be properly applied.

→→ *More mechanisms.* Sometimes a slippery slope comes about in a different way: earlier decisions change the *conditions* in which later ones are made. Perhaps the early decision will change the costs and benefits associated with the ones to come. Thus people who want long-term spending start by arguing for some temporary spending; it seems harmless but can make the case for more of it hard to resist later.

> If we are to incur that expenditure in this time of profound peace for the purpose of being prepared for war, as they say, for an attack from foreign nations, then you will not stop after this year with an appropriation of $3,000,000, but on the contrary you will have to increase it tenfold from year to year. The appropriations in this bill are but the entering wedge. The bill is drawn upon the idea that if you incur an expenditure of $3,000,000 this year you will be willing hereafter for the purpose of saving that amount to incur larger expenditures in future years.

Follett, speech in the House of Representatives (1884)

The first decision can also change the expectations and attitudes of the people subject to it, and increase their tolerance or demand for more of the same. An example from a debate about the federal role in local schools:

> If we once recognize Federal jurisdiction over the subject of education, that jurisdiction will always be asserted and necessarily maintained because the people of the States will become accustomed to depend more and more upon Federal taxation for the support of the public schools, and the result will inevitably be the abandonment of the local common-school system and the establishment of a grand national educational

Crain, speech in the House of Representatives (1886)

scheme maintained by the United States Treasury, regulated by the United States Congress, and managed by United States officials.

Or the first decision can affect the power of the parties affected by it, and thus change their ability to bring about the second decision, for better or worse.

Burdett, speech in the House of Commons (1828)

Never was there a grosser mistake in policy, than to yield such a power to the Irish Catholics, if it were intended to stop short and withhold from them equal rights with the rest of their fellow countrymen. By giving them the elective franchise, we gave them that which Archimedes required—a point from which to move the world.

➤➤ *Objections*. The standard objection to a slippery-slope argument: if you're worried that a good decision now will lead to a bad extension later, make an objection *then*. It makes no sense to injure yourself in the present out of fear that you can't be trusted to draw lines in the future.

Knatchbull-Hugessen, speech in the House of Commons (1876)

To concede to the demand now made is either right or wrong—just or unjust—and if it is right, I will not refuse to do that which is right today, for fear that if I do so, I may be asked to do something which I may think wrong tomorrow.

Eliot, *Daniel Deronda* (1876)

"I think that way of arguing against a course, because it may be ridden down to an absurdity, would soon bring life to a standstill," said Deronda. "It is not the logic of human action, but of a roasting-jack that must go on to the last turn when it has once been wound up. We can do nothing safely without some judgment as to where we are to stop."

Sometimes making an objection later works out fine. Some people once argued that allowing interracial marriages would lead to legal marriages that are polygamous or incestuous. It was said in reply that those other possibilities could be resisted when they came up, and they have been. In other cases, of course, an assurance like that has been made and turned out to be wrong.

The last objection which I shall notice is the favorite one that this is the thin end of the wedge, and that if women are allowed to vote, they will ask to sit in the House of Commons. Well, Sir, and suppose they do? Cannot we successfully oppose so preposterous a demand?

Forsyth, speech in the House of Commons (1876)

The sorites paradox. A problem related to the slippery slope is the *sorites paradox.* (Compare the different sense of *sorites* on p. 92.) The word *sorites* comes from the Greek word for *heap*, which produced the basic example of a famous problem: one stone doesn't make a pile; neither do two stones; it's hard to say that a third does it; and so on until you have a hundred stones but still haven't said that you have a heap. Yet everyone thinks you *do* have one. Again, metaphors besides the heap have been used to describe the pattern.

We seem to be proceeding on what is known as the "horse-tail" argument—that is, that you may take away a hair from the tail and still leave a horse's tail, and you may take away another and another, and so on, removing hairs, and still leave the tail; the only question is, when do you come to the point where there is no horse's tail?

Healy, speech in the House of Commons (1887)

The horse's tail is an allusion to Horace, *Epistles*, book 2, 43.

This problem is most familiar in arguments about numbers: if you would say yes to this many, why not to a few more or less? It's often hard to defend a line drawn between any two points in particular.

Boston will want these cutters next; and why not? It is a question of degree, and not of principle. Charleston will want them next; and why not? New Orleans will want them next; and why not? It is a question of degree, and not of principle. It is no answer to say, that because there are a thousand men in danger at New York, you will not protect nine hundred at Boston; and if nine hundred men are in danger there, why should you not protect against the danger of shipwreck five hundred at Norfolk, or one hundred at Savannah, or fifty at Charleston?

Toombs, speech in the Senate (1856)

Guinness, speech
in the House of
Commons
(1914)
The argument which has been brought forward from the other side has been that troops must be used in aid of the civil power to maintain order in the case of trade disputes and the riots which occasionally arise therefrom, and that if you are justified in using troops in such riots, you are therefore equally justified in using them in Ulster. I think that that is an example of sophism which, I believe, is known as a sorites. You get somebody to admit something which is obviously true, and you lead up by imperceptible steps to something which is manifestly false.

Sometimes a sorites gets solved by a crude line drawn *somewhere* because the errors produced by it are of no great concern. Putting up with them is better than having no lines at all.

Palmer, speech
in the House of
Commons
(1856)
The noble Lord says—"See what you allow now. How can you justify that without going on and allowing this?" The noble Lord is far too able a man not to know that in all these questions there must always be a debatable ground. We must have a line drawn somewhere. It cannot be drawn with perfect theoretical accuracy; but there is no great practical harm as long as it is so drawn as neither to offend nor corrupt the public conscience.

Balfour, speech
in the House of
Commons
(1887)
If you draw the line at one number of years, why not just above or below that number? But this is an argument always held in contempt by practical legislators. You must draw a line somewhere, and there will always be on either side of that line cases that differ from cases on the other side of the line chosen by very small and almost imperceptible distinctions. But that is no reason for not drawing the line.

⇥ *Untenable lines.* We've seen how a slope can become slippery when it's hard to draw lines between two points. Those line-drawing problems can be severe on their own, not just as a reason why one thing leads to another. The difficulty of drawing a line between two cases can make it hard to address them at all.

I should like to vote for a bill which would destroy all oppressive and injurious trusts, but I have never seen one which had
that tendency, and I do not believe the ingenuity of man can
draw the line between legitimate combinations and oppressive
trusts. It is very difficult even to get legislation to draw a line
between good and bad men.

Stewart, speech
in the Senate
(1900)

If a line can't be drawn cleanly, of course, discussion need not stop.
You might just have to decide which is worse: treating both cases
like the first one, both like the second, or both in some middle way.
A humble example:

It is very difficult to draw the line between brushes and
brooms. There are many kinds of brushes made from broom-
corn which are in a certain sense brooms, and vice versa, and
it is very difficult to distinguish between them. There should
be a uniform rate upon the two articles, and as the duty upon
brushes can not be reduced without injury to American manufactures, the committee have placed the duty on both brushes
and brooms at the same rate.

Aldrich, speech
in the Senate
(1889)

A more dramatic example came up after the Civil War. Citizens of
rebel states had suffered great losses at the hands of the Union army.
They wanted compensation from the federal government. Some of
the claimants had been active in the rebellion; some hadn't. What
to do?

If it were a practicable thing to draw a line of discrimination
between the guilty and the innocent, and the Government
were able to pay, I would feel it my duty to vote for the payment of this class of damages when the claimants are loyal
citizens. I beg leave, however, to suggest to the House the
utter impracticability of drawing this line of discrimination.

Delano, speech
in the House of
Representatives
(1866)

Congress rejected all the claims.

18

Consistency

➤ *Stare decisis* (lit., to stand by things decided). A well-known principle of law: past decisions ordinarily aren't reversed; they're binding in similar cases. Our interest here isn't primarily in the use of stare decisis by courts, which is an involved topic. It's in the broader use of the notion that past decisions should be respected and consistency with them valued.

The first usual rationale for leaving decisions alone, and holding to the principles they reflect, is that people have relied on them. Reversing course disrupts those expectations and makes it hard to form them going forward (because the same thing might happen again).

Allen, speech in the Senate (1898)

It is stare decisis in name and principle when we follow a case or a line of decisions of courts and apply the rules there recognized, conceded to be wrong in some cases in the first instance, but which we believe better to follow than to disturb them for technical accuracy, because they have become fixed and have established relations and conditions.

Or the point may be to avoid confusion: clarity is valuable, and we achieve it by staying consistent.

Logan, speech in the Senate (1872)

Some say this is a bad precedent. If it is a bad precedent, two precedents differing would be worse.

Sometimes stare decisis is valued because it's a kind of decision by rule. Past decisions may have been made at discretion. Still, once they're on the books, stare decisis means treating them as fixed. They then reduce discretion in the later cases. They force like cases to be treated alike.

Cullom, speech in the Senate (1884)

If we can disregard a construction settled by our predecessors we can not claim that we have a right to make a construction which will bind our successors.... No man could know his rights, duties, or obligations under the Constitution until those in power at the time shall have decided what they are; nor would the trouble end with such decision, for, if precedents are of no value, the same men might change their minds, as several Senators seem to have done on this very question, and afterward reach a different conclusion. As to questions pertaining to private rights and cognizable by the courts, such uncertainty would be intolerable. In such cases the uncertainty would amount to creating a government of men, not a government of the laws.

Stare decisis can be defended, finally, on the ground that past cases show the right way to decide a question. They amount to a body of wisdom more impressive than what anyone making a new decision is likely to have now. The mood behind this way of thinking is associated with Burke.

> We are afraid to put men to live and trade each on his own private stock of reason; because we suspect that the stock in each man is small, and that the individuals would do better to avail themselves of the general bank and capital of nations and of ages.

Burke, *Reflections on the Revolution in France* (1790)

→→ *Skepticism of precedent.* If one side in a debate wants to stick to past decisions, the other side probably doesn't. Some arguments against precedent are particular to the forum where the arguing takes place. The value of consistency is different in courts and legislatures, for example. The common law ordinarily treats the decisions of courts as irreversible; legislatures are at liberty to change their decisions (and the decisions of courts) in ways that courts aren't.

> From the very nature of legislation there can be no precedent. Each Congress is supreme, and each law must be passed upon its own merits. You may, indeed, refer to the proceedings of a former Congress, as expressing the opinions of gentlemen entitled to great weight, but surely you are not bound by them. Hence arises the difference between the effect of precedents

Spencer, speech in the House of Representatives (1818)

in a court of justice and in a Legislature. In the former some fixed rule is necessary, that suitors may know their rights; in the latter, when it is not a question of right, each case furnishes its own rule.

You can attack a specific precedent as weak or inapplicable because it was made in times or by people that ought to reduce its weight.

Burke, *Speech on Conciliation with the Colonies* (1775)

The irregular things done in the confusion of mighty troubles, and on the hinge of great revolutions, even if all were done that is said to have been done, form no example.... None of your own liberties could stand a moment, if the casual deviations from them, at such times, were suffered to be used as proofs of their nullity.

Lincoln, *Admission of West Virginia* (1862)

A measure made expedient by a war is no precedent for times of peace.

But the strongest general criticism of holding to past decisions is that it amounts to doubling down on mistakes. Note that stare decisis really has bite when the earlier decision seems wrong; if it's right, we can just follow it on *that* basis. So some people regard stare decisis as the last resort of someone whose position can't stand on its own. You defend a decision on the merits when you can; when you can't, you say the merits aren't the issue. The issue is consistency.

Thompson, speech in the House of Representatives (1848)

A sound precedent is only that which is sustained by sound reason, and which when followed works no injustice. Stare decisis is the cry and principle of a tyrant.

Allen, speech in the Senate (1900)

Whenever a man wants to fortify a thing which he can not fortify in logic or reason he always resorts to precedents. I have no doubt the man who taught the doctrine that the world was flat and rested upon a serpent invoked that precedent in subsequent discussion.

↦ *Resisting demands for precedent.* The word *unprecedented* can be a form of objection: you're making a novel proposal, and it's alarming to go into uncharted waters. Where's the precedent? One line of reply: you're solving a novel problem.

Gentlemen talk about precedent. I am ashamed to hear them. There may be no precedent on the subject. But are we always to act by precedent? There is scarcely a circumstance occurs in this House but what is different from any that was before it.

Nicholas, speech in the House of Representatives (1796)

This project cannot be met successfully by the assertion that there is no precedent for it. Sir, there is no precedent for our position in the history of the world.

Butler, speech in the House of Representatives (1869)

You can also suggest that calling for a precedent is questionable in general. Precedent is what lawyers worry about; if we aren't in court, who cares whether there's a past case on point? The situation calls for a broader perspective.

A case lawyer in court, instead of reasoning upon the principles of the law, is always looking back after an old case, and it sometimes happens in politics that statesmen instead of confronting the situation before them and seeing what is required, are looking back for a rusty precedent to find what somebody else has said under other circumstances, and in different times.

Morton, speech in the Senate (1870)

Some men do not dare reach any conclusion unless they find some precedence, some authority, some fellow who has reasoned things out for them. These men always look for paragraph 2, section 5, subdivision 4, on page 297 of volume 2, or some other paragraph or section of a textbook. Why not come down to fundamental principles?

London, speech in the House of Representatives (1917)

→→ *Setting precedents.* Arguments about precedent can matter in a forward-looking way: a bad decision will turn into a precedent that we regret. It'll be used to justify worse things, or what's done for someone now will have to be done later for others or for everyone.

I call upon Senators to reflect before they proceed further in this business. I tell you this record will be brought up in future time, just as the records of our ancestors are brought up now; and our descendants will be told that, because we did this today, they may do it in all time to come.

Brown, speech in the Senate (1854)

Or if others treat our decision as a precedent that gives them the right to do the same thing, *we* will be hurt.

Stanley,
speech in the
House of
Commons
(1855)
Is the House prepared to accept that theory? Is it prepared to affirm that peace shall never be made except after decisive victory? Because if so, understand it clearly, you are declaring that there shall be one law for England and another for all other Powers. If you allow that what is necessary for the honor of this country may be necessary also for that of Russia, if she too is to lay down the same principle and abide by it, then peace at any time becomes impossible, and the war is rendered interminable.

And maybe the precedent you make will be turned against you directly.

Voorhees,
speech in the
House of
Representatives
(1863)
Let the advocates of this monstrous doctrine beware.... Your day is drawing near the close, and that which you may seek to exercise for temporary purposes, while you yet linger in power, for the destruction of political opponents, or as a power upon which the Executive is to ride through this Hall triumphant, may all come back to haunt you hereafter.

↠ *The incriminating shift.* Your adversaries haven't stuck to precedent or have changed position in some other way. This may show that they don't believe either thing they've said.

Smith,
Address to the
People of
New York
(1788)
The advocates for the constitution have shifted their ground. When men are uniform in their opinions, it affords evidence that they are sincere. When they are shifting, it gives reason to believe, they do not change from conviction.

Or they're trimming their positions for bad reasons, such as conformity to popular opinion.

Smith,
Address to the
People of
New York
(1788)
It is only too true, as was said by the noble Lord the Member for Marylebone, that the First Lord of the Admiralty is nothing but a weather-cock, and that he changes his position day after day, week after week, and month after month as events occur.

Even if the change means nothing so specific, it might suggest that the people who made it shouldn't be taken too seriously.

He came here at the commencement of this rebellion a strong Union man; and he says now that he hugs to his very soul a platform that disunionists have made. I merely suggest these things to show that where next he may be found, the Lord only knows.

Nye, speech in the Senate (1868)

⇥ *Defending a change.* You've changed *your* position and have to defend the shift. One route: the change is justified by changes in the world.

It will be asked, if such was then my opinion of the mode of pacification, how I came to be the very person who moved, not only for a repeal of all the late coercive statutes, but for mutilating, by a positive law, the entireness of the legislative power of Parliament, and cutting off from it the whole right of taxation. I answer, Because a different state of things requires a different conduct.

Burke, Letter to the Sheriffs of Bristol (1777)

Sometimes you can go further: you're proud to have changed positions. A good expression of this has been (mis)attributed to Churchill: "When the facts change, I change my mind. What do you do, sir?" (Something like that was probably once said by Keynes.) Other examples:

MR. NORWOOD. Why has the Senator changed his position since he made that report?

MR. ALCORN. I simply changed my position in obedience to law; what every man should do.

Exchange in the Senate (1876)

I am not consistent with my record of that time, and if there is anything I am proud of, it is that I am never consistent two years at a time amid changing events such as we have.

Grosvenor, speech in the House of Representatives (1906)

Or you just changed your mind. Very good: you aren't afraid to rethink your position. Confessing error is frightening to those who do it, but often makes an appealing impression on everyone else.

Cobb, speech in
the House of
Representatives
(1858)

I am ashamed to say that I have myself often neglected the Territories because they have no votes. But it was wrong; and I censure my own action on former occasions, and admit that it was wrong.

Saying you've changed your mind can encourage others to change theirs. You describe your earlier view in sympathetic terms that they will recognize as their own. Then you guide them away from it.

Essays of
an Old Whig
(1787)

When the constitution proposed by the late convention made its appearance, I was disposed to embrace it almost without examination; I was determined not to be offended with trifles or to scan it too critically. "We want something: let us try this; experience is the best teacher: if it does not answer our purpose we can alter it: at all events it will serve for a beginning." Such were my reasonings;—but, upon further reflection, I may say that I am shaken with very considerable doubts and scruples.

↠ *Hypocrisy.* The words and doings of people on the other side aren't consistent. They criticize others for things of which they're as guilty or worse, and so shouldn't be heard on the subject.

Ransdell, speech in
the Senate (1916)

Surely with his record his tongue should be forever silent upon questions of national honor.

Mann, speech in the
House of Represen-
tatives (1919)

It does not lie in the mouth of any gentleman on that side of the House to lecture this side of the House about wasting time.

Or if they haven't done the same things, their choices disqualify them in other ways from judging the choices of others. They have no standing.

Hoar, speech
in the Senate
(1893)

It comes with very ill grace from Senators who peer out of their luxurious carriage windows drawn by elegant spans of horses to sneer at the man who finds his recreation in the bicycle.

Another version of the point is what lawyers call estoppel: you won't be heard to complain now because you didn't speak up when the time was right. If someone is silent when it counts but becomes a critic afterwards, it can put their credibility or motives into doubt.

> The famine found the people of Ireland in the midst of their vicious system of potato culture and potato reliance. It was all very well to point out retrospectively the defects of any measures adopted in such an emergency; but when they were introduced, no voice was raised against them. Where was the hon. Gentleman then?

Somerville, speech in the House of Commons (1849)

You can make it a warning: *we'll* be discredited as hypocrites if we act as you propose.

> How can this Government as one of the civilized nations of the earth say to foreign nations with whom we may engage in war hereafter: "When you tread our soil, our institutions of learning are safe even from the incendiarism of war;" how can we say that when we have burned down an institution of our own in civil war, and then refuse to pay for it?

Tucker, speech in the House of Representatives (1879)

For more discussion of this theme, see chapter 14 (*ad hominem* arguments).

⤳ *Double standards.* A debate is carried out on certain terms—A, B, and C. Then the criteria are changed to X, Y, and Z. This makes it an unfair fight. One side is judged by different standards than the other. The issue may be what body of knowledge is treated as relevant to a question.

> Let us use one weight and one measure. Let us not throw history aside when we are proving a theory, and take it up again when we have to refute an objection founded on the principles of that theory.

Macaulay, *Westminster Reviewer's Defence of Mill* (1829)

Suppose the issue is the style of argument that's allowed. Should we use a wide lens or a narrow one? Should we debate principles or details? Whatever the answer, let it be the same for everyone.

> "You deal in general, in vague declamation," said the noble Lord; "no facts have you to mention, not one: I challenge you

Peel, speech in the House of Commons (1837)

to come forward with the details; and I will brand you with disgrace, unless you produce your facts." Well, four hours did not elapse before the discussion became very inconvenient; and then the House was told, that it would be infinitely better to confine themselves to the great question, which was the proper object of our debate—that the detail of small facts was more inconvenient than a statement of general principles.

The same can happen when one side makes an unannounced change in how costs and benefits will be reckoned.

Mackintosh, speech in the House of Commons (1831)
They use the probability of future evil from Reform as their main stay. But when we employ the probability of future evil from Non Reform, in support of our opinion, they call it menace, and they charge us with intimidation. They do not allow to us the same fair mode of reasoning on which they exclusively rely; and they do not seem to perceive, that the proofs of evil likely to issue from the measure are of no avail if they are not attended by the proof that they are probably greater than those likely to flow from its rejection.

Apples should be compared to apples.

19

Abuses and Exceptions

↠ *Risks of abuse*. The ability to do right is usually joined to an ability to do wrong. This is a frequent objection to the conferral of any power or liberty: the risk of abuse is too great. The distrust is typically said not to be personal. It's just the lesson of experience.

> Let the disposition of a man be what it may, I will not consent to invest him with extraordinary, unconstitutional powers, for this plain reason, that it is subject to abuse. The virtue of a man is therefore no argument with me in favor of such grants; because I learn from the history of mankind, because particularly the history of the constitution, and my own experience, forbid such grants.

O'Connell, speech in the House of Commons (1804)

> I may be told that this privilege or prerogative may be sparingly exercised, and that we must not object to a good thing because it may be abused. I do not give way to that delusion. I do not accede to that position in what I call constitutional policy. I will give no power that is capable of being abused, unless where I think it necessary for some great object.

Lyndhurst, speech in the House of Lords (1856)

↠ *Abusus non tollit usum*. That worry can bring back standard replies: just about anything can be abused, including whatever is good and necessary. So the risk has to be treated as a problem to manage, not a disqualifier. The Latin for this idea is *abusus non tollit usum*: abuse does not remove use. Thus Hamilton's reply to people who opposed public banks:

> Like all other good things, they are subject to abuse, and, when abused, become pernicious…. The truth is, in human affairs there is no good, pure and unmixed; every advantage has two sides; and wisdom consists in availing themselves of the good, and guarding as much as possible against the bad.

Hamilton, letter to Robert Morris (1781)

Abuse may be so unlikely that it isn't worth worrying about. That was Madison's defense of letting Congress set the pay of its members:

Madison, speech at Virginia Ratifying Convention (1788)

There is no instance where this power has been abused. In America, legislative bodies have reduced their own wages lower, rather than augmented them. This is a power which cannot be abused without rousing universal attention and indignation.

Or abuse, if it does happen, can be caught and corrected.

Webster, *The Weaknesses of Brutus Exposed* (1787)

Brutus all along founds his objections and fears on extreme cases of abuse or misapplication of supreme powers, which may possibly happen, under the administration of a wild, weak, or wicked Congress; but 'tis easy to observe that all institutions are liable to extremes, but ought not to be judged by them; they do not often appear, and perhaps never may; but if they should happen in the cases supposed, (which God forbid), there is a remedy pointed out, in the Constitution itself.

(The remedy Webster had in mind was amendment.) Or you say that we should accept some abuse as the price of good things.

Burke, *Speech on American Taxation* (1774)

It is the nature of all greatness not to be exact; and great trade will always be attended with considerable abuses. The contraband will always keep pace in some measure with the fair trade. It should stand as a fundamental maxim, that no vulgar precaution ought to be employed in the cure of evils which are closely connected with the cause of our prosperity.

And perhaps we can write rules to separate use from abuse. An application to flogging:

Norton, speech in the House of Lords (1889)

I rather think the noble and learned Lord's feelings with regard to this particular punishment arise simply from recollections of the excessive degree in which it was administered in former times; but the abuse of anything is no argument against the moderate use of it, especially when it has proved to be in peculiar cases deterrent.

The classic riposte to all such claims is a denial that abuses can be prevented or separated from the supposedly good uses of a rule. This can be a factual challenge to some of the arguments just seen: abuse is inevitable, not something from which we might hope to escape.

It was not the Constitution, according to him, which was the cause of the evils but the abuses which had crept into the Constitution. One might suppose from this, that the abuses were of recent origin and that there was a time when the Constitution existed in all its purity, and made manifest its goodness by the beauty of its effects. When was this time? Never.

Mill, speech on parliamentary reform (1824)

The thrust can also be conceptual: the bad features are so pervasive, or so inherent in the enterprise, that it's pointless to talk about suppressing or avoiding them.

In vain you tell me that artificial government is good, but that I fall out only with the abuse. The thing! the thing itself is the abuse!

Burke, A Vindication of Natural Society (1756)

The apologists for slavery often speak of the abuses of slavery; and they tell us that they are as much opposed to those abuses as we are; and that they would go as far to correct those abuses and to ameliorate the condition of the slave as anybody. The answer to that view is, that slavery is itself an abuse; that it lives by abuse; and dies by the absence of abuse.

Douglass, speech at Rochester (1850)

➻ *Exceptions.* The most famous thing said about exceptions—that the exception proves the rule—is often misunderstood. You're shown to be wrong about something; you say that your mistake is the exception that proves the rule, which is that you're generally right. That's foolishness. But the saying has a better meaning that becomes clear from the long Latin form of it: *exceptio probat regulam de rebus non exceptis*: an exception proves the rule concerning things not excepted. In other words, the *need* for an exception proves the *existence* of the rule.

"Sewing silk" is excepted; and in such a case the exception of one thing is equivalent to an affirmation of the exclusion of all other manufactures of silk in the same paragraph.

Adams v. Bancroft, 3 Sumn. 384 (D. Mass. 1838) (Story, J.)

Merrick, speech
in the Senate
(1838)

Special enactments are only necessary to take a case out of a general rule, and such special enactment, such exception proves the rule, does not reverse it, sir!

There's also a hostile view of exceptions: a *good* rule doesn't need them, or at least not many. Every exception shows that a rule was badly written, or that it's an effort to look like a rule without having the uniformity of one.

Money, speech in the
House of Commons
(1907)

Any legislation which contained so many exceptions as this Bill stood condemned on the face of it.

Bailey, speech in
the Senate
(1911)

I have little patience with any man who has so little confidence in his doctrine that he is always making exceptions to it. A man who believes in the soundness of his doctrine is always ready to apply it, and every time he admits the necessity of making an exception to it he acknowledges its unsoundness to that extent at least, or else he acknowledges his own insincerity.

Regardless of whether exceptions are good or bad in general, too many can make a rule useless or nearly so. The exceptions may then be said to have swallowed the rule.

Canning, speech in
the House of Com-
mons (1807)

We have heard it said that *exceptio probat regulam*: but when the proofs of the rule are nothing but exceptions, the rule itself may reasonably be thought to be in some danger.

Brown, speech
in the Senate
(1885)

Everything that is shipped from one point in North Carolina to another is excepted by the Constitution; everything that is shipped by express of course is excepted; and then every other thing where the freight is less than $20 on the shipment is subject to have 10 per cent. added, which destroys the equality. Then what is left? To what does the amendment apply?

When the exceptions to a rule are more prominent than the applications, there's a chance for rhetorical fun.

Mill, *The British
Constitution*
(1826)

When England, Sir, is called a free country, a slight mistake is made of a part for the whole: we are free as Sparta was free: the Helots are overlooked. If, Sir, I could overlook the whole of our peasantry, and all who are unhappy enough to need any service at the hands of what are denominated courts of justice, I might admit that we are on the whole subject to less oppression than any other nation in Europe.

The late Attorney General for Ireland—whose speeches always displayed a genuine ring of that Irish humor which softens the acerbities of life, and saves the Saxons from the painful fate of boring one another to death—once voted for the Bill, but on informing a lady of it was told he might have been much better employed; and he afterwards, in opposing it, remarked that nobody knew what it meant, comparing it to a Highlander's gun, which would have been a very good one if it had only a new stock, a new lock, and a new barrel.

> Scourfield, speech in the House of Commons (1873)

↞ *Maxim skepticism.* Sometimes an argument is supported by maxims, or rules of thumb. There's a tradition of contempt for such rules as a source of guidance. The elegance of a saying can give it more weight than it deserves. Thus Burke's view of maxims:

They are light and portable. They are as current as copper coin; and about as valuable. They serve equally the first capacities and the lowest; and they are, at least, as useful to the worst men as the best. Of this stamp is the cant of *Not men, but measures*; a sort of charm, by which many people get loose from every honorable engagement.

> Burke, *Thoughts on the Cause of the Present Discontents* (1770)

A literary comment:

All people of broad, strong sense have an instinctive repugnance to the men of maxims; because such people early discern that the mysterious complexity of our life is not to be embraced by maxims.

> Eliot, *The Mill on the Floss* (1860)

Maxims are sometimes thought to be less useful than they sound because for any such rule on point, another one cuts the other way.

We are told it is dangerous to trust power anywhere; that power is liable to abuse,—with a variety of trite maxims of

> Hamilton, speech in New York Assembly (1787)

the same kind. General propositions of this nature are easily
framed, the truth of which cannot be denied, but they rarely
convey any precise idea. To these we might oppose other
propositions, equally true and equally indefinite. It might be
said that too little power is as dangerous as too much; that
it leads to anarchy, and from anarchy to despotism. But the
question still recurs: What is the too much or too little?

Conkling,   We are told that "fraud vitiates everything," and therefore
speech   we may undo corrupt elections. As a popular saying, this
in the Senate   trite maxim is of some value; as a legal saying, it is far from
(1873)   accurate…. As an offset to this maxim, I offer another: Fraud
vitiates nothing, except in the forum and in the proceeding in
which it can legally be tried.

The legal scholar Karl Llewellyn once argued that for every legal
maxim there is another that seems to offset it. He made a list of 28
"thrusts" one can make with maxims and their corresponding "par-
ries." One maxim says that a statute can't go beyond its text; another
says that a statute can go beyond its text to give effect to its purpose.
But Llewellyn's argument wasn't that maxims are worthless. It was
that you need something more than a maxim to know how the maxim
should be applied.

20

Abduction and Related Forms of Inference

→→ *Inferring a design.* You don't know why others did what they've done, or anyway you can't prove it. It's only clear *what* they did. So you have to guess at their reasons or infer them. Perhaps you can devise an account of their intentions that at least fits the facts.

> I am forced to look for some common principle that shall explain the meaning of these Gentlemen going all round the compass in this manner; one time assuming one ground, and at another time another; and I do find that there is one principle common to all, and that that is a great desire to protect the West India interest.

Macaulay, speech in the House of Commons (1845)

Reasoning of this general kind is sometimes called *abductive* (as opposed to *deductive* or *inductive*), or "inference to the best explanation"—i.e., drawing the inference that best explains the evidence you see. Abductive reasoning resembles inductive reasoning, and indeed they're sometimes hard to tell apart (and not always distinguished in the same way). Both involve drawing probable inferences from observed facts. But inductive reasoning usually means making multiple observations and then drawing a generalization from them. Abductive reasoning is narrower: you're typically trying to *explain* one particular event or action by positing a cause, perhaps of someone's behavior or symptoms, etc. You consider the facts and come up with an inference that fits them. An abductive inference thus can be drawn from a single observation: the case we see is explained best in *this* way. Other possible explanations are less economical or less consistent with the facts or have other such shortcomings.

Someone who draws an abductive inference will sometimes give a disclaimer: maybe the other side's intentions aren't as I suggest, but they might as well be.

Burke, *Letters on the Proposals for Peace with the Regicide Directory of France* (1796)

Whatever may be the intention (which, because I do not know, I cannot dispute) of those who would discontent mankind by this strange pity, they act towards us, in the consequences, as if they were our worst enemies.

Lincoln, debate with Stephen Douglas at Galesburg (1858)

He is also preparing (whether purposely or not) the way for making the institution of slavery national! I repeat again, for I wish no misunderstanding, that I do not charge that he means it so; but I call upon your minds to inquire, if you were going to get the best instrument you could, and then set it to work in the most ingenious way, to prepare the public mind for this movement, operating in the free States, where there is now an abhorrence of the institution of slavery, could you find an instrument so capable of doing it as Judge Douglas, or one employed in so apt a way to do it?

⤞ *Why do we see this?* The reverse pattern. Somebody makes a claim and you want to challenge it. Consider its implications: assume the claim is true and ask how the rest of the world would then be expected to look. Perhaps it doesn't look that way.

Madison, speech at Virginia Ratifying Convention (1788)

He informs us that the people of the country are at perfect repose—that is, every man enjoys the fruits of his labor peaceably and securely, and that every thing is in perfect tranquility and safety. I wish sincerely, sir, this were true. If this be their happy situation, why has every state acknowledged the contrary? Why were deputies from all the states sent to the general Convention?

Davitt, speech in the House of Commons (1898)

The Home Secretary in his speech tonight put forward the strongest argument for the retention of this punishment by flogging—the theory that it was necessary for the safety of the warders. Very well; we all desire, Sir, that those men who have to perform very difficult and onerous duties in prisons should be safeguarded in every rational way. But warders are as much open to assault in Ireland and Scotland as in England, and yet they are protected amply in those two countries without the infliction of the "cat" upon prisoners.

We are told we should forget politics in considering this bill; that it is a patriotic measure to preserve the honor and dignity of our common country, and that Democrat and Republican alike can debate and amend it. If that is true, why is it that the plates from which to print the bonds and the paper they are to be engraved on are already prepared, even before this bill has been read in the House? Sir, the Republican party knows it has the votes and intends to pass this bill just as it is, no matter what Democrats may say.

Wheeler, speech in the House of Representatives (1898)

↣ *Falsus in uno, falsus in omnibus* (false in one thing, false in all things). Saying that someone who was wrong once has lost credibility in general. This was originally a legal maxim: a witness who testifies falsely on one point is not to be believed about others. But the spirit of the idea is used in other kinds of arguments—for example, to say that someone who made bad predictions before shouldn't be heard to make more now. The best inference is that he's unreliable.

Have your prophecies been fulfilled? The answer is the negative from all sources. Then they must be all false prophets, and in the olden times false prophets were stoned to death, but in this case it is not so. On the contrary, here we have the same prophets not only still living, but again prophesying, and in accordance with the legal adage, "Falsus in uno, falsus in omnibus," we will take it for granted that their sayings in regard to the bill now before us are as illogical, false, and misleading in this case as the one above mentioned.

Talbert, speech in the House of Representatives (1894)

An extension: if your adversary makes mistakes of one kind, maybe other kinds are likely, too. Someone careless with facts no doubt is careless in reasoning, etc.

Pardon me for reminding him that his historical references and quotations are not accurate. If he errs so much with respect

Randolph, speech at Virginia Ratifying Convention (1788)

to his facts, as he has done in history, we cannot depend on his information or assertions.

Grattan, *Answer to a Pamphlet of Lord Clare* (1800)

The work proceeds to state, but not to state fairly or fully, the propositions; and I cannot but again observe, that these frequent mistakes in fact must create a prejudice against its logic.

↠ *Inferences from haste.* When you see the other side in a hurry, you can draw inferences about why. Rushing may be an effort to avoid discussion or discovery.

Lee, *Letters from the Federal Farmer* I (1787)

It is natural for men, who wish to hasten the adoption of a measure, to tell us, now is the crisis—now is the critical moment which must be seized or all will be lost; and to shut the door against free enquiry, whenever conscious the thing presented has defects in it, which time and investigation will probably discover.

Pakington, speech in the House of Commons (1861)

Her Majesty's Government must, surely, have some very special reason for pressing the reception of the Report. And we have some ground to suspect this when we find them endeavoring to hurry over in this indecorous manner this stage of the proceeding, in order to prevent my hon. and learned Friend from stating his views.

↠ *Inferences from silence.* If you won't speak, the audience may assume the worst about what they would hear if you did. The most famous example is the criminal defendant who refuses to testify. It's natural to think that the silence is a sign of guilt; that conclusion is usually forbidden in American courts but sometimes allowed in the courts of the United Kingdom and elsewhere. The argument in stylized form:

Williams, speech in the trial of Queen Caroline (1820)

If this suspicion that hangs round the prisoner so close, be unfounded—if it be really untrue—if that which appears from the circumstances of the case, to amount to guilt be in effect only suspicion that has unjustly attached upon innocence, why has he been silent upon exculpatory proof? The day is recent; his memory fresh called to it; an opportunity was given to him; in that opportunity he has failed.

You don't have to be completely silent to earn the bad inference. It's often enough if you won't explain something or can't. This was Burke's reasoning when he was prosecutor in the trial of Warren Hastings, who had served as a British Governor-General in India.

Explanation he was called upon for, over and over again; explanation he did not give, and declared he could not give. He was called upon for it when in India: he had not leisure to attend to it there. He was called upon for it when in Europe: he then says he must send for it to India. With much prevarication, and much insolence too, he confesses himself guilty of falsifying the Company's accounts by making himself their creditor when he was their debtor, and giving false accounts of this false transaction.

Burke, argument in the impeachment of Warren Hastings (1789)

The same logic can apply when nobody is accused of anything. Someone just fails to address a point in dispute—whether X is good or bad or likely or unlikely and so forth. The point is the same: if they haven't addressed an argument, it's because they can't.

I readily perceive the reason why Mr. Burke declined going into the comparison between the English and French constitutions, because he could not but perceive, when he sat down to the task, that no such a thing as a constitution existed on his side the question.... It was the strongest ground he could take, if the advantages were on his side, but the weakest if they were not; and his declining to take it is either a sign that he could not possess it or could not maintain it.

Paine, *The Rights of Man* (1791)

Why draw so strongly marked a line between social and legal penalties? Mr. Mill asserts the existence of the distinction in every form of speech. He makes his meaning perfectly clear. Yet from one end of his essay to the other I find no proof and no attempt to give the proper and appropriate proof of it. His doctrine could have been proved if it had been true. It was not proved because it was not true.

Stephen, *Liberty, Equality, Fraternity* (1873)

A more daring use of the idea: the other side has failed to prove X, so we can conclude that X is false. This can easily become the fallacy known as *argumentum ad ignorantiam*: supposing that something is false just because it hasn't been proven true (or true because it hasn't been proven false). A sample warning:

Mill, *Catiline's Conspiracy* (1826)

The absence of evidence against him is not evidence in his favor: though it were not proved that his designs were bad, this is no proof that they were good.

But if they fail to prove X, sometimes that *does* suggest X is false. The natural question is whether the adversary has the means to offer proof if it exists. If so, a failure to make the case can put it into doubt.

King, speech in the House of Lords (1821)

If the charge preferred by the petitioner were true, a proof of it might easily be given. No proof has been given and under such circumstances the absence of proof shows the impossibility of proof.

Dunnell, speech in the House of Representatives (1879)

Gentlemen, in talking upon the point of order, claimed that the change of system would necessarily produce a cheaper method; but that has not been demonstrated. It has not even been said here that this new system is to be a cheaper one than the old system. Gentlemen have not the data wherewith to prove it. If they had been able to prove it we should have had the evidence long since before us.

21

Causation

➤➤ *Post hoc ergo propter hoc* (after this, therefore because of this). The fallacy of assuming that when one event follows another, the first causes the second. It's a typical way for correlation to be mistaken for causation. Something bad happened when you wore those shoes, so now they're your bad-luck shoes. A president assumes office and the economy takes a dive; many think it's no coincidence, but perhaps it is. The same thing can happen when laws are passed and good or bad things happen afterwards.

It would seem that every unpropitious event, social or political, moral, or even physical, which has occurred to this country since restrictions were first put upon the trade in corn, are attributed to the malign influence of the Corn-laws.

Hampden, speech in the House of Commons (1843)

Here are the Democrats tinkering with the tariff. Here are the men out of work. Post hoc, ergo propter hoc—after this, therefore on account of this. You can not argue with a man on a street corner or in a hall when a third or a fourth or one-half of men are out of work. Men are moved by conditions and not by ideas, and the fact of the depression in business following the tariff law is conclusive in their minds.

Whitacre, speech in the House of Representatives (1915)

➤➤ *Counterfactuals*. If you want to challenge the idea that X caused Y, you can give counterfactuals: what would have happened *without* X? (Perhaps Y would have happened anyway.)

I have heard it asserted by some, that as America hath flourished under her former connection with Great Britain that the same connection is necessary towards her future happiness, and will always have the same effect…. I answer roundly, that America would have flourished as much, and probably much more, had no European power had anything to do with her.

Paine, *Common Sense* (1776)

{ 157 }

Or it looks like X caused Y, but we should ask what would have happened if another cause—Z—hadn't also been present. X may be getting too much credit.

Mill,
speech on
parliamentary
reform
(1824)

A country with the natural resources, and with the capital of Great Britain, in a period of profound peace, and when commerce is subjected only to moderate restraints, must be ill governed indeed, if it does not rapidly increase in wealth; and before we ascribe any part of its prosperity to the goodness of its government, we must ascertain what are likely to be the effects of that government when no other causes of prosperity exist.

Or X *did* cause Y, but Y could have been produced by a less costly or more agreeable means.

Burke,
*Reflections on
the Revolution
in France*
(1790)

They who destroy everything certainly will remove some grievance. They who make everything new have a chance that they may establish something beneficial. To give them credit for what they have done in virtue of the authority they have usurped, or to excuse them in the crimes by which that authority has been acquired, it must appear that the same things could not have been accomplished without producing such a revolution.

↦ *Reverse causation.* Cause and effect run in a direction opposite to what has been supposed. These reversals are common when there's an obvious fact in the foreground and a pattern in the background. The immediate fact is seen as a cause of the distant result; in fact the prominent thing we see is produced by the subtler thing we don't. This sort of argument is a favorite of economists, as they often view local behavior as the product of larger influences.

Smith,
*Wealth
of Nations*
(1776)

Oatmeal, indeed, supplies the common people in Scotland with the greatest and the best part of their food, which is, in general, much inferior to that of their neighbors of the same rank in England. This difference, however, in the mode of their subsistence, is not the cause, but the effect, of the difference in their wages; though, by a strange misapprehension, I have frequently heard it represented as the cause. It is not because one man keeps a coach, while his neighbor walks a-foot, that the one is rich, and the other poor; but because the one is rich, he keeps a coach, and because the other is poor, he walks a-foot.

He calls our attention to the effect of the large importation of foreign goods upon our currency. He has mistaken the effect for the cause. He might as well have invited our attention to the effect produced by the flowing of a river upon the attraction of gravitation. Why, sir, it is the increase of the currency which has produced these large importations.

Millson, speech in the House of Representatives (1852)

⤖ *Your own fault.* Someone complains about a result but has created the very situation being criticized. This theme arises easily when populations are condemned by officials, inviting the reply that the populations act as they do because of how the officials treat them.

The people have always been and still are peaceably inclined. They seek not violence; they avoid it. May they avoid it ever, unless they are driven to it. But moderate means have been tried. Petitions without number have been poured into Parliament. If our rulers still persist in their resistance, it is they and not the Reformers, who endeavor to excite insurrection.

Mill, speech on parliamentary reform (1824)

The men who are responsible for revolutions are not the men who rise; they are the men of the obstinate, stupid, hard-hearted, hard-headed Governments who say *non possumus* to everything, and resist, resist, resist until resistance is too late.

Fowler, speech in the House of Commons (1888)

(*Non possumus = we cannot.*) Of course such assignments of blame can be refused. Identifying causation in such a case can't be done in isolation. You need a judgment about who owes what to whom.

If a malignant wretch will cut his own throat, because he sees you give alms to the necessitous and deserving, shall his destruction be attributed to your charity, and not to his own deplorable madness?

Burke, speech at Bristol (1780)

Lincoln,
speech at
Cooper Union
(1860)

You will not abide the election of a Republican President! In that supposed event, you say, you will destroy the Union; and then, you say, the great crime of having destroyed it will be upon us! That is cool. A highwayman holds a pistol to my ear, and mutters through his teeth, "stand and deliver, or I shall kill you, and then you'll be a murderer!"

↠*Baseline problems.* As the previous section shows, a judgment about what causes what can create controversy about the baseline from which the judgment occurs. Such cases arise routinely when one tries to explain the difference between a subsidy and relief from a requirement to pay this or that. Calling something a subsidy (or using other such relative judgments; "paternalism" is another favorite) requires a decision about what's normal—the baseline—from which you can make the measurement of "extra" (the subsidy).

Myers,
speech in
the Senate
(1914)

The idea of taking by law money out of the pockets of the masses of the people and paying it over perforce to the rich owners of a few coastwise ships would be staggering; yet what is the difference between that and toll exemption?

McCumber,
speech in the
Senate
(1915)

What is the difference between a subsidy that is paid directly to the owner of a vessel who can operate a private vessel cheaper than the Government can operate a Government-owned vessel and going down in your pockets to pay the deficit caused by the more expensive operation by the Government? It is a subsidy in either way, because in both cases you get back into the people's pockets to cover the deficit.

A similar problem often arises when the same result can be reached by a direct or indirect route or by an active or passive one. Should those who take one of those routes be viewed the same way as those who use the other? It's hard to say without a judgment in the background about what's right or expected. If that judgment is skipped over, it becomes easy—maybe too easy—to put people in the same moral category because they produce the same outcomes.

Suppose he shall succeed in preventing ten men from joining the Army, has he not rendered the enemy much more service than if he had actually joined the ranks of the enemy and raised the sword in his favor? To my mind, it is impossible to draw a line of distinction between adding to the strength of the enemy and taking from the strength of his own country.

Grundy, speech in the House of Representatives (1813)

→→ *The self-fulfilling prophecy.* Sometimes making a prediction increases its chance of coming true (or guarantees that it will). The point may be psychological: expecting the best or worst can create a mindset that makes those results more likely. It affects your confidence or the confidence of others.

It had been well observed, that to believe anything difficult or impossible was the surest way to make it so. Such predictions, too, had always a tendency to their own fulfilment. They suggested weakness. They invited attack.

Shaw, speech in the House of Commons (1845)

The Under Secretary said it appeared to him that this negotiation, as he called it, would not be completed. Such a statement seemed not only ominous but prophetic. Their Lordships knew that there were prophecies which led to, and perhaps, insured their own fulfilment....The hon. Gentleman very well knew what he was saying, and could not have been wholly unconscious that he was verifying his prediction at the moment he uttered it.

Thirlwall, speech in the House of Lords (1857)

A self-fulfilling prophecy comes true in a more or less automatic way as a result of being made. A related problem is the maker of a bad prediction who then works deliberately to bring it about.

The Under Secretary of State for India had declared that Lord Salisbury had had the gift of prophecy, and had foretold the attempt of Russia to establish influence in Afghanistan. But he was reminded by that statement of that astrologer who prophesied long life to an English King. The King having died immediately, the astrologer, in disgust, prophesied his own death upon a given day, and killed himself in order to make

Dilke, speech in the House of Commons (1878)

his prophecy come true. Lord Salisbury, by his instructions to Lord Lytton, had made his own prophecies come true—that the Ameer would be thrown into the arms of Russia.

See also Paine's comment:

Paine, *The Age of Reason* (1795)

As certainly as a man predicts ill, he becomes inclined to wish it. The pride of having his judgment right hardens his heart, till at last he beholds with satisfaction, or sees with disappointment, the accomplishment or the failure of his predictions.

➤➤ *Complex machinery.* Urging people to be cautious when they're about to tamper because it can have consequences they didn't intend. This may amount to a plea for humility.

Burke, *Thoughts on the Cause of the Present Discontents* (1770)

Every project of a material change in a government so complicated as ours, combined at the same time with external circumstances, still more complicated, is a matter full of difficulties : in which a considerate man will not be too ready to decide; a prudent man too ready to undertake; or an honest man too ready to promise.

A common variation: leave things alone because tampering might do more harm than good. We can't tell; the workings of the system are too subtle.

Nicholl, speech in the House of Commons (1817)

You will pause the more when you reflect upon the frame and character of the constitution. It is not a simple machine, but one of delicate movements, complicated and difficult to be understood; in which one spring works upon or checks another almost imperceptibly; a machine, therefore, with which it is dangerous to meddle, since the alteration or removal of the slightest part may derange the whole, and either by impeding stop it, or by accelerating its velocity, urge it to destruction.

Reed, speech in the Senate (1917)

Let no man incautiously interfere with that vastest and most intricate machine in all the world, the great industrial machine that has a million brains that think; a million eyes that see; a million pairs of hands to feel and grasp; a million stomachs

to fill, that must always produce because it always must con-
sume; that can not stop lest it starve, and so must always be
kept in condition to never stop. That is the most intricate
machine there is in the world. You had better let it alone.

⇥ *Perverse consequences*. Sometimes a measure has effects that are the
opposite of what was intended. The efforts may be said to backfire
because, as under the previous heading, the understanding of the
reformer is no match for the complexity of the system.

> The Poor-laws were intended to prevent mendicants; they
> have made mendicancy a legal profession; they were estab-
> lished in the spirit of a noble and sublime provision, which
> contained all the theory of virtue; they have produced all the
> consequences of vice. Nothing differs so much from the end
> of institutions as their origin.... The Poor-laws, formed to
> relieve the distressed, have been the arch-creator of distress.

Lytton,
*England and
the English*
(1874)

Unintended consequences aren't always bad. The results can indeed
be good, as in Smith's famous argument that efforts to follow one's
own self-interest can promote the welfare of the community. Smith's
businessman

> intends only his own gain; and he is in this, as in many other
> cases, led by an invisible hand to promote an end which was
> no part of his intention. Nor is it always the worse for the
> society that it was no part of it. By pursuing his own interest,
> he frequently promotes that of the society more effectually
> than when he really intends to promote it.

Smith, *Wealth
of Nations*
(1776)

This idea has been adapted to many other cases.

> The man who works from himself outwards, whose conduct
> is governed by ordinary motives, and who acts with a view to
> his own advantage and the advantage of those who are con-
> nected with himself in definite, assignable ways, produces in
> the ordinary course of things much more happiness to others
> (if that is the great object of life) than a moral Don Quixote
> who is always liable to sacrifice himself and his neighbors.

Stephen,
*Liberty, Equality,
Fraternity*
(1873)

Chesterton,
Heretics
(1905)

In the *fin de siècle* atmosphere every one was crying out that literature should be free from all causes and all ethical creeds. Art was to produce only exquisite workmanship, and it was especially the note of those days to demand brilliant plays and brilliant short stories. And when they got them, they got them from a couple of moralists. The best short stories were written by a man trying to preach Imperialism. The best plays were written by a man trying to preach Socialism. All the art of all the artists looked tiny and tedious beside the art which was a byproduct of propaganda.

III

Judgments and Tradeoffs

THIS SECTION considers practical problems in making and judging arguments, particularly as they move from disputes about logic and principle to matters of fact: who has to prove what, how to weigh evidence and interpret words, the analysis of trade-offs, the use of illustrations to make points more persuasive, and knowing when argument isn't going to work.

22

Burden of Proof

If you have the burden of proof in an argument, the presumption is against whatever you claim. You lose if you aren't persuasive; the other side wins by refuting your points even if they have nothing better to say. In court the burden of proof is assigned by rules. We're interested here in less formal cases where the burden may itself be assigned by argument.

➤➤ *Access to proof.* Suppose the other side has control of evidence or information that the argument depends on. That's a reason for giving them the burden of proof. Having the burden will force them to show what they know or can easily find out.

> If the burden of proof is upon the railroad company to make this showing, it has all the facts and it can do so speedily. Where the burden of proof is transferred to the shipper, he has not the facts with which to show that the rate is unreasonable. He is in no position to disprove it if the railroad company sets up that any less rate than the one they have advanced would be confiscatory of their property.

La Follette, speech in the Senate (1910)

➤➤ *The affirmative claimant.* It often makes sense to put the burden of proof on the side that makes an affirmative claim, not the side that's denying it. If you say something is true, you're ordinarily expected to back it up; otherwise the other side can dismiss it as easily as it was said. This point used to be expressed as a Latin maxim: *quod gratis asseritur, gratis negaturi:* what is asserted for nothing is going to be denied for nothing.

> Some people speak as if we were not justified in rejecting a theological doctrine unless we can prove it false. But the burden of proof does not lie upon the rejecter. I remember a conversation in which, when some disrespectful remark was

Bury, *A History of Freedom of Thought* (1913)

made about hell, a loyal friend of that establishment said triumphantly, "But, absurd as it may seem, you cannot disprove it." If you were told that in a certain planet revolving around Sirius there is a race of donkeys who speak the English language and spend their time in discussing eugenics, you could not disprove the statement, but would it, on that account, have any claim to be believed?

This way of thinking about the burden of proof makes obvious sense when the claim is an accusation. An accusation can be damaging whether or not it's proven, so we expect it to be made with good support or not at all. This idea, too, was the subject of a maxim: *semper necessitas probandi incumbit ei qui agit* (the necessity of proof always lies with he who makes a charge).

Burlingame, speech in the House of Representatives (1856)

There have been general and specific charges made against old Massachusetts. The general charge, when expressed in polite language, is, that she has not been faithful to her constitutional obligations. I deny it. I call for proof. I ask when? where? how?

Usually an accusation or other claim isn't quite bare. It at least comes with arguments, and the arguments call for a response. But keeping the burden on the party making the claim still matters. It means that the side playing defense does its job by just shooting down whatever is said by the side with the burden.

Macaulay, *Westminster Reviewer's Defence of Mill* (1829)

The affirmative of the issue and the burden of the proof are with Mr. Mill, not with us. We are not bound, perhaps we are not able, to show that the form of government which he recommends is bad. It is quite enough if we can show that he does not prove it to be good.

↠ *Proving a negative.* People sometimes say that you can't prove a negative. This is a standard objection when someone demands evidence that something *isn't* true. But the saying is too strong. Suppose you're asked to prove that you weren't at the scene of a crime. That's a negative, but proving it might be easy. (Maybe you can show you were somewhere else.) Yet sometimes the point is fair, as with Bury's

donkeys noted above. And even when it's possible to prove a negative, it may be hard; it's easier to prove there *is* a fly in the building
than to prove that there isn't one. So instead of saying that you can't
prove a negative in general, it's better to explain why it's hard in this
case and why the burden of proof shouldn't be yours.

Thus suppose you're accused of something you could have done
anytime. You can't offer an alibi; all you can do is deny having done
it, and perhaps point out the unreasonable predicament that the accusation creates.

> It is certainly a most ingenious device—that of putting into the
> mouth of political opponents that which they never said and
> never intended to say. The beauty of the thing is you cannot
> disprove it. Nobody knows who wrote those articles; they
> may all have been written by my noble Friend at the head of
> the Government; but it would be perfectly impossible, unless
> we could produce the persons who wrote them, to prove that
> they were not written by Members of the Cabinet.

Cecil, speech
in the House
of Lords
(1878)

A humble example: a military widow had been drawing a pension
from the government, but it was stopped because she was found to
have remarried, which she denied. This resulted in a debate in the
Senate about whether to reinstate her pension.

> MR. SAULSBURY. Ought she not to be required to prove af-
> firmatively that there had been no remarriage before we can
> be justified in reversing the judgment of the Commissioner
> of Pensions?
>
> MR. EDMUNDS.... You might bring the whole neighborhood
> to say, "We never attended any wedding;" you might bring
> all the clergymen in the neighborhood to say, "We never
> celebrated a marriage;" but that would not prove that there
> had not been a remarriage. So the difficulty lies in the fact
> that she is called on to show, on the suggestion of my friend
> from Delaware, a negative, which can never be proved by
> anything that amounts to a demonstration or to anything else
> than a probability.

Exchange in
the Senate
(1888)

(The matter was sent back to committee without resolution.) So it's fair to argue that accusations of this type generally need evidence behind them before they deserve a response.

Lincoln, debate with Stephen Douglas at Ottawa (1858)

About this story that Judge Douglas tells of Trumbull bargaining to sell out the old Democratic party, and Lincoln agreeing to sell out the old Whig party, I have the means of knowing about that: Judge Douglas cannot have; and I know there is no substance to it whatever.... I have no means of totally disproving such charges as this which the Judge makes. A man cannot prove a negative; but he has a right to claim that when a man makes an affirmative charge, he must offer some proof to show the truth of what he says.

The same problem can arise without an accusation. Someone just makes any claim that X happened, and it's much easier to prove than disprove. So you don't try to disprove it. You put the burden on the other side.

Lincoln, speech at Peoria (1854)

I deny that the public ever demanded any such thing—ever repudiated the Missouri Compromise, ever commanded its repeal. I deny it, and call for the proof.

This general pattern can also come up in debates about policy. The issue isn't what happened. It's that one side of a claim is hard to refute because it would call for endless inquiry or exposition. Explaining this can help even out the ground on which an argument goes forward. Thus Hamilton's argument about taxes:

Hamilton, *Address to the Electors of New York* (1801)

It is always easy to assert that they are heavier than they ought to be, always difficult to refute the assertion, which cannot ever be attempted without a critical review of the whole course of public measures. This gives an immense advantage to those who make a trade of complaint and censure.

↠ *Demands for change.* The burden of proof is often put on whoever wants a change of some kind. People readily treat the status quo as entitled to weight, especially if it has seemed bearable.

When a certain policy has obtained in this country for a half a century and over, and Senators want to change that policy in the twinkling of an eye, it is not for me to show that the bill is a bad one. It is for them to show that the bill is a good one.

Husting, speech in the Senate (1917)

In hard times it may seem that *something* has to change. The burden might then be shifted to whoever wants to leave things alone. You can also attack the presumption against change by asking about the motives of those who want to keep everything the same. Maybe they're just protecting their interests. That's an *ad hominem* point, but it's relevant if you're arguing about whether their wishes should get weight.

[Monopolists] are afraid of every movement in the direction of tariff reduction, fearing that the tide might run on until it beat against their own fortress. Hence they are against everything that tends to disturb the status quo and menace the strongly protected and opulent privileges they enjoy and have enjoyed for so many years.

Stone, speech in the Senate (1911)

→→ *Attacking the popular.* If you contradict a principle that's popular or widely accepted, expect to be assigned the burden of proving that you're right. Of course this basis for assignment depends on the understandings of the time and place where it's invoked.

The gentleman called upon gentlemen on this side of the House to prove the justice of the war. That is not necessary; it has been often done before. The burden of proof, on the presumption that our country is always in the right till the contrary be proved, now certainly rests with the gentleman from New Hampshire, and his friends on that side of the House.

Calhoun, speech in the House of Representatives (1814)

Every man has a right to all that may conduce to his pleasure, if it does not inflict pain on any one else. This is one of the broadest maxims of human nature, and I cannot therefore see how its supporters can be fairly called upon to defend it—the *onus probandi* lies, not on the advocates of freedom, but on the advocates of restraint.

Macaulay, speech in the House of Commons (1830)

23

Bias

➤➤ *The biased tribunal.* You can't expect a fair decision if the judge is too closely identified with one of the advocates.

Lyndhurst, speech in the House of Lords (1856)

I find that no person shall be allowed to return who has exhibited a spirit of hostility against the Russian Government; and who is to decide upon what may be a spirit of hostility against the Russian Government? The officers of the Russian Government.

Likewise if those who pass judgment on a claim are rooting for its success or against it. The decision may then owe less to the arguments or evidence than to the sympathies of the judges.

Sheil, speech in the House of Commons (1834)

The speech just spoken by the member for the county of Wexford has been received with acclamations, and if it were less able, the acclamation would not, perhaps, have been less enthusiastic, or less loud. Fortunate advocate, whose success depends as much at least on the predilections of the tribunal, as upon the merits of the cause!

Walbridge, speech in the House of Representatives (1858)

It was the duty of the Chair to appoint a committee from members of the House who favored the investigation, not from those who were opposed to it. But the Speaker not having done so, it was the business and duty of the committee to investigate just to the extent that the House ordered it. Sir, this child was put to a nurse, in my judgment, predisposed and predetermined to strangle it; and I trust this House and the country will hold that nurse to a just responsibility for the deed.

➤➤ *Judicial standards.* People care about the standards that judges use even when they aren't in front of judges. The idea isn't necessarily that legal rules should apply outside of court. It's that judicial standards of fairness are appropriately high, and that the standards in use *now* are sloppy by comparison: we would never allow there what we find here.

> Were the gentleman a judge or juror, could he find in this sufficient to convict, or even to cast a well grounded suspicion upon the meanest wretch who crawls in the filth of society? And yet this is offered as ground of inquiry against your President! Sir, is it liberal, is it candid, is it charitable, is it magnanimous? Sir, who are we?

Holmes, speech in the House of Representatives (1819)

> In private life, if one man instigates a prosecution against another for an offense, and it turns out upon investigation that there is no foundation for it, and not even a probable cause for its commencement, the prosecutor is liable to an action of damages for the injury done to individual reputation. Are the characters of public men less valuable to them than those of private citizens? Are they not equally under the protection of the law?

Hamer, speech in the House of Representatives (1837)

↠ *Excessive agreement.* It smells like partisanship or worse when people agree too much.

> When men exercise their reason coolly and freely on a variety of distinct questions, they inevitably fall into different opinions on some of them. When they are governed by a common passion, their opinions, if they are so to be called, will be the same.

Madison, *Federalist* 50 (1788)

This view makes it a rightful point of pride for a group to have dissenters within it, and the absence of them a fair basis for taunts.

> He said, "Don't, I beg of you, don't let us have any partisanship in this matter." Well, let me say to gentlemen here that we are somewhat divided over on this side of the House; there is no partisanship over here. How is it, General, over there with you? How many Democrats are going to vote against this bill? Are there fifty of you; are there twenty of you; are there ten of you; are there five of you? Is there one who is going to vote against this bill? Come, do not all speak at once.

Horr, speech in the House of Representatives (1884)

The same theme has been used to criticize partisanship in courts, where politics are supposed to be absent and voting on party lines might seem good cause for embarrassment. Hence this claim about the Supreme Court's efforts to settle matters of federal election law:

Ewing, speech in the House of Representatives (1880)

The public mind in this country will never accept as final a decision on a disputed question of constitutional law when the decision is obtained by a party division of that tribunal. Such a decision, so reached, is lasting only as a melancholy instance of the fact, of which the action of certain judges in the electoral commission three years ago convinced the people, that the fires of partisanship burn beneath the ermine just as fiercely as under the jackets of the people.

Suspicious agreement can also be produced by self-interest. That's how it looks when the self-interest and the agreement stop at the same time.

Burke, *Thoughts on the Cause of the Present Discontents* (1770)

What shall we think of him who never differed from a certain set of men until the moment they lost their power, and who never agreed with them in a single instance afterwards? Would not such a coincidence of interest and opinion be rather fortunate?

↠ *Motivated reasoning.* Reasoning tends to seem impressive when it leads to conclusions we like. The mind then looks harder for the strengths of a supporting argument than for its flaws, and so finds what it wishes. Or perhaps the judgment of the argument is made impressionistically, and without careful analysis: it just *seems* convincing—and that's because it ends where we had hoped.

Burke, *Further Reflections on the Revolution in France* (1790)

When people see a political object which they ardently desire but in one point of view, they are apt extremely to palliate or underrate the evils which may arise in obtaining it.

Mill, speech on aristocracy (1825)

This morality they preach to the people, aye! and believe it themselves, and teach it to their children; for it is wonderful how easy a matter it is to believe that to be right which we know to be pleasant.

I have no doubt that the able and versatile gentleman from Virginia will be able this morning to give excellent reasons why this addition to the Birney School should not be constructed. It is always perfectly patent that any gentleman can give reasons when he is determined to find reasons.

Mann, speech in the House of Representatives (1912)

The same tendency naturally causes the mind to *reject* arguments when it's predisposed against them.

When, on the contrary, we peruse a skillful writer, with whom we do not coincide in opinion, how attentive is the mind to detect fallacy…. We never allow ourselves to be warmed; and, after contending with the writer, are more confirmed in our opinion; as much, perhaps, from a spirit of contradiction as from reason.

Wollstonecraft, *A Vindication of the Rights of Men* (1790)

These points are strongest when you can note a specific incentive that might lie behind the conclusions.

It is not with much credulity I listen to any when they speak evil of those whom they are going to plunder. I rather suspect that vices are feigned or exaggerated when profit is looked for in their punishment.

Burke, *Reflections on the Revolution in France* (1790)

The slaveholder does not like to be considered a mean fellow for holding that species of property, and hence, he has to struggle within himself and sets about arguing himself into the belief that slavery is right. The property influences his mind.

Lincoln, speech at Cooper Union (1860)

↦ *Declarations against interest.* The prior theme was self-serving reasoning. This pattern is roughly the reverse: when people say things that make themselves less popular or otherwise worse off, we reasonably give more credit to their statements.

When a man says that he was bribed, his admission is entitled to credence, even in a court where the strictest rules of the common law prevail, because it is not natural that a man would make a declaration of that kind unless he was impelled to do so by its truth, and probably by the fact that he believed that his crime had been discovered.

Poindexter, speech in the Senate (1911)

Rucker, speech in
the House of Repre-
sentatives (1917)

I believe when a man in writing admits the paternity of a child the presumption is so strong against him that any court would accept it. It is a declaration against his interest.

As those examples suggest, this point is a famous part of the law of evidence. But the sense of it carries over to other settings.

Mill, *The British
Constitution* (1826)

I at least shall be acquitted of having anything to gain by my opinions: unquestionably they are not the road either to preferment or to popularity.

Smith, speech in the
House of Represen-
tatives (1854)

I will admit, however, for the sake of the argument, that my proposition is unpopular. Happily for me, I have no popularity to jeopard.

↠ *Preferring candor.* Saying to your adversaries: wouldn't it be better to just admit your rooting interests and what you're doing to advance them? We prefer forthright depravity to the concealed kind.

Mill, speech on
parliamentary
reform
(1824)

I pity the man who can see any thing to admire in all this. I should prefer even the straightforward despot, who is not imbecile enough to be duped by his own fallacies but feels and acknowledges the power of sinister interest.

Roebuck, speech
in the House of
Commons
(1837)

It is plain that you love those exclusive privileges more than you love good government for the people, and that when the two things come into collision you in reality side not with the people, but with their enemies. Let the world know this—be honest in the matter, and do not pretend to be Liberals with such feelings predominant.

You can say the same to your own group: if we're going to do X, let's just admit that it is (whatever terrible thing I say it is). It's a way to shame others into doing better.

Vest,
speech in
the Senate
(1892)

Let us be frank with each other. If we propose to trample down the rule in order to do what we want to do, let us do it, but do not let us do it under the miserable pretense that we are observing the rule, for we are doing nothing of the kind.

➤➤ *Preferring ignorance.* Saying that you'd prefer not to know something. If you're judging others, for example, it might be best not to be aware of things that could influence your thinking but shouldn't.

> My first duty as a Senator upon a question of legal and consti-
> tutional right like this is to guard myself against the influence
> of any partisan bias, to know nothing of the political opinions
> or party affiliations of the man who is seeking admission here.

Christiancy,
speech in the
Senate
(1876)

Likewise, if you're trying to make a decision in the public interest, it might be best not to know how it would bear on *you.*

> I would rather not know the precise and immediate conse-
> quence or results to my individual interest when I have to
> pass upon a case any more than as a judge I would ask to
> know what was the personal result to me of a decision which
> I should give under my oath.

Bayard, speech
in the Senate
(1876)

The same thing—*I'd rather not know*—can be said for humbler reasons.

> He did not ask for their names; he had rather not know them.
> Such knowledge would only give him the pain of despising
> his fellow-creatures, which was at all times a disagreeable
> feeling, though sometimes inevitable.

Brougham, speech
in the House
of Lords
(1847)

24

Weighing Evidence

➤➤ *Seriatim comparisons.* Many arguments are about how two things compare: one candidate or proposal or philosophy vs. another. Sometimes it helps to make a quick statement of contrasts between them—a series of *this vs. that* points. Thus Burke's approach in comparing his proposal for dealing with the colonies to the government's plan of taxation:

Burke, *Speech on Conciliation with the Colonies* (1775)

This I offer to give you is plain and simple: the other full of perplexed and intricate mazes. This is mild: that harsh. This is found by experience effectual for its purposes: the other is a new project. This is universal: the other calculated for certain colonies only. This is immediate in its conciliatory operation: the other remote, contingent, full of hazard. Mine is what becomes the dignity of a ruling people: gratuitous, unconditional, and not held out as matter of bargain and sale.

Here's the pattern with the elements filled in by figures of speech—metaphorical flourishes, synecdoche (the use of a part to suggest the whole), and antonomasia (the use of a proper name to suggest a class):

Packard, speech in the House of Representatives (1870)

There is a new spirit and an old. The hope of the one is in the future, the other clings to the past. The one is young and vigorous, moving onward with the stride of a giant; the other is old, and loves its age, and rattles its dry bones, and loves the sound, and scatters ashes on every growing thing, and calls itself "Conservative." The one is Rome, the other is Carthage; the one is Luther, the other is the pope; the one is Cromwell, the other is Charles; the one is Washington, the other is George III; the one is freedom, the other is human bondage; the one is Grant, the other is Lee; the one is the Republican party, the other is modern Democracy.

⤳ *Audi alteram partem* (hear the other side). An elementary point about careful judgment that needs to be made often because it frustrates human nature: decide nothing before hearing both sides of a question.

> I pray you, gentlemen of the House of Representatives, as you value your liberties and each his own fair name, which may be attacked in the very next resolution presented here, to interpose to prevent anything like a snap judgment. *Audi alteram partem* should be, of all things in this world, the motto of every deliberative assembly, as it is the motto of every just judge.

Butler, speech in the House of Representatives (1873)

A lighter version:

> I should be sorry to see the Earl of Aberdeen's Government in the position of the celebrated Welsh judge who always thought it convenient to decide when he had heard one side only, knowing that he was unable to grapple with the difficulties of the case when he heard both sides.

Bright, speech in the House of Commons (1853)

Sometimes hearing only one side of a dispute is worse than hearing neither. It creates greater prospects for misjudgment. People then imagine that their views have been informed by a discussion when they've really just heard half of one.

> I am willing the Senate should decide these questions without debate, and I am sorry if we should not decide them sufficiently well without debate; but I am not willing there should be debate on one side and not on the other.

Badger, speech in the Senate (1851)

The same idea can be used to censure those who show signs of deciding too early.

> You say you want discussion; that the same is necessary to elucidate the truth; that you are not sufficiently informed to decide the case; and yet, before you have heard the whole case, before you have considered it, you cheer every sentiment which looks to the seating of one of the litigants as against the other.

Atherton, speech in the House of Representatives (1882)

↦ *Omitting half the case.* Here the problem isn't that only half the case has been heard. It's that only half is being *told* by the other side. Maybe they're emphasizing the bad (or good) points of a thing while downplaying or ignoring the others.

Macaulay, *Mill on Government* (1829)

We know that every man has some desires which he can gratify only by hurting his neighbours, and some which he can gratify only by pleasing them. Mr. Mill has chosen to look only at one-half of human nature, and to reason on the motives which impel men to oppress and despoil others, as if they were the only motives by which men could possibly be influenced. We have already shown that, by taking the other half of the human character, and reasoning on it as if it were the whole, we can bring out a result diametrically opposite to that at which Mr. Mill has arrived. We can, by such a process, easily prove that any form of government is good, or that all government is superfluous.

Scarlett, speech in the House of Commons (1830)

His learned friend had conducted himself like a lawyer; he had exaggerated whatever told in favor of his client, and had extenuated whatever told against him.

Or they're citing some facts and skipping others. From Webster's defense of the 1842 treaty that adjusted the border between the United States and (as we now know it) Canada:

Webster, speech in the Senate (1846)

The gentleman states concessions made by the United States, but entirely forgets, "in his researches after truth," to state those made on the other side. He takes no notice of the cession of Rouse's Point; or of a strip of land a hundred miles long, on the border of the state of New York. His notion of historical truth is to state all on one side of the story, and forget all the rest.

This tendency can deceive oneself as well as others; it's a classic source of confirmation bias.

Coleridge, *A Sailor's Fortune* (1840)

"Oh, what a lucky fellow! Well, Fortune does favor fools— that's certain! It is always so!"—and forthwith the exclaimer relates half a dozen similar instances. Thus accumulating the one sort of facts and never collecting the other, we do, as poets in their diction, and quacks of all denominations do in their reasoning, put a part for the whole, and at once soothe our envy and gratify our love of the marvelous.

The general pattern Coleridge talks about is common. Instead of comparing the pros and cons of both sides, it's tempting to look at the pros of one side and the cons of the other because that's all one wants to see.

The Secretary for the Treasury has quoted every bad act passed by the Irish—he has quoted every good one passed by an Imperial Parliament. Why did he omit the least mention of any one of the beneficial measures enacted by the parliament of his country?

> Sheil, speech in the House of Commons (1834)

An antidote to this tendency: expose its workings or potential use on *both* sides and ask for better. People admit their own fallacies more easily when their use by others is acknowledged.

On all sides there is a certain amount of insincerity in the language too often used on this subject. When we speak of a war which we approve we talk of its glories. When we speak of a war of which we disapprove we talk of its horrors. Can we not be honest with ourselves on this matter?

> Campbell, speech in the House of Lords (1879)

↦ *Asymmetrical evidence.* A similar trap in reasoning: one side of a comparison is easier to see than the other. No one is hiding anything. It's just that (for example) the evidence on one side is impossible to gather.

It was a good answer that was made by one who, when they showed him hanging in a temple a picture of those who had paid their vows as having escaped shipwreck, and would have him say whether he did not now acknowledge the power of the gods,—"Aye," asked he again, "but where are they painted that were drowned after their vows?"

> Bacon, *Novum Organum* (1620)

That example shows a common reason why people come to believe in magical thinking. As Coleridge observed a moment ago, they only count the cases where it works. They can't see the cases where it doesn't work, or they don't pay as much attention to them.

James Fitzjames Stephen once said that coercion by religions can have value because Christianity and Islam would never have established themselves without it. The reply of John Morley used our current theme:

Morley, *Mr. Mill's Doctrine of Liberty* (1873)

To this one might reply by asking how we know that there might not have been something far better in their stead. We know what we get by effective intolerance, but we cannot ever know what possible benefactions we lose by it.

The same problem can come up in judging how a policy will work in the future. It might prevent bad things that are easy to see but also good ones that aren't.

Hamilton, *Federalist 22* (1787)

When the concurrence of a large number is required by the Constitution to the doing of any national act, we are apt to rest satisfied that all is safe, because nothing improper will be likely to be done, but we forget how much good may be prevented, and how much ill may be produced, by the power of hindering the doing what may be necessary, and of keeping affairs in the same unfavorable posture in which they may happen to stand at particular periods.

Another variation: the person judging a question has experience of one side of it but not the other. Mill once called the result a fallacy of non-observation, and he came back to it often in different settings.

Mill, *Utilitarianism* (1863)

It is better to be a human being dissatisfied than a pig satisfied; better to be Socrates dissatisfied than a fool satisfied. And if the fool, or the pig, is of a different opinion, it is because they only know their own side of the question. The other party to the comparison knows both sides.

Mill, *Considerations on Representative Government* (1861)

We know how easily the uselessness of almost every branch of knowledge may be proved, to the complete satisfaction of those who do not possess it.

It will not do, for instance, to assert in general terms, that the experience of mankind has pronounced in favor of the existing system. Experience cannot possibly have decided between two courses, so long as there has only been experience of one.

Mill, *The Subjection of Women* (1869)

Mill had an especially keen eye for cases of this kind where people's incapacities prevent them from realizing that the incapacities exist.

Originality is the one thing which unoriginal minds cannot feel the use of. They cannot see what it is to do for them: how should they? If they could see what it would do for them, it would not be originality.

Mill, *On Liberty* (1859)

⤚ *Silent evidence of efficacy*. It's natural to judge a rule by looking at cases where it gets used. But sometimes the more important cases are those where a rule *doesn't* get used, at least not explicitly, because it prevents things from happening rather than causing them.

It would really seem as if gentlemen imagined that the end and object of law was punishment. The end and object of law is the prevention of evil…. [Laws] live in the manners, habits, and opinions of the people; they live in the rules and maxims of their life; the silent, invisible operation of the law is much more effectual for good, than the busy and bustling activity, which would keep them always in sight and in motion.

Frankland, speech in the House of Commons (1811)

A simple application of the idea, however dated:

You must not judge the effect of a flogging by its effect on the boy himself. The great value of flogging is to the people who are not flogged; the great value is the deterrent it offers to others, who see what evil courses lead to.

Cecil, speech in the House of Lords (1900)

The same point can be made at higher levels of abstraction. Mill once said that society had made progress away from domination by the law of force. Stephen replied that that force was as important as ever. It was just less visible because it did its work by deterring crime, not by punishing it.

Stephen,
Liberty, Equality,
Fraternity
(1873)

Society rests ultimately upon force in these days, just as much as it did in the wildest and most stormy periods of history.... The reason why it works so quietly is that no one doubts either its existence, or its direction, or its crushing superiority to any individual resistance which could be offered to it.

The same kind of argument can attack a practice: it's worse than it seems because the evidence is largely silent.

Mill, *The*
Subjection of
Women
(1869)

There is never any want of women who complain of ill usage by their husbands. There would be infinitely more, if complaint were not the greatest of all provocatives to a repetition and increase of the ill usage.

↠ *Evidence that hints at more.* The evidence that we see might suggest more that we can't see. An example is the prisoner awaiting execution who is found to be innocent. What does that tell us about others with less luck?

Dickens,
Capital
Punishment
(1846)

But for the exertions, I think, of the present Lord Chief Baron, six or seven innocent men would certainly have been hanged. Such are the instances of wrong judgment which are known to us. How many more there may be in which the real murderers never disclosed their guilt, or were never discovered, and where the odium of great crimes still rests on guiltless people long since resolved to dust in their untimely graves, no human power can tell.

Mill applied this point to the topic we saw a moment ago: the abuse of wives when only the worst violence was addressed by the law. The most egregious examples came to light—but then how many more examples were slightly less severe and never known?

Mill, *The*
Subjection of
Women
(1869)

When we consider how vast is the number of men, in any great country, who are little higher than brutes, and that this never prevents them from being able, through the law of marriage, to obtain a victim, the breadth and depth of human misery caused in this shape alone by the abuse of the institution swells to something appalling. Yet these are only the extreme cases. They are the lowest abysses, but there is a sad succession of depth after depth before reaching them. In domestic as in political tyranny, the case of absolute monsters chiefly illustrates the institution by showing that there is scarcely any horror which may not occur under it if the despot pleases, and thus setting in a strong light what must be the terrible frequency of things only a little less atrocious.

25

Costs and Benefits

↦ *Judgment ex ante.* When a decision produces a bad result, it's important to ask whether it was wise when it was made—that is, to judge it *ex ante*. Judging a decision by its outcome is a bad habit that often needs resistance.

Johnson, *The Adventurer* No. 99 (1753)

It has always been the practice of mankind, to judge of actions by the event. The same attempts, conducted in the same manner, but terminated by different success, produce different judgments: they who attain their wishes, never want celebrators of their wisdom and their virtue; and they that miscarry, are quickly discovered to have been defective not only in mental but in moral qualities.

Burke, *Letter to a Member of the National Assembly* (1791)

The conduct of a losing party never appears right: at least, it never can possess the only infallible criterion of wisdom to vulgar judgments,—success.

The same pattern can run in reverse: a decision that turns out well might have been a bad one—a foolish gamble that *did* pay off.

Macaulay, *Life and Writings of Addison* (1843)

If a friend were to ask us whether we would advise him to risk his all in a lottery of which the chances were ten to one against him, we should do our best to dissuade him from running such a risk. Even if he were so lucky as to get the thirty thousand pound prize, we should not admit that we had counseled him ill.

This was Burke's reasoning when decisions that he thought were bad produced war with America. After a year of the war had passed and disaster hadn't ensued for Britain (yet), he wrote:

Burke, *Letter to the Sheriffs of Bristol* (1777)

Wise men often tremble at the very things which fill the thoughtless with security.... Even if I were certain of my safety, I could not easily forgive those who had brought me into the most dreadful perils, because by accidents, unforeseen by them or me, I have escaped.

The same idea can be an argument for action: it's costly to wait to fix a problem until the harm from it is evident. If it has harmful tendencies visible in advance, those tendencies should be taken as seriously as bad results actually produced.

> If no mischiefs at all had as yet resulted from the Constitution, the obligation to reform it, if it were proved to have a tendency to evil, would not be a whit less imperative. Contrivance, combination, foresight, are the characteristics of the philosopher: to wait for specific experience is that of the man who is incapable of doing more than groping in the dark.

Mill, speech on parliamentary reform (1824)

↠ *Expected costs and benefits.* There are typically two things to think about when sizing up the risks of a decision: the good and bad results it might produce, discounted by the likelihood of each. Those points are useful and natural to compare even when they can't be quantified. Sometimes, for example, the gravity of the harm offsets the small chance that it will happen.

> Admit that in our case invasion is upon the whole improbable; yet, if there are any circumstances which pronounce that the apprehension of it is not absolutely chimerical, it is the part of wisdom to act as if it were likely to happen. What are the inconveniences of preparation compared with the infinite magnitude of the evil if it shall surprise us unprepared? They are lighter than air, weighed against the smallest probability of so disastrous a result.

Hamilton, *The Stand* No. 6 (1798)

> In the management of an Army no danger is to be treated as inconsiderable, and no jealousy as excessive. The chance may be small, the object of fear may be distant, but the magnitude of the evil makes up for the smallness of the risk.

Mackintosh, speech in the House of Commons (1815)

But behind those claims, note the risks caused by quirks of judgment in either direction. A chance of large harm can sound scary regardless of its likelihood; the fear if it does happen can swamp judgments about whether it will.

Hume,
A Treatise of
Human Nature
(1739)

A man cannot think of excessive pains and tortures without trembling, if he be in the least danger of suffering them. The smallness of the probability is compensated by the greatness of the evil; and the sensation is equally lively, as if the evil were more probable.

And there's the opposite temptation: underrating harm because, even if it's likely or certain, it looks small. Maybe it *is* small. Some forces of destruction operate in little ways that add up.

Lowe, speech
in the House of
Commons
(1856)

I, however, agree with Bentham, who says there is no injury so slight or small that its multiplication may not become intolerable. Give me the power of taking a farthing from a man with impunity, farthing by farthing, I will find the bottom of his purse; let me let fall a drop of water on his head—*gutta cavat lapidem*—the power of striking off his head would be subject to less abuse.

Gutta cavat lapidem = a drop hollows a stone.

↦*Distortions of distance.* Another pitfall in thinking about risk: giving too much weight to costs and benefits when they're nearby. Gains right now can easily seem more attractive than benefits of waiting that take effort to imagine, or harms that may or may not ever happen.

Burke, Letter
to the Sheriffs
of Bristol
(1777)

Partial freedom seems to me a most invidious mode of slavery. But, unfortunately, it is the kind of slavery the most easily admitted in times of civil discord: for parties are but too apt to forget their own future safety in their desire of sacrificing their enemies. People without much difficulty admit the entrance of that injustice of which they are not to be the immediate victims.

Madison,
Federalist 42
(1788)

The mild voice of reason, pleading the cause of an enlarged and permanent interest, is but too often drowned, before public bodies as well as individuals, by the clamors of an impatient avidity for immediate and immoderate gain.

→ *Concentration vs. diffusion.* And energies that are concentrated often win out over those that are spread thinly. People who will directly be made better or worse off by a proposal will mobilize, make noise, and have an effect out of proportion to their numbers. Less is heard from those who will be affected indirectly even if there are more of them. Burke tried to preempt this pattern, too:

> The individual good felt in a public benefit is comparatively so small, comes round through such an involved labyrinth of intricate and tedious revolutions; whilst a present, personal detriment is so heavy where it falls, and so instant in its operation, that the cold commendation of a public advantage never was, and never will be a match for the quick sensibility of a private loss: and you may depend upon it, sir, that when many people have an interest in railing, sooner or later, they will bring a considerable degree of unpopularity upon any measure.

Burke, speech in the House of Commons (1780)

A congressman likewise defending his defiance of noisy constituents:

> [If] the measure be one which excites an interest equal to, or perhaps even beyond its importance, if it touch the feelings of any particular class in the community, or rouse into opposition the adherents of a political party, he will be liable to be led astray by the overheated exertions of its opponents, and to mistake the noisy clamor of a few zealous partisans, for the real, sober, and permanent sense of the community.

Osgood, speech in the House of Representatives (1834)

→ *External costs.* It's best for the costs and benefits of a choice to be felt by the person who makes it. When your choices have effects on others that you don't feel, you don't make them as carefully. Economists call those effects externalities, but the fancy name isn't needed to make the point. Thus Mill's remark on the Duke of Wellington:

> I grudge nobody his glory, if he would pay for it himself. I have a great respect for Sir Arthur Wellesley, and *ceteris paribus* I would much rather that he should be, as he is, a hero

Mill, *The British Constitution* 2 (1826)

and a duke, than not: but when I consider that every feather in his cap has cost the nation more than he and his whole lineage would fetch if they were sold for lumber, I own that I much regret the solid pudding which we threw away in order that he might obtain empty praise.

Hill, speech in the House of Representatives (1890)

Every dollar that the rich man calls his own remains his by the protecting arm of the Government. Let him pay for this protection.

Gibson, speech in the House of Lords (1898)

Nothing could be more conciliatory or frank than the speech of my noble friend, which I am not surprised at, because people are very often frank and generous with the money of others.

Of course some decisions *can't* be felt by the people who make them; that may be true whether a legislator votes for a just war or a bad one. Burke thought that if you have to make such a decision without skin in the game, this ought to at least be grounds for humility.

Burke, *Letter to the Sheriffs of Bristol* (1777)

A conscientious man would be cautious how he dealt in blood. He would feel some apprehension at being called to a tremendous account for engaging in so deep a play without any sort of knowledge of the game.... I cannot conceive any existence under heaven (which in the depths of its wisdom tolerates all sorts of things) that is more truly odious and disgusting than an impotent, helpless creature, without civil wisdom or military skill, without a consciousness of any other qualification for power but his servility to it, bloated with pride and arrogance, calling for battles which he is not to fight.

↠ *Zero-sum games.* Sometimes every gain to one side of a case is a loss to the other. Spotting a pattern like this is important because it may mean that what's good for the other side can be opposed on that ground alone.

Crisp, speech in the House of Representatives (1886)

What benefits the one injures the other; what helps one hurts the other. Their interests then are not the same, and as a representative from the South I look with some degree of suspicion

upon suggestions as to financial legislation coming from the
East…. They are looking after their own interest. Acting on
the same principle, looking after the interest of the people that
I represent, I suspect their policy. They may do the same as
to mine if they please.

And fine qualities may not be welcome if they're serving the interest
of the wrong side.

> We are told that there is talent and education in the House
> of Commons. And of what use to the people are talent and
> education which are sure to be directed against them? It is
> not customary for a player at cards to congratulate himself
> upon the trump card in his adversary's hand. A man of talent
> in parliament is a trump card in your adversary's hand.

Mill, *The British Constitution* (1826)

But the appearance of a zero-sum game is sometimes an illusion.
People are quick to imagine that what's good for one side of a give-
and-take relationship is bad for the other when that isn't true.

> There are but two parties to production—the laborer and his
> employer. If one has been benefited by Government inter-
> ference, the other must have suffered.

Cockran, speech in the House of Representatives (1906)

So then it's important to dispel the impression of a zero-sum game,
and to show that solutions might be found that help both sides.

> It is hard to persuade us, that everything which is *got* by an-
> other is not *taken* from ourselves. But it is fit that we should
> get the better of these suggestions, which come from what is
> not the best and soundest part of our nature.

Burke, *Two Letters to Gentlemen in Bristol* (1778)

> I deny altogether the doctrine, that commerce has a selfish
> character—that it can benefit one party without being advan-
> tageous to the other. It is twice blessed—it blesses the giver
> as well as the receiver.

Mackintosh, speech in the House of Commons (1824)

> Of all the mischievous fallacies which have been propounded
> in the course of this great discussion, it seems to me that the
> most mischievous is the assumption that the measure of the
> foreigner's loss is necessarily the measure of our gain.

Crewe, speech in the House of Lords (1904)

↦ *Sunk costs.* A sunk cost is a cost already spent that can't be recovered. It'll stay the same no matter what you decide now. It's easy to let sunk costs influence decisions about the future; it's hard to walk away from a project once you've started spending on it. But a good analysis of what to do next—a rational one, anyway—generally treats the current state of things as a given. It doesn't matter what it cost to get here. Suppose you pay a lot of money for a concert ticket but decide that you hate the concert halfway through. The ticket is a sunk cost. Its price shouldn't affect whether you stay for the rest of the show. It's best to think of yourself as just having been offered the chance to watch the rest of the concert for free; if that's not an appealing thought, leave. You avoid the sunk-cost fallacy, in other words, by just comparing the cost of *going forward* (in money, time, anything) with the benefits.

Fessenden, speech in the Senate (1861)

The friends of this work wish that the board we have appointed to examine and spend money with regard to small steamers comparatively, shall have the power, if they see fit, to spend more than half of it in completing this vessel. I will give no such power to anybody on a work which was begun twenty years ago and has been abandoned almost as long. As to the fact that we have spent $500,000, and therefore ought to complete it, it is an old rule that no wise man sends good money after bad; and if we have wasted $500,000, it is no reason why we should now throw away $1,000,000 on this work.

An example of going forward that sounds suspicious (but it's hard to be sure):

Quezon, speech in the House of Representatives (1914)

We found a road already built, for which we had expended several million dollars, and it was a question of either throwing away all the money already spent or of spending a little more for its maintenance. We had to choose the lesser evil. If we had had the decision in the first place, we should never have built that road.

It's especially tempting to worry about sunk costs when they're measured in struggle and pain. Then walking away might seem to show disrespect for the suffering that got us here. In fact that suffering probably *should* be disregarded before more of it is caused for bad reasons. But any country that has been stuck in a war knows this is more easily said than done.

> I deny that we should put both feet into a vise because we have one there; I deny that we should throw good money after bad money; I deny that two wrongs or a perpetuated wrong can ever make a right. Let us get out of those islands and leave those millions of people to govern themselves.

Brewer, speech in the House of Representatives (1900)

He was speaking of the Philippine-American War.

26

Choice of Evils

➤➤ *Necessary evils.* It's natural to imagine that the best amount of a bad thing is none. But people don't think that way when they run their own lives, because bad things are costly to avoid; and the same is true in the rest of the world.

Burke, *Present Discontents* (1770)

It is no inconsiderable part of wisdom, to know how much of an evil ought to be tolerated.

Bringing up simple examples can help an audience see why allowing some of a bad thing is often better than a zero-tolerance policy. An easy one is the use of speed limits. They could be set low enough to put an end to all accidents, but nobody wants that now, or ever did.

Houghton, speech in the House of Lords (1873)

If the English people chose to have all the trains, including the expresses, slow, and to have comparatively few trains, no doubt they might have an almost complete immunity from railway accidents. But he believed that was not what the English people wanted. He believed they were well satisfied to run a small risk of accident for the great convenience of frequency and celerity.

A similar argument against certain uses of undercover informants:

Cowen, speech in the House of Commons (1882)

He maintained that it was discreditable to any Government to have to use such means. They did not use them in England, because the people were in sympathy with the law of the land; and rather than use them in Ireland, and rather than use these exceptional measures, he should think it would be better to tolerate a certain measure of crime.

You might say these are cases in which the cure is worse than the disease. There was a Latin expression for that idea: *aegrescit medendo* (adapted from the *Aeneid*; more literally, *he grows worse by being healed*). Metaphors of disease and cure are a familiar way to talk about cases where a problem is solved at too great a cost.

> It would be an effective way to get rid of one's corns to chop off the feet, but the remedy would be worse than the disease. No doubt, by the recommendations of the Committee, you might stamp out foot-and-mouth disease; but you are likely to stamp out the farmer at the same time by the severity of the measures applied against him.

Playfair, speech in the House of Commons (1878)

You can apply the same point to giving things up (or refusing to give them up) in a *debate*. There are arguments you're better off not winning—because to win them, you have to say things that are worse than losing.

> To prove that the Americans ought not to be free, we are obliged to depreciate the value of freedom itself; and we never seem to gain a paltry advantage over them in debate, without attacking some of those principles, or deriding some of those feelings, for which our ancestors have shed their blood.

Burke, *Speech on Conciliation with the Colonies* (1775)

➤➤ *Too much of a good thing.* The reverse is also true: more of a good thing may be a bad one. Sometimes the point is that a good thing *becomes* bad in excess.

> There is no more common error among unthinking persons than to imagine, that whatever is good in a certain quantity must be good in any quantity: and the admirers of aristocratic rule, who are in general very little alive to any political evils except those which emanate from a seditious rabble, are apt to imagine, or to talk as if they imagined, that we never could by possibility have enough of so very good a thing.

Mill, speech on aristocracy (1825)

Or good things are expensive, and here they aren't worth having. So in the same way that allowing an evil may reflect good judgment, the presence of seemingly good things can be just cause for embarrassment. There are garish houses of this kind, and victories in war.

Chamberlain, speech in the House of Commons (1884)

We boast of our national prosperity, take pride in the development of our national wealth and national enterprise. These things, good as they are, may be bought too dear; and, in my opinion, they are bought too dear if they cannot be bought without a sacrifice of life such as I have described.

➻ *Compared to what?* It's a mistake to carry on about the bad side of anything without looking at the bad side of the alternative. This pattern arises easily when people complain about the status quo but aren't thinking as clearly about what might replace it. They can directly see the problems they *don't* like, but not the problems they *won't* like.

Henry, speech at Virginia Ratifying Convention (1788)

Before you abandon the present system, I hope you will consider not only its defects, most maturely, but likewise those of that which you are to substitute for it. May you be fully apprised of the dangers of the latter, not by fatal experience, but by some abler advocate than I!

These points can be hard to make when the problems we have now are definite and the problems with the alternative are merely things that *might* happen. Warnings about them have to compete with wishful thinking. Burke regarded this as a starting point for trouble.

Burke, *Reflections on the Revolution in France* (1790)

No difficulties occur in what has never been tried. Criticism is almost baffled in discovering the defects of what has not existed; and eager enthusiasm and cheating hope have all the wide field of imagination, in which they may expatiate with little or no opposition.

But it can work the other way around, too: someone trashes the bad side of an alternative while ignoring the cost of leaving things alone. Perhaps problems with the status quo are familiar and don't stand out. New problems have the force of novelty. So pointing out flaws in a proposal for change can sink it, even if it would be better than the way things are. Why try something new when everyone can see that it will go badly? Maybe because it won't go *as* badly as what they know now.

It is a matter both of wonder and regret, that those who raise so many objections against the new Constitution should never call to mind the defects of that which is to be exchanged for it. It is not necessary that the former should be perfect; it is sufficient that the latter is more imperfect. No man would refuse to give brass for silver or gold, because the latter had some alloy in it.

Madison, *Federalist* 38 (1788)

This theme can sometimes be advanced with comparisons to others: you complain, but is anyone doing better than we are?

What government has not some law in favor of debtors? The difficulty consists in finding one that is not more unfriendly to the creditors than ours. I am far from justifying such things. On the contrary I believe that it is universally true, that acts made to favor a part of the community are wrong in principle. All that is now intended is, to remark that we are not worse than other people in that respect which we most condemn.

Winthrop, *Agrippa* III (1787)

Or indeed, is anyone doing better than *you* are?

You (suffer me respectfully to say so) of all the members of the union, appear to have the least cause of complaint. Permit me to remind you of the objections made on this ground by Mr. Martin, of Maryland. The opposition there asserted that the great states had too large a share of power, and you have the most of all. The same sentiments were urged in the Connecticut Convention. Is it probable then that an allotment of power more favorable to you would be made by a new Convention?

Coxe, *Virginia's Power Under the Constitution and the Dangers of Failing to Ratify* (1788)

Other comparisons are possible, too—between two past states of things, for example:

The right hon. Gentleman made a very eloquent discourse on the calamities of war. Everybody agrees about that, but it should be remembered that, altering a word of the poet, "Peace has its miseries as well as war;" and that whatever calamities have fallen on a part of Italy in consequence of the war which has just terminated, the miseries which the Italians

Palmerston, speech in the House of Commons (1859)

have suffered through peace for a great number of years are
matters of no light consideration, and ought not to be viewed
as if belonging to a condition which it was a crime to disturb.

(The line he adjusts is from Milton: peace hath her victories no less
renowned than war.) Or one proposal for the future can be compared
to others that have been made (or that *haven't* been made). If you
don't like the idea on the table, what exactly *would* you like?

Hanson,
*Remarks
on the Proposed
Plan of a Federal
Government*
(1788)

You have been told that the proposed plan was calculated
peculiarly for the rich. In all governments, not merely despotic, the wealthy must, in most things, find an advantage,
from the possession of that, which is too much the end and
aim of mankind. In the proposed plan, there is nothing like a
discrimination in their favor. How this amazing objection is
to be supported, I am at a loss to conjecture. Is it a just cause
of reproach, that the constitution effectually secures property?
Or would the objectors introduce a general scramble?

→→ *Choice of evils.* If the only solution to a bad thing has bad points of
its own, the result is a choice of evils. Framing it that way can take
the edge off the criticisms; you accept them. The question is just how
they compare to the alternative. So you no longer have to argue, for
example, that the people you support for office are *good.*

Mill,
*The British
Constitution* 2
(1826)

We must resign ourselves to be governed by incapables of
some sort: do what we may, our only choice is whether we
will be governed by incapables who have an interest in good
government, or incapables who have an interest in bad.

It's the same if you're talking about policies rather than people. When
you're arguing about a tax, for example, it doesn't matter whether it
comes with problems. Any tax does. The question is how it compares
to other options.

Gregg, *Principles
of Taxation*
(1853)

All taxes are objectionable.... Almost every one we ever
heard of is either inequitable in its nature, or fetters commerce, or stimulates to fraud, or is costly in the collection, or

is irritating to the temper, or combines several or all of these objections. All that is left to us is a choice of evils. It is no sufficient reason, therefore, for rejecting or repealing a tax, that it is open to one or more of the above charges.

Maybe everyone sees evils, but *different* ones:

> It is absurd for a man to oppose the adoption of the constitution, because *he* thinks some part of it defective or exceptionable. Let every man be at liberty to expunge what *he* judges to be exceptionable, and not a syllable of the constitution will survive the scrutiny. A painter, after executing a masterly piece, requested every spectator to draw a pencil mark over the part that did not please him; but to his surprise, he soon found the whole piece defaced.

Webster, *An Examination into the Leading Principles of the Federal Constitution* (1787)

Another choice-of-evils problem arises when a risk simply can't be eliminated by any solution.

> If all this will not produce a Congress fit to be trusted, and worthy of the public confidence, I think we may give the matter up as impracticable. But still we must make ourselves as easy as we can, under a mischief which admits no remedy, and bear with patience an evil which can't be cured: for a government we must have.

Webster, *The Weaknesses of Brutus Exposed* (1787)

It can then be useful to move from arguments about how to solve the problem (which can't be done) to arguments about how to make it less likely to arise.

> Should it be asked, what is to be the redress for an insurrection pervading all the States, and comprising a superiority of the entire force, though not a constitutional right? The answer must be, that such a case, as it would be without the compass of human remedies, so it is fortunately not within the compass of human probability; and that it is a sufficient recommendation of the federal Constitution, that it diminishes the risk of a calamity for which no possible constitution can provide a cure.

Madison, *Federalist* 43 (1788)

And when even the best decision you can make isn't appealing, that might be a good argument for delay. Maybe one of the options will get better or another will arrive.

Churchill,
*Liberalism and the
Social Problem*
(1909) It sometimes happens that the politics of a Party become involved in such a queer and awkward tangle that only a choice of evils is at the disposal of its leader; and when the leader has to choose between sliding into a bog on the one hand and jumping over a precipice on the other, some measure of indulgence may be extended to him if he prefers to go on marking time.

→ *The better mistake.* A debate may be full of claims about what *will* happen, when the real question is what *might* happen. You can describe a case like that as a choice of risks, similar to the choice of evils just shown but now a matter of probability. We may have to err on the side of this or that. Which is safer?

Smith, speech at
New York Ratifying
Convention
(1788) I will not declaim, and say all men are dishonest; but I think, in forming a constitution, if we presume this, we shall be on the safest side. This extreme is certainly less dangerous than the other.

The argument can also focus on the likelihood of each risk coming to pass. A claim that you should "err on the side of" this or that often depends on a view about the chance of one result or another (*that'll probably never happen*). Those views can be attacked (*oh yes it might*), as was done by Patrick Henry when he protested against federal tax collectors.

Henry, speech at
Virginia Ratifying
Convention
(1788) When these harpies are aided by excisemen, who may search, at any time, your houses, and most secret recesses, will the people bear it? If you think so, you differ from me. Where I thought there was a possibility of such mischiefs, I would grant power with a niggardly hand; and here there is a strong probability that these oppressions shall actually happen. I may be told that it is safe to err on that side, because such regulations may be made by Congress as shall restrain these

officers, and because laws are made by our representatives, and judged by righteous judges: but, sir, as these regulations may be made, so they may not; and many reasons there are to induce a belief that they will not. I shall therefore be an infidel on that point till the day of my death.

We've been talking about risks as if they all involve bad things. But suppose you're trying to achieve something *good*—a victory. Then you compare the upsides of your choices, or the chances of winning as well as losing. It's often said that one should err on the side of caution, but in these cases the opposite may be true. Thus Burke's comment about how England might best approach the French revolutionaries he hated:

> Distrust is a defensive principle. They who have much to lose have much to fear. But in France we hold nothing. We are to break in upon a power in possession; we are to carry everything by storm, or by surprise, or by intelligence, or by all. Adventure, therefore, and not caution, is our policy. Here to be too presuming is the better error.

Burke, *Remarks on the Policy of the Allies* (1793)

> Beware, my dear sir, of magnifying a riot into an insurrection, by employing in the first instance an inadequate force. 'Tis better far to err on the other side. Whenever the government appears in arms, it ought to appear like a Hercules, and inspire respect by the display of strength.

Hamilton, letter to James McHenry (1799)

↠ *Cancellation.* A final variation: both sides to a dispute dislike a proposal or result; perhaps their shared unhappiness is a sign of the proposal's merit. The complaints of two adversaries (or of the same one) cancel each other out, or suggest that both are wrong.

> Charles Fox made in the British Parliament exactly the same objections to the treaty as the patriots in this country have made. It was humiliating to Great Britain, he said. Unfortunate, indeed, must be the negotiators who have made a treaty humiliating to both the contracting parties! Mr. Fox's censure is the best comment in the world on that of the American patriots, and theirs on his.

Cobbett, *A Little Plain English* (1795)

Hamilton, *Federalist 77* (1788)

To this union of the Senate with the President, in the article of appointments, it has in some cases been suggested that it would serve to give the President an undue influence over the Senate, and in others that it would have an opposite tendency, a strong proof that neither suggestion is true.

Henry, speech at Virginia Ratifying Convention (1788)

That honorable gentleman, and some others, have insisted that the abolition of slavery will result from it, and at the same time have complained that it encourages its continuation. The inconsistency proves, in some degree, the futility of their arguments.

27

Compromise and Degree

↦ *Against compromise.* "Never compromise" doesn't work well as an approach to human affairs. But *sometimes* it's best not to meet halfway, and useful to be skeptical of compromises broadly—e.g., because they cause trouble later.

> I believe that this compromise, like compromises in general, will leave behind it an amount of unsatisfied principle from which, some day or other, mischief is certain to accrue.

Borlase, speech in the House of Commons (1881)

The point can be a matter of principle: compromise and concession are bad habits because they amount to doing less than the right thing.

> I am an enemy to concession; I object not only to the principle, but I believe the word itself to be radically an improper word; it ought to be expunged from the political dictionary. If it means anything it means this, the departing from the line of just principle, and to that, I for one, will never concede.

Poulter, speech in the House of Commons (1836)

Hatred of compromise thus can be made a point of pride.

> I do not remember a more thrilling incident in history than the story of the French war vessel which, when it had been surrounded by the enemy and knew that it had no chance of escape, nailed colours to the mast and went down with colours flying. That is what Unionists will do if they are to be beaten—they will be beaten thoroughly, but they will have nothing to do with compromise.

Rentoul, speech in the House of Commons (1893)

Or compromise with *these* parties may be a mistake.

> He could understand that many hon. Members were anxious that the matter should be dealt with in the nature of a compromise. He, however, had carefully watched the course of the debate, and had noticed that the Opposition, instead of being

Healy, speech in the House of Commons (1902)

satisfied when Amendments were made, like the horse-leech simply asked for "more;" they divided against the Amendments as amended, and the Government, instead of gaining anything from yielding to the Opposition, simply involved themselves in further entanglements.

↦ *Matters of principle.* Refusing to compromise for reasons specific to this case: a principle is at stake *here* that doesn't lend itself to addition and subtraction.

Shaw, speech in the House of Commons (1835)

To return to the real question before us. It is not one of degree, but of principle—not of the more or the less—not of a part, but of the whole; not whether there is a surplus, or if so, how it should be applied—but divested of all party tactics, of all ingenious obscurity, of all dexterous covering—the real question is, shall the Protestant Church be suffered to exist in Ireland?

Treating an issue as a matter of principle can force the audience to take a position. That works well if the listeners are likely to divide favorably when they commit.

Rapier, speech in the House of Representatives (1875)

I have no compromise to offer on this subject; I shall not willingly accept any. After all, this question resolves itself into this: either I am a man or I am not a man. If I am a man, I am entitled to all the rights and privileges and immunities that any other American citizen is entitled to. If I am not a man, then I have no right to vote, I have no right to be here upon this floor; or if I am tolerated here, it is in violation of the Constitution of our country. If the negro is not a man, and has no right to vote, then there are many occupying seats here in violation of law. Sir if any man is entitled to the protection of the laws of his country, I hold that the colored man is that man.

Matters of principle can make a small case as important as a big one.

Pelham-Clinton, speech in the House of Lords (1853)

Sacrilege cannot be a question of degree. If a man breaks into a church and steals one piece of the communion plate, he just as much commits sacrilege as a man who takes the whole service.

Of course I admit the difference in degree; but, surely, liberty of conscience is not a question of degree. It is one of principle if anything is; nor, I think, does this House desire or claim to oppress consciences any more in small than in great matters.

Errington, speech in the House of Commons (1878)

↦ *For compromise.* Appealing to the value of compromise, and fending off refusals to bend.

The right hon. Gentleman indeed says, that the moment the people pass the line of just and reasonable demand, that moment we should refuse to concede anything ... we should make no concession, lest it should be supposed that we had conceded every thing to fear. What, Sir, shall I answer to such an argument? What shall I say more than this—take care that you concede in time? Seasonable concession is the only means by which you can either put down just or prevent unjust demands.

Stanley, speech in the House of Commons (1831)

If the period for compromising is past, this Republic will soon pass away with it. The Constitution of this country itself was but a compromise. We have been told by the fathers of the country that no one man came out of the convention which formed that Constitution who had not opposition to some section or clause in it. Sir, the whole world is full of compromises, and chaos would come again without them. Every law we pass is but a compromise. No man in civil society—no man even in a despotic Government—has ever yet been permitted to have everything his own way.

Clayton, speech in the Senate (1856)

↦ *Matters of degree.* Turning a debate into a matter of degree affects how it continues. Some positions are much more easily pressed once they're matters of marginal analysis rather than a choice between absolutes. This is done most easily by thinking first of a case that both sides agree about; then you show it to differ from the case in dispute only in extent. An example is this defense of a general right to seize goods from neutral ships that were destined for enemy hands—not just when the goods were weapons, but when the ship was carrying food or anything else:

Phillimore,
speech in the
House of
Commons
(1856)

If a neutral were found carrying contraband you might seize contraband. That right was admitted, and why? Because the neutral might thereby minister to the force of the enemy. But did not furnishing food administer to his force, equally as supplying him with arms. Was it not a mere question of degree, and not a question of principle?

Another example: Mill said that adults shouldn't be forced to do anything for their own good, but that compulsion of children wasn't a problem. Stephen replied that the concession about children made Mill's whole claim a matter of degree rather than principle (so sometimes the state *should* be able to coerce adults):

Stephen,
*Liberty, Equality,
Fraternity*
(1873)

[Mill's concession] admits the whole principle of interference, for it assumes that the power of society over people in their minority is and ought to be absolute, and minority and majority are questions of degree, and the line which separates them is arbitrary.... One person may be more mature at fifteen than another at thirty.

The procedure can also be turned around: treating this as a matter of principle would mean X, and *nobody* thinks X is true; so let's talk about where to stop short of X, which is a question of degree. From a defense of laws that forbade selling liquor on Sundays:

O'Conor,
speech in the
House of
Commons
(1874)

Is there any man who would propose in this House that there should be unrestricted sale of liquors at every hour on every day, by every man who chose to sell them? We know that such a proposal as that would not be listened to for a moment.... The question with regard to a further restriction on Sundays is not a question of principle but singly a question of degree, and that degree is to be arrived at by ascertaining what, in the general opinion of the country, would be best for the public good.

↠ *A middle way.* There's a question on the table. You point out two possible answers. Both are bad because they're too extreme. Now an answer in the middle sounds more sensible even if there's something arbitrary about it. Thus Hamilton's argument about how many members ought to be in the House of Representatives:

> I acknowledge that ten would be unsafe; on the other hand, a thousand would be too numerous. But I ask him, Why will not ninety-one be an adequate and safe representation? This, at present, appears to be the proper medium.

Hamilton, speech at New York Ratifying Convention (1788)

> It must be confessed that in this, as in most other cases, there is a mean, on both sides of which inconveniences will be found to lie. By enlarging too much the number of electors, you render the representatives too little acquainted with all their local circumstances and lesser interests; as by reducing it too much, you render him unduly attached to these, and too little fit to comprehend and pursue great and national objects. The federal Constitution forms a happy combination in this respect; the great and aggregate interests being referred to the national, the local and particular to the State legislatures.

Madison, *Federalist* 10 (1787)

Describing answers that are too extreme isn't just a gimmick to make a middle way sound reasonable (though of course it *can* be that). Asking *why* the extreme answers don't work can make the interests at stake more clear. Sometimes those interests are hard to see clearly except in extreme cases. From an argument for letting members of the House of Representatives serve for two years:

> It is apparent that a delegation for a very short term, as for a single day, would defeat the design of representation. The election, in that case, would not seem to the people to be of any importance, and the person elected would think as lightly of his appointment. The other extreme is equally to be avoided. An election for a very long term of years, or for life, would remove the member too far from the control of the people, would be dangerous to liberty, and in fact repugnant to the purposes of the delegation. The truth, as usual, is placed somewhere between the extremes, and I believe is included in this proposition: The term of election must be so long, that the representative may understand the interest of

Ames, speech at Massachusetts Ratifying Convention (1788)

the people, and yet so limited, that his fidelity may be secured by a dependence upon their approbation.

Of course poles that seem too extreme don't tell you where the right landing spot is between them. The two-year answer from Ames seems familiar to Americans now but is unusual worldwide.

28

Moderation and Concession

➻ *Not this but that.* To continue from where the last chapter left off: debates about a claim can be affected by framing it as more or less moderate. You can compare your adversary's view to what would be moderate and reasonable (your own position, perhaps) and profit from the contrast.

> It is one thing to say at any given moment—"We will not try to mediate, because our interposition would probably do no good," and it is quite another to lay down as a general rule that we have nothing to do with the matter, and will let events take their course. The former course may be one dictated by reason and prudence; the latter is the language, as it seems to me, not of statesmanship, but of mere indolence and despair.

Derby, speech in the House of Lords (1876)

The moderate claim is put in measured language. The opponent's position is stated with words (*general*, *rule*, *nothing*) that are absolute and thus unattractive.

The same idea can be used on your own behalf: *you* aren't saying X (and concede that it would be a problem). You're just saying Y, a more moderate thing. Contrasting your view with extreme ones makes it seem more reasonable. It also reassures the audience that you aren't taking a position they wouldn't like and with which yours might be confused.

> I certainly do not desire that there should be no rich men. I heartily wish that there were no other sort of men. I by no means agree with that tribe of moralists who would have us believe that great riches are an evil. But we ought to look at both sides of the question: if the law and custom of primogeniture make a few rich, it ought not to be forgotten that they make many poor.

Mill, speech on primogeniture (1826)

Lincoln, debate with Stephen Douglas at Ottawa (1858)

The Bible says somewhere that we are desperately selfish. I think we would have discovered that fact without the Bible. I do not claim that I am any less so than the average of men, but I do claim that I am not more selfish than Judge Douglas.

Stephen,
Liberty, Equality, Fraternity
(1873)

It is one thing to say, as I do, that after careful consideration and mature study a man has a right to say such and such opinions are dishonest, cowardly, feeble, ferocious, or absurd, and that the person who holds them deserves censure for having shown dishonesty or cowardice in adopting them, and quite another thing to say that everyone has a right to throw stones at everybody who differs from himself on religious questions.

This approach can be used to shake off extreme claims attributed to you. You explain precisely what you're saying and not saying.

Lincoln, debate with Stephen Douglas at Galesburg (1858)

Judge Douglas also makes the declaration that I say the Democrats are bound by the Dred Scott decision, while the Republicans are not. In the sense in which he argues, I never said it; but I will tell you what I have said and what I do not hesitate to repeat today. I have said that as the Democrats believe that decision to be correct, and that the extension of slavery is affirmed in the National Constitution, they are bound to support it as such.

A minor correction can add emphasis to the part you leave uncorrected.

Exchange in the House of Representatives (1902)

MR. LANDIS. My distinguished friend from Missouri said on the floor of this House just a few weeks ago that Grover Cleveland was the greatest calamity that had been visited upon this country since the days of Adam.

MR. CLARK. Mr. Chairman, I wish the gentleman from Indiana would quote me correctly, because I do not want to be put in the attitude of saying something I did not say. What I did say was that the second election of Grover Cleveland was the greatest calamity that has happened to the human race since the fall of Adam.

➤ *The cracked foundation.* You might concede that the other side's argument would be valid if the first step were right. But a mistake at the start runs like a crack through the whole thing and makes it all infirm.

> Your reasoning against the New Constitution resembles that of Mr. Hume on miracles. You begin with some *gratis dicta*, which are denied; you assume premises which are totally false, and then reason on them with great address.

Webster, *Reply to the Pennsylvania Minority* (1787)

> "The Republican party believes that we should never tax our own people so long as we can have other people to tax." Hon. William McKinley, April 2, 1892. If McKinley is right then protection is right, if we look at it from a purely selfish standard. But if the major is wrong in his premises, then both his argument and his theory fall down.

Hudson, speech in the House of Representatives (1894)

Macaulay said the same about the political system urged by utilitarians. He thought their model had subtracted away too many features of reality to be relevant even if their reasoning was internally sound.

> It is no longer a practical system, fit to guide statesmen, but merely a barren exercise of the intellect, like those propositions in mechanics in which the effect of friction and of the resistance of air is left out of the equation; and which, therefore, though deduced from the premises, are in practice utterly false.

Macaulay, *Utilitarian Theory of Government* (1829)

➤ *Be it so.* Your case is strong even after you concede what the other side says about it. This gains you some credit for admitting the force of the other side's claims, and it prevents them from being used to gain more points. It might be better than pushing back against everything they say. Assume they're right about some of it; so what?

> But then it is said that Palmer is not to be credited; that by his own confession he is a felon; that he has been in the State prison in Maine; and, above all, that he was intimately associated with these conspirators themselves. Let us admit these

Webster, argument for the prosecution in the murder trial of John Knapp (1830) facts. Let us admit him to be as bad as they would represent him to be; still, in law, he is a competent witness. How else are the secret designs of the wicked to be proved, but by their wicked companions, to whom they have disclosed them?

Attwood, speech in the House of Commons (1833) They were told, that in the evidence taken before the Committee, there were many exaggerations. Be it so. Make what allowance it was thought fit for exaggeration, and still an immense mass of evidence would remain, which showed beyond question that a great body of the infant population of the country was subject to a system prejudicial to health and even destructive of life.

You can concede predictions, too. Suppose the other side objects to some result that might be produced by an idea. Assume it *does* happen; perhaps it would be tolerable or even good.

Pearce, speech in the Senate (1854) Now, I introduce a bill separately for the payment of Maryland, and I am told that it may open the door for all other States that have similar claims. What if it does? If other States have such claims, they have just claims which this Government ought to satisfy and adjust without regard to money. If it took every dollar in the Treasury, it ought to be done.

When Mill argued for giving the vote to women, it was said that they would just vote the way they were told by the men in their families. Mill replied *so what?* If that were to happen, we'd be no worse off than we are now.

Mill, *Considerations on Representative Government* (1861) Nobody pretends to think that woman would make a bad use of the suffrage. The worst that is said is that they would vote as mere dependents, the bidding of their male relations. If it be so, so let it be. If they think for themselves, great good will be done; and if they do not, no harm.

↠ *Concessions for the sake of argument.* Conceding a point *arguendo*— not for real, but to see where the concession leads and (typically) to show that it doesn't change the result.

MR. MEEKER. May I ask if this is not the only project of that sort whereby the Government gives its money away and thereafter has no control whatever?

MR. SAUNDERS. I am not prepared to say, but I will admit it, pro arguendo. The statement, if true, does not detract at all from the merits of the proposition.

Exchange in the House of Representatives (1916)

This approach lets you say what would follow if X *were* true, while suggesting—perhaps strongly—that it isn't. If the underlying argument survives anyway, X can be eliminated from the debate no matter who's right about it. Speaking *arguendo* also lets the point at issue be attacked without quite provoking a defense of it (because it is, after all, being conceded—provisionally).

The supposition is, that absolute power, in the hands of an eminent individual, would insure a virtuous and intelligent performance of all the duties of government.... I am willing, for the sake of the argument, to concede all this, but I must point out how great the concession is, how much more is needed to produce even an approximation to these results than is conveyed in the simple expression, a good despot. Their realization would in fact imply, not merely a good monarch, but an all-seeing one.

Mill, *Considerations on Representative Government* (1861)

Take the very first argument that is frequently put forward by the defenders of this institution—namely, that the existing Protestant Church in Ireland is the identical old Catholic Church established there long before what we call the Reformation, and in ancient times the Church of the majority of the people. Why, Sir, admitting this to be the case for argument's sake, and only for argument's sake, for I for one do not believe in it, what does it show?

Pollard-Urquhart, speech in the House of Commons (1866)

↠ *Arguing from concessions.* Using the premises, positions, or words of your adversaries against them, thus causing them to seem trapped in the result. Perhaps their concessions make your case complete.

Williams, speech in the Senate (1884)

The Senator denies that there is any disease among his cattle in Texas, but he admits that at certain seasons of the year they are capable of communicating a disease which kills all other cattle that graze with them on the same pastures. That admits the whole question. I do not want a stronger argument for my side.

Or you can stitch what the other side has said into conclusions that you like. You aren't the author of the result, just the presenter of it.

Burke, Speech on Conciliation with the Colonies (1775)

My resolution, therefore, does nothing more than collect into one proposition what is scattered through your journals. I give you nothing but your own; and you cannot refuse in the gross what you have so often acknowledged in detail.

And sometimes this pattern can be used without any stitching. You just hold up what the other side has said and add nothing. It's bold and effective if you can count on the right reaction.

Douglass, speech at London (1846)

I think no better exposure of slavery can be made than is made by the laws of the states in which slavery exists. I prefer reading the laws to making any statement in confirmation of what I have said myself; for the slaveholders cannot object to this testimony, since it is the calm, the cool, the deliberate enactment of their wisest heads, of their most clear-sighted, their own constituted representatives. "If more than seven slaves together are found in any road without a white person, twenty lashes a piece; for visiting a plantation without a written pass, ten lashes."

29

Interpretation

↦ *Considering the purpose.* Suppose an argument depends on words that might mean more than one thing. The problem isn't necessarily that the other side is being unclear. (Compare *equivocation* in chapter 15.) It's that you're arguing about something—a law, a proposal, a goal—and it's ambiguous. You can make headway by asking about the purpose of the words at issue.

> When they charge against some Democrats that they have failed in the past to vote for large navies and large armies, for preparedness, what a stupid slogan to catch fools with it is. The word "preparedness" has no meaning unless you know the purpose of the preparedness. You prepare for a certain purpose. If I were preparing to follow the career of a minister, I would study theology; if I were preparing to be a pugilist, I would develop myself physically. Preparedness should be measured by the policy of the country. It was not the policy of the United States to prepare for a war with any country.

London, speech in the House of Representatives (1918)

This idea isn't just useful for arguing about words. The purpose of any enterprise can shed light on arguments about it.

> We ought to consider what is the end of government, before we determine which is the best form. Upon this point all speculative politicians will agree, that the happiness of society is the end of government, as all divines and moral philosophers will agree that the happiness of the individual is the end of man.

Adams, *Thoughts on Government* (1776)

> You interpose the objection "paternalism." ... Do you say that this is not the function of government? What is the function of government, anyway? My conception of government is that government began when the citizen could not aid himself

Murray, speech in the House of Representatives (1914)

and that government was created to do any and all things for the people which they cannot do for themselves.

↠ *What they could have said.* The meaning of a text is in dispute—a rule, an agreement, anything. You ask how else the language could have been written. Perhaps if the authors *meant* to say X, it would have been easy for them to say it more clearly.

Pettit, speech in the House of Representatives (1861)

The argument of the minority of the committee amounts to this: that the fathers meant to make slavery national, to invigorate it, and protect it, and perpetuate it. If they had meant this, they would have said it frankly in the Constitution, for they were frank men.

Good arguments like this show that the alternative phrasings—the words that *would* have made X clear—were easier to use than the ones used in fact.

Hardwick, speech in the House of Representatives (1909)

The constitutional provision in question does not mean, as our opponents in this debate would have the House and the country believe, that no Member of Congress shall be appointed to an office the salary of which is higher at the time of such appointment than it was when his congressional service began. If it had meant that, it would have been a very simple matter to have said just that, and in fewer words than were employed in the provision that was adopted.

Often both sides can make this argument. If a text is unclear enough to call for imaginary rewriting, it probably could have been written more clearly either way. Pointing this out can help the discussion go elsewhere.

Bragg, speech in the Senate (1861)

If they intended to recognize slavery, they could have said so in one word. If they intended not to recognize it, they could have said it in another word. If they intended to mystify and leave in doubt, then they have been very successful in accomplishing their purpose.

↠ *Membership in sets.* You want to apply a label to something. If the fit is strong, you can emphasize it by saying that if the label doesn't apply to your case, it doesn't apply to any case. This is mostly a dramatic way to say that yours is an ultimate instance of whatever quality is at issue.

> The noble Earl steps in at the close of the debate, and says that he is willing to affirm the principle of the Bill; but that he will in Committee move an Amendment to abandon one-half of it and keep the other. I do not know what vacillation means if there is not vacillation on the part of the noble Earl.

Pelham-Clinton, speech in the House of Lords (1853)

> I am naturally anti-slavery. If slavery is not wrong, nothing is wrong.

Lincoln, letter to Albert Hodges (1864)

You're inviting the listeners to think: if this case doesn't count, is there anything that does? They search for an answer among other terrible things, and then the game is largely won; you've at least put the subject into bad company. Be careful, though: if thinking of a worse case is easy, that hurts your credibility.

> Britain, with an army to enforce her tyranny, has declared that she has a right (not only to tax) but "to bind us in all cases whatsoever," and if being bound in that manner, is not slavery, then is there not such a thing as slavery upon earth.

Paine, *The American Crisis* (1783)

You can reverse the claim: if this is a case of X, what *isn't* a case of X? George Grote was an MP who argued for secret ballots in general elections. Some said that secret ballots would hurt the ability of people to legitimately influence how others voted. Grote pointed out that landlords could use an open ballot to pressure tenants to vote a certain way or be ousted:

> If this be what is meant by legitimate influence, I stretch my imagination in vain to discover what influence can possibly be illegitimate; for the most barefaced bribery could not produce worse political effects than this degrading vassalage.

Grote, speech in the House of Commons (1835)

Douglass, speech
at Rochester
(1850)

The relation of master and slave has been called patriarchal, and only second in benignity and tenderness to that of the parent and child.... Now, if the foregoing be an indication of kindness, *what is cruelty*? If this be parental affection, *what is bitter malignity*?

Still another variation: if you call *this* X, we'll need another word for real cases of X or worse cases of it. That might have been a good reply to Paine in the example a moment ago: if you want to call that "slavery," we'll need a new word for the things currently labeled that way. This was the argument made by Charles Sumner about guerillas who fought against the adoption of slavery in Kansas. Stephen Douglas said they were traitors. Sumner's view: in that case, we'll need new terms for those who commit violence on the other side.

Sumner, speech
in the Senate
(1856)

If the word "traitor" is in any way applicable to those who refuse submission to a tyrannical usurpation, whether in Kansas or elsewhere, then must some new word, of deeper color, be invented, to designate those mad spirits who could endanger and degrade the Republic, while they betray all the cherished sentiments of the fathers and the spirit of the Constitution, in order to give new spread to Slavery.

In response to other remarks in this speech, Senator Preston Brooks famously beat Sumner with a cane.

A final possibility: if a case of X doesn't have this property, it *isn't* a case of X.

Hume, *Dialogues
Concerning Natural
Religion*
(1779)

A mind, whose acts and sentiments and ideas are not distinct and successive; one, that is wholly simple, and totally immutable, is a mind which has no thought, no reason, no will, no sentiment, no love, no hatred; or, in a word, is no mind at all.

Madison, speech at
Virginia Ratifying
Convention
(1788)

There never was a government without force. What is the meaning of government? An institution to make people do their duty. A government leaving it to a man to do his duty or not, as he pleases, would be a new species of government, or rather no government at all.

Compare:

> The French Revolution, say they, was the act of the majority   Burke, *An Appeal*
> of the people; and if the majority of any other people, the peo-   *from the New to*
> ple of England, for instance, wish to make the same change,   *the Old Whigs*
> they have the same right. Just the same, undoubtedly. That   (1791)
> is, none at all.

↦ *Expressio unius.* This is a shortening of a longer maxim, which
may be rendered in full: the expression of the one is the exclusion of
the other. It means that if some things are included in a list or other
statement, the omission of other things is presumed to be deliberate.
A sign on a business that says "Closed on Sundays" implies that it's
open on other days. This is a famous principle in law, where it's used
to interpret statutes, contracts, and other documents. A nice application of the idea from a different age:

> A covenant to marry the covenantee, doth carry along with   *Low v. Peers*, 97
> it a covenant not to marry any one else, "expressio unius est   E.R. 138
> exclusio alterius;" but the converse of the proposition is not   (K.B. 1770)
> true; for a promise to marry no person but the covenantee,
> is not a promise to marry the covenantee.

The example is charming but unorthodox because it uses the maxim
to find a *promise*. But it suggests the idea well enough.

The logic of the maxim, and also its limits, are also useful to understand when arguing about words in less formal (nonlegal) settings.
If a sign says *No Dogs Allowed*, does it imply that other animals are
welcome? Nobody thinks so, and various theories have been offered
to explain why. For now just view the maxim as a resource, not a rule.
It's a shorthand way to express a common-sense point, and indeed
the point can be invoked without the maxim, as in this challenge to
an early draft of the Constitution.

> In criminal cases this new system says, the trial shall be by   Leonidas,
> jury. On civil cases it is silent. There it is fair to infer, that as   *Antifederalist* 48
> in criminal cases it has been materially impaired, in civil cases (1788)
> it may be altogether omitted.

➤➤ *Noscitur a sociis* (it is known by its associates). Another famous Latin maxim. It attributes to any given subject the properties of things nearby. The most literal application is to people who are presumed to have the same qualities as their friends, for better or worse.

Sumner, speech in the Senate (1862)

[I add] that the writer had been for a long time in notorious personal relations with the notorious authors of the rebellion, especially with Jefferson Davis and with John Slidell; that he had notoriously sympathized with them in those barbarous pretensions for slavery which constitute the origin and mainspring of the rebellion, and that he had always voted with them in the Senate. All this is notorious, and if the old maxim, *noscitur a sociis*, or, according to our familiar English, "a man is known by the company he keeps," be not entirely rejected, then this inquiry must commence with a presumption against such an intimate associate of the rebels.

But the better-known application of the idea is figurative: an ambiguous *word* should be given the meaning suggested by the other words that are used with it. If a regulation refers to "cows, horses, and other animals," those last words—"other animals"—don't include humans and probably don't include lions, because neither would be in natural company with the animals named. A more consequential example:

Simpson, argument in the impeachment of Robert Archbald (1912)

At the very basis of all constructions, whether of constitution or of statutes or of contracts, is the maxim *noscitur a sociis*, which says neither more nor less than that words are to be taken in their meaning in conjunction with the other words with which they are, in fact, associated.... General words, like the word "misdemeanor" in this case, are to be construed in accordance with the words which precede; and under the constitutional provision that is particularly emphasized by the use of the word "other" in the phrase "treason, bribery, or other high crimes and misdemeanors."

We shouldn't overlook the offensive use of *noscitur a sociis*: besmirch a word, and the things it represents, by putting it in the company of others less savory. To gain the full benefit of the device, you don't *say* that two things are alike. You just refer to them together and let the maxim do the work.

> I am not in the least provoked at the sight of a lawyer, a pickpocket, a colonel, a fool, a lord, a gamester, a politician, a whoremonger, a physician, an evidence, a suborner, an attorney, a traitor, or the like.

Swift, *Gulliver's Travels* (1726)

Borges comments that "certain words, in that good enumeration, are contaminated by their neighbors."

30

Words

‑‑ *Empty words*. We turn from the interpretation of ambiguous language to arguments (and complaints) about the use of words as such. Sometimes, for example, an argument can be attacked for its dependence on words that lack a clear meaning. This happens readily when people throw around abstractions without explaining them.

Hobhouse, speech in the House of Commons (1821)

He favored us with the usual charges against the reformers, and the favorite phrases of office rang through all his declamatory periods. I noted some of them: here they are—"measures of overt violence,"—"crisis of disaffection,"—"apparatus of republicanism and sedition,"—and lastly, "overthrow of government." Sir, these are all mere words, meaning nothing and good for nothing. It is an insult to our understandings to suppose that we will accept them as an indemnification for the blood of our fellow-citizens, poured out like water.

You can also attack a vague expression by going over what it *might* mean. This may help listeners realize that they aren't sure which possibility is right, or whether any of them are.

Cobbett, *On Two Pamphlets Lately Published* (1803)

As it is the talent of Mr. Pitt so it seems to be that of his defender, to wrap himself round in terms which will bear any meaning, or, if necessary, no meaning at all. What is meant by *general measures*? Does this phrase mean measures in general? Or measures of a general nature? Or measures general in their effect? There is no catching him: he slips through your fingers like an eel; and then you stand and stare as I now do, knowing not what to say, or what to think.

Unclear words sometimes come into a debate without being noticed and hide the hard questions. (See the related discussions on pp. 99 and 115.) A claim sounds strong, but all the action lies in how we define some term or phrase within it that's taken for granted.

Congress, say our political jugglers, have no right to meddle
with our internal police. They would be puzzled to tell what
they mean by the expression. The truth is, it has no definite
meaning; for it is impossible for Congress to do a single act
which will not, directly or indirectly, affect the internal police
of every State.

*Hamilton,
Letter from
Phocion
(1784)*

➻ *Define the words.* If someone uses words that don't have a clear
meaning, you can ask for definitions of them. Suggesting that people
define their terms is an old but effective way to slow them down.
Defining an abstraction often turns out to be harder than expected.

The hon. and learned Gentleman who has just sat down has
said he objects to cynical materialism in political questions.
What does he mean by that? I should like to have a translation
of that expression. I do not understand it; we are not cynics;
nor are we materialists.

Whiteside, speech
in the House of
Commons
(1866)

The gentleman from Alabama also said that we must also meet
what he was pleased to call the issue of "Cannonism." ... But
I notice the gentleman failed to define this issue. What does he
mean by it? I have heard men roll "Cannonism" like a sweet
morsel under their tongues. I have read lurid and lying articles
in sensational newspapers and magazines, but I have never
yet read any definition of what was meant by "Cannonism."

Fassett, speech
in the House of
Representatives
(1910)

Suppose the other side does offer a definition of a word or phrase.
You can probably give examples of cases that the definition covers
but shouldn't, or cases that it doesn't cover but should. If you can't
go back and forth with your adversary about this, you can create a
little dialogue of your own.

The honorable gentleman has laid much stress on the maxim,
that the purse and sword ought not to be put in the same
hands.... Does it mean that the sword and purse ought not to
be trusted in the hands of the same government? This cannot
be the meaning; for there never was, and I can say there never
will be, an efficient government, in which both are not vested.

Madison,
speech at Virginia
Ratifying
Convention
(1788)

The only rational meaning is, that the sword and purse are not to be given to the same member.

Webster,
speech in
the Senate
(1834)

The President declares that he is "responsible for the entire action of the executive department." Responsible? What does he mean by being "responsible"? Does he mean legal responsibility? Certainly not. No such thing. Legal responsibility signifies liability to punishment for misconduct or maladministration.... What then, is [his] notion of that responsibility which [he] says the President is under for all officers, and which authorizes him to consider all officers as his own personal agents? Sir, it is merely responsibility to public opinion.

Different definitions can produce conditional responses: if the word means X, I say *this*; if it means Y, I say *that*.

Stephen,
*Liberty, Equality,
Fraternity*
(1873)

Therefore, to the question, "Admitting the existence of God, do you believe him to be good?" I should reply, If by "good" you mean "disposed to promote the happiness of mankind absolutely," I answer No. If by "good" you mean virtuous, I reply, The question has no meaning.

Ashbourne,
speech in the
House
of Lords
(1906)

What did he mean by the word "compromise"? Where is the compromise? If compromising is taking all on one side, and giving nothing to the other, he is right; but if the word is to be taken in the ordinary sense, no one except a person who thought he was addressing a lunatic asylum would venture to adopt any such phrase.

↦ *Bill of particulars.* Sometimes words or claims are unclear because they're too general. They don't call for definitions; they call for *specifics*. This often happens when someone makes claims or criticisms stated broadly. A good response: let's hear details and examples of what you mean.

Sinclair, speech
in the House of
Commons (1836)

Why do not the Gentlemen who, out of doors, are the Bombardinians and Bombastes Furiosos of reform in the House of Lords, come forward at this moment with their specific propositions? The Order Book is before them, pen and ink

are at their service; and I challenge any one of them to place
a definite motion on the table.

The passage refers to *Bombastes Furioso*, a satirical opera by Thomas
Rhodes. The title character used big words. Bombardinian was a
character in *Chrononhotonthologos*, an eighteenth-century satirical
play by Henry Carey.

> I challenge gentlemen to specify; I challenge them to come
> out from behind the coward's fort of broad and unqualified
> denunciation, and name the facts upon which they rely.

Lahm, speech in
the House of Repre-
sentatives (1849)

> He said—"When we come to re-organize the Army the ques-
> tion of purchase meets us at every point." When my right hon.
> Friend has occupied a seat in this House for a little longer
> time I think he will learn that in discussing subjects of great
> national importance opinion cannot be changed by vague
> declarations. We want something a little more specific—we
> want to be told what are those points.

Pakington,
speech in the
House of
Commons
(1871)

↠ *Inflation and restatement.* A related problem: big words or long
sentences to say things that could have been put more simply. The
problem isn't quite *euphemism* (we'll get to that). It's the use of con-
voluted phrasing, often in words derived from Latin. The result has
meaning; it just takes too much work to make out what it is, and it
sounds daunting in the meantime. You can respond by boiling the
claim down into plain language.

> The words are "representatives and direct taxes, shall be ap-
> portioned among the several states, which may be included
> in this union, according to their respective numbers, which
> shall be determined by adding to the whole number of free
> persons, including those bound to service for a term of years,
> and excluding Indians not taxed, three fifths of all other per-
> sons."—What a strange and unnecessary accumulation of
> words are here used to conceal from the public eye, what
> might have been expressed in the following concise man-
> ner. Representatives are to be proportioned among the states

Brutus III
(1787)

respectively, according to the number of freemen and slaves inhabiting them, counting five slaves for three free men.

Big or vague words sometimes don't serve a tactical purpose. They may just show that their author is pompous, insecure, or inept. Those possibilities create tempting chances for ridicule.

Mencken, *Professor Veblen* (1919)

The next paragraph is even worse. In it the master undertakes to explain in his peculiar dialect the meaning of "that non-reverent sense of aesthetic congruity with the environment which is left as a residue of the latter-day act of worship after elimination of its anthropomorphic content." Just what does he mean by this "non-reverent sense of aesthetic congruity"? I have studied the whole paragraph for three days, halting only for prayer and sleep, and I have come to certain conclusions. I may be wrong, but nevertheless it is the best that I can do. What I conclude is this: he is trying to say that many people go to church, not because they are afraid of the devil but because they enjoy the music, and like to look at the stained glass, the potted lilies and the rev. pastor.

➤➤ *Specific substitution.* Replacing a big word with a simple one can do more than make a point clear. It can help analysis. Sometimes a claim sounds attractive because the word used to express it has good connotations. Swapping out that word for a homelier one with the same meaning can expose the claim in less varnished form.

Stephen, *Liberty, Equality, Fraternity* (1873)

Liberty is a eulogistic word; substitute for it a neutral word— "leave," for instance, or "permission"—and it becomes obvious that nothing whatever can be predicated of it, unless you know who is permitted by whom to do what. I would ask Mr. Morley whether he attaches any absolute sense whatever to the word liberty, and if so, what it is? If he attaches to it only the relative sense of "permission" or "leave," I ask how he can make any affirmation at all about it unless he specifies the sort of liberty to which he refers?

Or you can substitute one word for another for the sake of correction. The new word isn't a synonym for the old one; it's more accurate.

Instead of the people, they talk of the country: the wealth, power, and glory of the country: by which is to be understood the wealth, power, and glory of one man in a hundred, and the misery of the remaining ninety-nine. By this word country, they always mean the aristocracy. Whenever they talk of the prosperity of the country, it is the prosperity of the aristocracy that is meant. When they say country read aristocracy, and you will never be far from the truth.

Mill, *The British Constitution* 2 (1826)

→→ *Euphemism*. A euphemism is a nice or delicate word used in place of another that would be more natural or a better fit. Some euphemisms are used just to be polite. You want to refer to an unpleasant or private subject, but doing it bluntly would be in bad taste. So you use delicate language—"intimate relations," etc.—and everyone knows what you mean. In argument, though, a euphemism can do more; it puts a mild or upbeat face on bad facts. The best response is usually to pull off the mask.

The Prime Minister put the matter very euphemistically yesterday when he said that nobody grudges us the performance of our duty in Egypt. The fact is nobody will lift a little finger to help us.

Hicks-Beach, speech in the House of Commons (1885)

Calling something a euphemism amounts to a judgment about whatever it describes. "Enhanced interrogation" or "sex work" sound like euphemisms to people who hate what the words describe, but seem merely accurate to those who don't. Complaining about euphemisms, then, can just be a way to criticize something: the way its friends talk about it is too flattering. In this next example, the government said it needed "men of independent thought" to try a case. That wasn't meant as a euphemism, but a skeptic of the proceedings treated it that way.

I do not believe that in the racy and exuberant history of Irish humor there is a nobler euphemism than this. A man of independent thought is a man to whom the Crown can trust to give you a conviction.

Morley, speech in the House of Commons (1887)

The opposite of euphemism is sometimes called *dysphemism*: the use of ugly words for something that might have been named more neutrally.

Barlow, speech in the House of Representatives (1898)

And yet these cormorants, these vampires, have the effrontery to call this an "honest-money" movement and prate of "sound financiering." Financiering, indeed! Its true title is deliberate swindling—coolly planned and deliberate robbery. These are titles the cool-headed, indignant, plain people apply to such trickery and treason.

The speaker doesn't think he's engaged in dysphemism. He thinks he's exposing euphemisms used by others. So euphemism and dysphemism are two sides of the same coin: the use of strong words, good or bad, to color the facts described by them. Either label is relative. Noting the equivalence can nudge a debate beyond disputes about words.

Bartlett, speech in the House of Representatives (1824)

I know this is called "cold-hearted, pence-calculating policy." These are easy epithets; and must pass as substitutes for reason, for argument, if nothing better can be offered. While a disregard of consequences is termed generous, noble, glorious.

Hunter, speech in the House of Representatives (1841)

I know, sir, that in this House the term "abstraction" means that it is the opinion of an adversary, and that "good common sense" always designates one's own.

➤ *Appropriation.* You've been slapped with a bad label. Instead of resisting it, you embrace it. A charge can gain power when it's fought; the greater the resistance, the worse it seems. Accepting it leaves your adversary with fewer resources for attack. Accepting it can also move debate away from the label and toward facts behind it that make a better topic.

And there are ways to reduce the sting of a label in the course of agreeing to it. First, you can redefine the label in ways that are favorable. Some labels meant to be insulting don't have a fixed meaning. Then a good response to being called X might be to say: if X means *this*, count me in.

I am charged with being an American. If warm affection towards those over whom I claim any share of authority be a crime, I am guilty of this charge.

Burke, *Letter to the Sheriffs of Bristol* (1777)

Second, you can drain a charge of its force by showing that it applies to lots of people. You might start by giving examples of others who've been charged with the same thing. Or define the charge a certain way and then show how many it fits. Maybe it should be a point of pride. (*If X is wrong, I don't want to be right*, etc.)

If the Ulster delegates are incendiaries, if the Connaught delegates are incendiaries—if all the societies who joined in that opinion throughout this kingdom are incendiaries,—then, in the name of God, let me be added to the number, let me be an incendiary too!

Flood, speech in the Irish Parliament (1783)

This way of reversing an insult can occur on a larger scale over time. The word *tory* originally meant *robber* or *rebel*. The word *whig* was also an insult before being claimed for use. When William Henry Harrison ran for president in 1840, he was ridiculed by his enemies as fit for a log cabin. He took hold of the idea and it became a rallying cry.

What was intended as reproach was immediately seized on as merit. "Be it so! Be it so!" was the instant burst of the public voice. "Let him be the log cabin candidate. What you say in scorn, we will shout with all our lungs."

Webster, speech at Saratoga (1840)

The same has happened to the word *queer* and others in more recent times.

↦ *Words vs. things.* An old point of contention: whether one side or the other is talking about words or about things. Everyone wants to be on the side of things, not mere words. Of course both sides to the debate are probably using words and nothing else. The contrast at issue isn't really between words and things; it's between kinds of words and their uses. Saying that you prefer things to words is sometimes a way to downplay style: you like plain speaking better than rhetorical fireworks.

Wollstonecraft,
A Vindication of the
Rights of Woman
(1792)

I shall not waste my time in rounding periods, nor in fabricating the turgid bombast of artificial feelings, which, coming from the head, never reach the heart.—I shall be employed about things, not words!

This response can help when your adversaries use impressive language: they're showing an unseemly interest in words at the expense of things. (The more beautiful their words, the worse it gets.) Saying that you prefer things also sets the expectations of the audience lower: you won't be offering much in the way of words. (See the related discussion at pp. 60–61.) A disclaimer like that, followed by powerful rhetoric, is a time-honored strategy. Its most famous use is Mark Antony's: "I come to bury Caesar, not to praise him"—things, not words—followed by words that move the crowd to riot.

Preferring things to words can also mean that you don't like treating statements as if they were action. Sometimes saying things looks like doing something useful when it isn't. During the Greek War of Independence against the Ottoman Empire, Congress considered a resolution in favor of the Greeks that was said to have symbolic value. It brought on this protest:

Bartlett, speech
in the House of
Representatives
(1824)

I deprecate such a mode of aiding friends, or annoying enemies. We are too justly reproached already for our wordy valor; too deservedly nicknamed a logocracy. If a nation insult us, we send a proclamation! If an enemy is to be vanquished, or a province captured, we send a proclamation! If our Capitol is attacked, we run for our lives, but we send back a proclamation! Enough already, more than enough, have we had of this.

There's also a tradition of response against this entire theme: the defense of words as things in their own right. They have consequences.

Webster, speech
in the Senate
(1833)

Was it Mirabeau, Mr. President, or some other master of the human passions, who has told us that words are things? They are indeed things, and things of mighty influence, not only in addresses to the passions and high-wrought feelings of mankind, but in the discussion of legal and political questions also; because a just conclusion is often avoided, or a false one reached, by the adroit substitution of one phrase, or one word, for another.

"Words are things" is an expression also attributed to Byron; it's in his poem *Don Juan*.

The Senator from Georgia says these amendments are all "verbal." ... In law words are things, and take or give life, liberty, and property. The Senator has only altered words, and that is exactly what fixes my attention.

Benton, speech in the Senate (1851)

This line of reply can be made a form of offense: a distrust of words and of theory (they're related) is an excuse for people who lack the patience to understand the implications of an idea. Thus Mill once said it was hard to find anyone in Parliament who was able to clearly see how laws affected the happiness of the public as a whole.

Occasionally, indeed, this sort of talent is accidentally met with in the House of Commons and how is it treated? It is called theory—abstraction—metaphysics—and the other cant words by which the many who do not think are in the habit of expressing their contempt for the few who do.

Mill, *The British Constitution* (1826)

31

Illustration

↬ *The eyes of strangers*. We turn to devices that make points more vivid, starting with this: You ask how a situation would look if it were viewed through the eyes of a stranger—the proverbial man from Mars, or just someone unfamiliar with the case. This helps the audience see the problem from a fresh point of view. It can also show that appearances created by the other side are misleading.

Hamilton, *Federalist* 24 (1787)

A stranger to our politics, who was to read our newspapers at the present juncture, without having previously inspected the plan reported by the convention, would be naturally led to one of two conclusions: either that it contained a positive injunction, that standing armies should be kept up in time of peace; or that it vested in the *Executive* the whole power of levying troops, without subjecting his discretion, in any shape, to the control of the legislature. If he came afterwards to peruse the plan itself, he would be surprised to discover, that neither the one nor the other was the case.

You can use this theme when a shocking problem no longer causes shock because the audience is used to it. Looking at it through foreign eyes can refresh the perception of its character.

Paine, *The Rights of Man* (1791)

Could we suppose a spectator who knew nothing of the world, and who was put into it merely to make his observations, he would take a great part of the old world to be new, just struggling with the difficulties and hardships of an infant settlement. He could not suppose that the hordes of miserable poor with which old countries abound could be any other than those who had not yet had time to provide for themselves. Little would he think they were the consequence of what in such countries they call government.

↦ *Voices of ancestors.* Speculating about what the dead would say if they could see and speak. Summoning such figures can summon values in the minds of the listeners; they store idealistic feelings in their thoughts of heroes from the past. The device can throw discredit on lines of argument that the shades from the past wouldn't approve.

> I wish that the spirits of the departed heroes could rise in this assembly during the discussion of this question. If they had addressed you, would they tell you of your weakness, or appeal to your fears by proclaiming your inability to protect your rights? They would banish such idle stuff from this hall.

Mumford, speech in the House of Representatives (1810)

> Many of my race, the representatives of these men on the field of battle, sleep in the countless graves of the South. If those quiet resting-places of our honored dead could speak today what a mighty voice, like to the rushing of a mighty wind, would come up from those sepulchral homes! Could we resist the eloquent pleadings of their appeal? Ah, sir, I think that this question of immediate and ample protection for the loyal people of Georgia would lose its legal technicalities, and we would cease to hesitate in our provisions for their instant relief.

Revels, speech in the Senate (1870)

> Many of the brave sons of your State and mine fought and suffered there, and many of them are sleeping in lonely graves in those distant lands. I wonder what they would say if they could come back to earth and hear these things. They at least believed they were fighting for a just cause.

Steenerson, speech in the House of Representatives (1914)

↦ *What would you have said?* Another thought experiment: imagine what you would have said in the past about the situation now in front of us. This is useful when someone complains about an outcome they once would have considered a success. Thus Trollope's comment on the American Constitution:

> Let those who now say that it is insufficient, consider what their prophecies regarding it would have been had they been called on to express their opinions concerning it when it was

Trollope, *North America* (1862)

proposed in 1787. If the future as it has since come forth had then been foretold for it, would not such a prophecy have been a prophecy of success?

Or what happened later would have been considered outrageous shortly beforehand.

Kahn, speech in the House of Representatives (1910)

If any soothsayer had predicted in 1897 that in the year 1898 the United States would become enmeshed in a war with Spain he would have been laughed to scorn as a rattlepated madman. And yet in the year 1898 the order was given by the Congress of the United States to let slip the dogs of war, and we found ourselves engaged in a mighty struggle in the sacred cause of humanity.

Thinking this way can show that a new proposal should seem more startling than it does. It reflects an abrupt change in sensibility that we shouldn't trust.

Green, speech in the House of Representatives (1917)

If anyone had said here last year that he proposed to raise a sum equal to the amount of our national debt and pay it off with one year's taxation he would have been thought to have been insane or a fit candidate for an asylum for feeble minded, and yet in this bill we propose to raise, in addition to the taxes which were already levied, an amount equal to about twice what our national debt was before the breaking out of this war.

A stronger variation when it's possible: remember what we *did* say.

Hamilton, speech at New York Ratifying Convention (1788)

In 1779 and '80, when the state, from the ravages of war, and from her great exertions to resist them, became weak, distressed, and forlorn, every man avowed the principle which we now contend for—that our misfortunes, in a great degree, proceeded from the want of vigor in the Continental government. These were our sentiments when we did not speculate, but feel.

↦ *What X really means.* If the other side talks about a bad idea in the abstract, you can reduce it to consequences more concrete and alarming. (Compare pp. 225–227.) Examples of such translation:

What does that mean? It means that we shall pay high taxes upon almost everything we wear and every pound of iron or steel that we use in order to pay the interest upon an ever-enduring national debt. It means death to free trade or anything like it. That is what the perpetuation of the national debt means.

Thurman, speech
in the Senate
(1874)

This strategy has been invoked often in efforts to avoid war. On a bill proposing conscription for World War I:

The main purpose of this bill is to clothe one man with power, acting through emissaries and agents appointed by him, to enter at will every home in our country, at any hour of the day or night, using all the force necessary to effect the entry, and violently lay hold of 1,000,000 of our finest and healthiest and strongest boys, ranging in age from 19 to 25 years, and against their will, and against the will and wishes of their parents or family, deport them across the seas to a foreign land three thousand and more miles away, and to require them, under penalty of death if they refuse, to wound and kill other young boys just like themselves and toward whom they feel no hostility and have cause to feel none.

La Follette, speech
in the Senate
(1917)

A more extreme version:

War consists of the dead in convulsive states, groans and shrieking of wounded men, screams of dying horses; shrapnel ripping, tearing, lacerating, and penetrating human flesh; pierced bodies, exuding hogsheads of blood, maimed limbs, broken bones, glazing eyes, slow dying from exposure or starvation, inflammatory rheumatism from watery trenches, skulls smashed, brains oozing out, abdomens ripped open and bowels protruding, and so on ad infinitum, producing the most excruciating pains; and it is the healthy and strong who suffer most. If we must choose between war and peace, the lesser evil is peace.

MacDonald, speech
at Washington
(1917)

↠ *Visible numbers.* Numbers are easier to grasp when put into a form that the audience can visualize and compare. That's a classic way to make the size of an area vivid: not with figures, but by comparing it to other areas already understood.

Burrows, speech in the House of Representatives (1882)
The area drained by the Mississippi is but little less than eight hundred million acres of land surpassingly rich beyond the same amount to be found upon the inhabitable globe; more than enough to make one hundred and fifty States as large as Massachusetts—as large as England, France, Prussia, Austria, Spain, Turkey in Europe, and Italy combined, and if inhabited as densely as the most thickly populated countries of Europe would contain four hundred million souls.

Brumbaugh, speech in the House of Representatives (1914)
The shape of Alaska is that of a large rectangle with two long, broad wings. If Alaska were imagined to be placed upon the map of the United States, the first wing would begin at Columbia, South Carolina, and the body of Alaska would cover the States of Illinois, Missouri, Kansas, Iowa, Nebraska, Wisconsin, Minnesota, and North and South Dakota. The second broad, long wing would reach from Illinois down through the States, through Texas, and out into the Pacific Ocean…. It is one-half larger than the thirteen original States; it is as large as the United States east of the Mississippi River; it is twelve times the size of the State of New York.

If a number isn't already attached to a physical unit like that, you might be able to convert it into units that you can display in space. Thus an effort to help the listener envision $1.5 billion:

Hicks, speech in the House of Representatives (1918)
The cost of the war on August 1, 1917, was over three times the total deposits of all the banks in the United States…. If laid out in $1 bills placed end to end, it would make a chain of notes that would encircle the globe 404 times and would make 48 bands of money between the earth and the moon.

The same approach applied to deaths:

Church, speech in the House of Representatives (1916)
The killed, wounded, and missing in this war are already more than 13,000,000. Four million at least have been killed. If the bodies of all these dead were placed end to end in rows, one

could go more than twice the distance across the American Continent, walking on dead bodies every step of the way.

Instead of converting the number into units that take up space, you can turn it into units of time. There are 525,600 minutes in a year; that amounts *very* roughly to around a billion minutes since the birth of Christ, a fact that has been pressed into service many times.

> Our public debt is approximately $30,000,000,000; that is, our debt is $30 for every minute of time that has passed since Jesus walked upon the blue waters of deep Galilee.
>
> Thomas, speech in the House of Representatives (1919)

➻ *Opportunity cost.* You can measure the cost of anything by what else might have been done with the resources it consumed. Thus this argument about the cost of the Philippine-American War:

> I believe the war has already cost $600,000,000.... You could build with what you have spent and what you expect to spend in the near future two or three isthmian canals to the Pacific, equipped with harbors and defenses.... You could endow in every one of our 45 States a university which would equal Harvard in resources. You would have money enough almost to pension the entire old age of this country, if it were an expedient thing to do; so that not only the soldiers and sailors and civil servants, but every man who had done good work for the Republic in private life could enjoy an honorable and comfortable old age. That is what this miserable doctrine of buying sovereignty for gold, that is what this miserable pride that will not talk with men with arms in their hands, has cost the American people already.
>
> Hoar, speech in the Senate (1902)

> To visualize $98,500,000,000, that amount would construct 257 Panama Canals; it would build a railroad which would encircle the earth at the Equator 56 times; it would build such a vast number of standard steel ships that, placed bow to stern, they would make an unbroken floating bridge from New York to Liverpool and from New York to Panama; it would construct 2,042 stone highways of standard specifica-
>
> Hicks, speech in the House of Representatives (1918)

tions across the United States; it would purchase 221,000,000 Ford automobiles.

32

Futility

→→ *Argument is pointless.* Sometimes it isn't worthwhile or feasible to argue. The other side's position is hard to answer, for example, just because it's so weak. It can then be hard to know where to begin.

> In truth, that speech is the most difficult to answer of any— for the difficulty of refutation is usually proportional to the insignificance of the arguments, and it is not easy to reply, where nothing has been adduced.

Mill, speech on parliamentary reform (1824)

Or the argument is so bad that the natural reaction is disgust or ridicule rather than reason.

> A man is found to be a conspirator to commit a murder; he has planned it; he has assisted in arranging the time, the place and the means; and he is found in the place, and at the time, and yet it is suggested that he might have been there, not for cooperation and concurrence, but from curiosity! Such an argument deserves no answer. It would be difficult to give it one, in decorous terms.

Webster, argument in the trial of John Francis Knapp (1830)

> That which is inhuman cannot be divine. Who can reason on such a proposition! They that can, may! I cannot.

Douglass, speech at Rochester (1850)

Or responding would show respect to a claim that it doesn't deserve.

> The hon. Gentleman has used the opportunity, which might have been used in the interest of the poor and for the benefit of the unemployed, for the purpose of instructing and advising the Government, for wasting the time of the House with a *réchauffé* of weary, stale, flat, and unprofitable references to the President of the Local Government Board. To notice them would be to dignify them; to reply to them would give them a substantiality which they lack.

Burns, speech in the House of Commons (1906)

Plunkett, speech
in the House
of Lords
(1832)

He asks me, have I made any inquiry as to the source or authenticity of the statement? I answer him, no. I would not lower myself in my own estimation by treating it otherwise than with silent contempt.

This kind of reply can also be more personal: not that the claim is beneath your notice, but that the *adversary* is. That's what Mill said about people who argued that women shouldn't be given rights because they would be too unyielding in their use of them.

Mill,
*The Subjection
of Women*
(1869)

This would have been said by many persons some generations ago, when satires on women were in vogue, and men thought it a clever thing to insult women for being what men made them. But it will be said by no one now who is worth replying to.

It may not be worth replying just because your adversaries (or others) are beyond the reach of argument. Since it's apparent that nothing will persuade them, there's no point wasting time on it.

Lincoln, debate
with Stephen
Douglas at
Peoria
(1854)

If we do not know that the compromises of 1850 were dependent on each other; if we do not know that Illinois came into the Union as a free State,—we do not know anything. If we do not know these things, we do not know that we ever had a Revolutionary War or such a chief as Washington. To deny these things is to deny our national axioms,—or dogmas, at least,—and it puts an end to all argument. If a man will stand up and assert, and repeat and reassert, that two and two do not make four, I know nothing in the power of argument that can stop him.

↠ *Conjecture is pointless.* Refusing to speculate about "what if" or what might have been, because you can't say with enough confidence.

Gore, speech
in the Senate
(1915)

I shall not follow the Senator from Pennsylvania in his declaration that but for the European war this country would be immersed in calamities which have no precedent in all the industrial history of the Republic. Mr. President, that statement is easy to make. I do not undertake to say—nothing but infinite wisdom can say—what would have happened if what did happen had not happened. That is reserved for the senior Senator from Pennsylvania, who is never so happy as when he is miserable.

In an earlier entry (on asymmetrical evidence; see p. 182), John Morley said that coercion may have helped religions get started, but that we should compare those gains to what we might have had without the coercion—gains that are easy to overlook because we can't see them. Stephen replied with our current pattern:

> Surely the region of the "might have been" lies beyond the limits of sane speculation. If I show (and Mr. Morley has not attempted to deny it) that the agents by which in fact men have been improved have been mostly coercive I have proved my point. To ask what might have been if the world had had another history is like asking what might have been if men had had wings.

Stephen, *Liberty, Equality, Fraternity* (1873)

The difficulty of speculating can also be used to excuse imprecision. In the case below, a candidate for Senate (Davies) had made statements about World War I; a sitting senator (Williams) commented on how Davies likely *would* have voted if he had currently held office. This colloquy ensued:

> MR. GALLINGER. As Mr. Davies has never been a Member of either House of Congress, how does the Senator know what Mr. Davies would have done had he been a Member?
>
> MR. WILLIAMS. I do not, of course, know what he might or might not have said on the floor of either House.
>
> MR. GALLINGER. No; exactly.
>
> MR. WILLIAMS. Nobody except God knows what a man who has never been a pig would have said if he had been a pig.

Exchange in the Senate (1918)

↣ *Distinctions without a difference.* Different words are used to mean the same thing. One usually points this out to dismiss a distinction that amounts to nothing and isn't worth fussing about. Thus Macaulay was once arguing in favor of political rights for Jewish people. It was said that they already had civil rights but that political rights were another matter. He said that they were the same matter.

Macaulay, *Civil Disabilities of the Jews* (1831)   Privileges are power. Civil and political are synonymous words, the one derived from the Latin, the other from the Greek. Nor is this mere verbal quibbling. If we look for a moment at the facts of the case, we shall see that the things are inseparable, or rather identical.

Lopes, speech in the House of Commons (1871)   What was the difference between a rate and a tax to those who paid it? It was a distinction without a difference. The word "rate" was a synonym for the word "tax." Both were arbitrary—both were compulsory. Why, then, salve and gloss them over by calling them rates? Because it tended to divert public attention.

Sherman, speech in the Senate (1894)   When you come to talk about a tariff for revenue with incidental protection as distinguished from a protective tariff such as we Republicans are in favor of, the difference is between tweedledum and tweedledee; it is a mere question of detail; a mere question of amount, and not a question of principle.

➤➤ *De gustibus non est disputandum* (there's no disputing matters of taste). This saw can convey a few related ideas—that tastes aren't right or wrong, that they can't be changed by talking, and that they're different from one person to the next. For example:

Macaulay, *Utilitarian Theory of Government* (1829)   It is the grossest ignorance of human nature to suppose that another man calculates the chances differently from us, merely because he does what, in his place, we should not do. Every man has tastes and propensities, which he is disposed to gratify at a risk and expense which people of different temperaments and habits think extravagant.

Mill said that people have two kinds of interests: their interests as they understand them and as the rest of us do. There's no point in

imagining that we can change the first into the second. We just have
to decide which are entitled to weight.

> It would be vain to attempt to persuade a man who beats his
> wife and ill-treats his children that he would be happier if he
> lived in love and kindness with them. He would be happier
> if he were the kind of person who could so live; but he is
> not, and it is probably too late for him to become that kind
> of person.

Mill, *Considerations on Representative Government* (1861)

The *de gustibus* idea can also be used to belittle adversaries. In effect
you say: if the tastes of those on the other side are contemptible, so
be it. There's nothing the rest of us can do (except feel the contempt).

> I had hoped that when peace had returned, when passion had
> subsided, when the spirit of party had become calm, I never
> again in the Senate of the United States should hear the term
> "copperhead" drop from the lips of any Senator. But, sir, there
> is an old maxim, *de gustibus non disputandum est.* It may be
> the taste of honorable Senators to indulge in such epithets; I
> will not imitate the example.

Saulsbury, speech in the Senate (1866)

"Copperhead" was a term applied to senators from northern states
who opposed the Civil War.

> I consider it an extremely bad instance of ingratitude on the
> part of any Scotchman to take sides now against Ireland in its
> effort to achieve redress for herself in this very serious matter.
> Every man to his own taste, however; all I can say is that I
> do not admire the taste of Scotchmen.

Clancy, speech in the House of Commons (1900)

↣ *To ask the question is to answer it.* This is usually something to say
about a question *you've* raised. The question was rhetorical or nearly
so; it's put in a way that makes any answer but one seem foolish.

> Is it safe, is it right, that such cases should be disposed of
> without careful and thorough investigation, or that they be
> tried upon wholly *ex parte* proofs? To state the question is
> to give the answer.

Browne, speech in the House of Representatives (1882)

A question can answer itself in a different way: it shows itself to be bad or unanswerable. That's what Stephen said when ridiculing one of John Stuart Mill's arguments for utilitarianism—i.e., the effort to produce the greatest happiness for the greatest number. Mill talked about the kinds of happiness that one might try to maximize; he concluded: "Of two pleasures, if there be one to which all or almost all who have experience of both give a decided preference, irrespective of any feeling of moral obligation to prefer it, that is the more desirable pleasure." Stephen said in reply:

Stephen,
Liberty, Equality,
Fraternity
(1873)

It is perhaps a minor point that the application of Mr. Mill's test about the different kinds of happiness is impossible. Where are we to find people who are qualified by experience to say which is the happier, a man like Lord Eldon or a man like Shelley; a man like Dr. Arnold or a man like the late Marquis of Hertford; a very stupid prosperous farmer who dies of old age after a life of perfect health, or an accomplished delicate woman of passionate sensibility and brilliant genius, who dies worn out before her youth is passed, after an alternation of rapturous happiness with agonies of distress.... To ask these questions is to show that they can never be answered.

You can use the same approach without a question: the truth or falsity of a statement—or the absurdity of it, etc.—is simply plain on its face.

Redmond, speech
in the House
of Commons
(1890)

It is an extraordinary doctrine of the hon. Member that a Member of Parliament ought not to advocate the removal of grievances in which his own constituency is specially interested. To state the doctrine is to show its absurdity.

Williams, speech
in the Senate
(1913)

The higher the protection, then, that Canadians thought they needed against you, the higher would be the protection that you think you need against them. That is the logic of the argument. I leave it to fall by its own weight.

➻ *The problem solves itself.* When what seems to be a problem isn't one, so there's no need to argue about it.

To falsify a prophecy inspired by Divine Wisdom would be a most atrocious crime. It is, therefore, a happy circumstance for our frail species, that it is a crime which no man can possibly commit. If we admit the Jews to seats in Parliament, we shall, by so doing, prove that the prophecies in question, whatever they may mean, do not mean that the Jews shall be excluded from Parliament.

Macaulay, *Civil Disabilities of the Jews* (1831)

Some said it was better not to give women the right to vote because most women didn't *want* to vote. Again the problem takes care of itself.

The argument that women do not want to vote is no argument at all, because if the right to vote is conferred upon them they can exercise it or not as they choose.

Anthony, speech in the Senate (1866)

Others said women are best kept out of one or another line of work because they can't do it as well as men. The reply was the same: if so, the problem solves itself; if they don't do it as well, they won't do it as much.

What women by nature cannot do, it is quite superfluous to forbid them from doing. What they can do, but not so well as the men who are their competitors, competition suffices to exclude them from; since nobody asks for protective duties and bounties in favor of women; it is only asked that the present bounties and protective duties in favor of men should be recalled.

Mill, *The Subjection of Women* (1869)

↦ *Deep disagreement.* Argument won't go anywhere because the two sides disagree too fundamentally; they have no shared point of departure. Thus Parliament once debated whether a man whose wife had died should be permitted to marry her sister. Some treated religious reasoning as relevant, provoking this response:

Such reasons, if they exist, are no doubt binding on the consciences of those who believe in their existence; but they have no force for those who do not, and it is useless—it is merely

Coleridge, speech in the House of Lords (1880)

irritating—to attempt to silence an adversary by an authority which he does not acknowledge; it is a waste of time to argue except on common ground and from premises which are admitted.

Sometimes this is a way to suggest that the other side has become too extreme or perhaps gone crazy. Such was Burke's view of efforts at negotiation by the English with the revolutionaries in France:

Burke, Letters on the Proposals for Peace with the Regicide Directory of France (1796)

To talk of the balance of power to the governors of such a country was a jargon which they could not understand even through an interpreter. Before men can transact any affair, they must have a common language to speak, and some common, recognized principles on which they can argue; otherwise all is cross purpose and confusion.

Webster took a similar view of his famous debate with Robert Hayne. Hayne was against federal tariff policies; he said states could nullify laws on the subject that they thought were unconstitutional. Webster said later that Hayne's position had made it hard to argue with him.

Webster, speech at New York (1831)

Men cannot well reason, and confer, and take counsel together, about the discreet exercise of a power, with those who deny that any such power rightfully exists, and who threaten to blow up the whole Constitution if they cannot otherwise get rid of its operation.

↠ *The same might be said about anything.* You can meet a criticism by asking for cases where it *wouldn't* apply. If the class is empty, the criticism might likewise be empty: the same could be said about anything.

Webster, The Weaknesses of Brutus Exposed (1787)

'Tis vain, 'tis childish, 'tis contentious to object to a constitution thus framed and guarded, on pretense that the commonwealth may suffer by a bad administration of it; or to withhold the necessary powers of government, from the supreme rulers of it, lest they should abuse or misapply those powers. This is an objection which will operate with equal force against every institution that can be made in this world.

What does he mean by telling us that the rich are vicious and intemperate? Will he presume to point out to us the class of men in which intemperance is not to be found?

Livingston, speech at New York Ratifying Convention (1788)

You can apply this point to a whole line of attack: this or that *approach* to discrediting X is unimpressive because it can discredit anything.

The scorners of preaching would do well to consider, that this talent of ridicule they value so much is a perfection very easily acquired, and applied to all things whatsoever; neither is anything at all the worse, because it is capable of being perverted to burlesque.

Swift, *On Sleeping in Church* (1744)

This might be called an argument *a ridiculo*, and though it might produce laughter and pleasure, did it ever produce conviction? Was there ever a question of general reasonableness—was there ever a question of degree—was there ever a question including the ingredients of amount and number, in which such an argument might not be used? The very universality of it totally destroyed its force; for it might be used in every instance.

Poulter, speech in the House of Commons (1835)

⇥ *Criticism without remedy.* A good criticism isn't just *down with X.* It explains what would be better—not X, but Y—or how X might be fixed. So sometimes you can wave off criticism because the critic suggests nothing better.

The noble and learned Lord contented himself with general criticism, without condescending to tell their Lordships in what particular manner the evils of which he complained ought to be remedied.

Kingsdown, speech in the House of Lords (1861)

He complains of the action of the President, but never once does he declare that he would have acted differently. Throughout the entire speech nothing remedial is suggested, no reform is mentioned, no constructive legislation is advocated, and on the whole the distinguished gentleman seemed to be mortally afraid that he might directly or indirectly commit himself on some inconsequential proposition.

Clark, speech in the House of Representatives (1916)

This line of response can be used on offense as well as defense: criticism without remedy is destructive, so it's worse than pointless. It's shameful on the part of its maker.

Kearns, speech in the House of Representatives (1918)
A criticism that would tear down and at the same time blaze the way for a better and surer victory should not be withheld. A criticism that destroys and at the same time offers nothing better is treason against the American boys in uniform.

Or it's the kind of criticism you would expect of little people. Thus the following comment on the speech made by Charles Evans Hughes when he became the Republican nominee for president in 1916.

Clark, speech in the House of Representatives (1916)
Carping criticism and remediless complaint are both the products of the small brain.

A NOTE ON THE TYPE

This book is set in a digital version of Monotype Fournier (series 185), cut by the Monotype Corporation of Britain in 1925 under the direction of its typographical advisor, Stanley Morison. It follows a particular face found in Fournier's masterwork, *Maunel Typographique* (1764; 1766).

Pierre-Simon Fournier (1712–1768) not only cut an astonishing series of roman, italic, script, exotic, and music types, but introduced a standardization of type sizes that developed into the modern system of typographic points. Into the bargain, he created a veritable garden of typographical flowers that defined the Rococo style in French printing that blossomed throughout Europe and beyond. Fournier was called *le jeune* to distinguish him from his father, Jean-Claude, and brother, Jean-Pierre, who, in succession, managed and owned the Le Bé foundry, which included the work of the Parisian masters Claude Garamond and Robert Granjon.

*

DESIGNED AND COMPOSED BY

MARK ARGETSINGER

Library of Congress Cataloging-in-Publication Data

Names: Farnsworth, Ward, 1967– author.
Title: Farnsworth's classical English argument / Ward Farnsworth.
Description: Boston : Godine, 2024.
Identifiers: LCCN 2023030805 (print) | LCCN 2023030806 (ebook) | ISBN
  9781567927986 (hardback) | ISBN 9781567926835 (ebook)
Subjects: LCSH: English language—Rhetoric. | Persuasion (Rhetoric) |
  Reasoning. | Debates and debating.
Classification: LCC PE1431 .F38 2024 (print) | LCC PE1431 (ebook) | DDC
  808.53—dc23/eng/20230914
LC record available at https://lccn.loc.gov/2023030805
LC ebook record available at https://lccn.loc.gov/2023030806